D1589404

Kennedy

PROFILES IN **POWER**

General Editor: Keith Robbins

Kennedy

Hugh Brogan

Longman

An imprint of **Pearson Education**

Harlow, England · London · New York · Reading, Massachusetts · San Francisco
Toronto · Don Mills, Ontario · Sydney · Tokyo · Singapore · Hong Kong · Seoul
Taipei · Cape Town · Madrid · Mexico City · Amsterdam · Munich · Paris · Milan

Pearson Education Limited
Edinburgh Gate
Harlow
Essex CM20 2JE
England

and Associated Companies around the world

Visit us on the World Wide Web at:
www.pearsoneduc.com

First published 1996

© Hugh Brogan 1996

ISBN 0 582 43749 0

British Library Cataloguing-in-Publication Data
A catalogue record for this book can be obtained from the British Library

Library of Congress Cataloging-in-Publication Data
A catalog record for this book can be obtained from the Library of
Congress

10 9 8 7 6 5 4 3 2 1
04 03 02 01

Produced by Pearson Education Asia Pte Ltd.,
Printed in Singapore

CONTENTS

ACKNOWLEDGEMENTS

This book has been so long in the making that my first thanks are surely due to my patient publishers, and to the editor of *Profiles in Power*, Professor Keith Robbins. They have not only been patient, but encouraging, and every author knows how important that is.

I have also received encouragement, advice and assistance from many others, whom it is difficult to list equitably. At least there can be no doubt that pride of place goes to Richard E. Neustadt, who both at Harvard and at Essex has been immensely kind and, in his discourse, illuminating; and to Arthur Schlesinger, Jr., who has been equally helpful at our meetings in London and New York. I may add that this book has also benefited hugely from their sage and voluminous writings, as I hope the notes make clear.

The book could not have been written without labour at the John Fitzgerald Kennedy Library. I spent two agreeable months there in the autumn of 1990 and am grateful to the staff who made work so pleasant, particularly Maura Porter and June Payne. I am also indebted to the Charles Warren Center at Harvard, which appointed me a Fellow, gave me a warm welcome, and was useful to my researches in all sorts of ways, not least in the loan of a typewriter. My warm thanks to Bernard Bailyn, who made it all happen. But I must also pay tribute to the Fulbright Commission, which not only paid for my air-travel to the United States, but laid on some useful meetings at Harvard, from which I profited greatly. No one can understand John F. Kennedy without knowledge of Boston, and such knowledge as I have I owe to the Commission's patronage.

I also profited at various times and places from conversations with Donald Balmer, D.J.R. Bruckner, J.K. Galbraith, Nigel Hamilton, Anthony Lewis, David Nyhan, Eugene V. Rostow, Virginia Sapiro, William Sutton, Mark J. White and Graham K. Wilson. I am also grateful to Mike Gillette, of the National Archives, for his help, and to Don Bacon for introducing us. I was also helped by colleagues at the University of Essex, namely, Tim Hatton, Colin Samson and Eric Smith. Dr Smith read part of the book, and Anthony J. Badger, Sir Michael Howard, Hugh Tulloch and Ann Tusa read other bits, and between them saved me from many blunders (any that remain will be laid at my door). My heartfelt thanks to everyone.

I am also grateful to Eileen Fraser for permission to quote the poem 'Instead of an Elegy'.

And finally, thanks to the University of Essex, both for its excellent library and for its civilised arrangements for study-leave, without which this book would still be unfinished.

Hugh Brogan
Wivenhoe
22 May 1996

LIST OF ABBREVIATIONS

DD = The Pentagon Papers: *The Defense Department History of United States Decisionmaking on Vietnam* (Senator Gravel edn, Boston: Beacon Press 1971)

KOH = Kennedy Memorial Library, Oral Histories

LTW = John F. Kennedy, *'Let the Word Go Forth': the speeches, statements, and writings of John F. Kennedy, 1947 to 1963*, edited by Theodore Sorensen (New York: Delacorte 1988)

PC = John F. Kennedy, *Profiles in Courage* (New York: Pocket edn 1961)

PP = *Public Papers of the Presidents of the United States: John F. Kennedy*, 3 vols (Washington, DC 1962–64)

RK, *Words* = Edwin O. Guthman and Jeffrey Shulman (eds) *Robert Kennedy in his Own Words* (New York: Bantam 1988)

Schlesinger, *RK* = Arthur M. Schlesinger Jr, *Robert Kennedy and his Times* (London: André Deutsch 1978)

Schlesinger, *TD* = Arthur M. Schlesinger Jr, *A Thousand Days: John F. Kennedy in the White House* (New York: Fawcett Premier edn 1971)

SP = John F. Kennedy, *The Strategy of Peace*, edited by Allan Nevins (New York: Harper 1960)

WES = John F. Kennedy, *Why England Slept* (London: Sidgwick & Jackson 1962)

Chapter 1

THE KENNEDY PROBLEM

'Profiles in Power.' Irresistibly (for all I know, intentionally) the title of this series calls to mind *Profiles in Courage*, the book for which John Fitzgerald Kennedy was awarded a Pulitzer Prize in 1957. The echo suggests his unquestionable entitlement to a place in a catalogue which also includes Elizabeth I, Cardinal Richelieu and David Lloyd George; but in fact it is far from self-evident. As President of the United States Kennedy undoubtedly wielded great power, as much as the modern world can give to anybody, perhaps as much as anybody has exercised in all history; but it was his so briefly! Only two years and ten months separated his inauguration as President of the United States from his murder; as Theodore Sorensen said bitterly on hearing the dreadful news, 'they wouldn't even give him three years.'[1] Of the forty presidents, only six have served shorter terms than Kennedy's; only two in the twentieth century have done so (Harding and Ford: not names with which Kennedy would care to be associated). At his inauguration he said, 'Let us begin'; his successor, on inheriting his office, said, 'Let us continue'; but while it is clear that Kennedy finished little, it is not obvious that he started much. The great affairs of his time, it might be urged, were well advanced before he came to power. He passed his years in the presidency learning his job and mastering the issues, but was cut down before he could prove what he had learned or put it to use. I do not accept this view, but I have tried to face it.

A profile can only be a sketch. Short though Kennedy's life was, it was crammed with incident and great events, many of which I have had to leave out entirely. Readers wanting a full account will have to look elsewhere. But it has been my

1

purpose to provide enough information to justify the contention that Kennedy's was indeed a highly significant presidency, in which decisions were taken and choices made that, for good and ill, changed the course of history and still make themselves felt; that it was a lens through which the United States and the US presidency can effectively be studied; and that, because of the Kennedy personality and the fantastic circumstances of his death and its aftermath it was, so to say, a magical episode, the investigation of which carries the normally pedestrian political historian very far indeed from corridors of power and air-conditioned archives. Kennedy, in short, was important. (It does not need to be argued that he was interesting: the ever-growing library of books about him makes the point for me.)

In making my case I have been assisted by the mere lapse of time. In the last analysis, hindsight is the historian's only privilege, and where recent events are concerned it is, self-evidently, not available. Very little of the material in the Kennedy literature can be categorised as truly historical. This was not necessarily the writers' fault: the time was simply not ripe. Now it is ripening. More than thirty years have passed since Kennedy was president; thirty years is the conventional definition of a generation, though given modern rates of longevity forty might be a more realistic figure. At any rate, thirty years seems to be the period after which current affairs begin to become history: the presidency of Kennedy's immediate predecessor, Dwight D. Eisenhower, has already become the property of academic historians, and is debated by them with the right scholarly mixture of detachment and curiosity. Kennedy's turn (I thought and think) has surely come. There is no longer any justification (if there ever was) for adding to the high pile of tendentious pamphlets even if the author's experience is that of one who, when young, saw Shelley plain, greatly admired him, and was like all the world appalled by his assassination. True impartiality may be unattainable, but that need not impede the work of depicting Kennedy's performance as president, of defining the problems and choices that confronted him, and of trying, through examination of his record, better to understand his office, his country and his times. There has been enough outpouring of grief, anger, prejudice, eulogy and abuse. The time has come to try for the beginnings of a permanent judgement, that forever unattainable prize which historians are obliged forever to seek.

Time has already begun to change the most fundamental categories of interpretation. For instance, Kennedy was most evidently a Cold War president, and the Cold War is over. One of the minor consequences of this tremendous fact has been to make most studies of Kennedy's foreign policy obsolete: some are still valuable for the raw information which they contain, and for their authors' mental powers; but they are obsolete, past appeal, for their interpretation, and the historian, who, having lived through the Cold War, has most probably been bent to a view of the world which must now be discarded, has the additional burden of fighting free of other scholars' theories and assumptions, theories and assumptions which, only yesterday, seemed beyond question. It does not matter which school they belong to: left, right or centre, they must all be consigned to the dustbin. The same may be said, if perhaps less emphatically, of studies of Kennedy's domestic record: the Reagan years have come and gone and nothing behind them looks the same. Kennedy is no longer part of our present; he belongs to a definable historical period, and the task is to define it.

Yet not all the controversies in which he was involved are now dead. The Cold War is over, but argument continues about the United States' place in the modern world, and what new international order can and should be worked for. Thirty years have amply vindicated the wisdom of the policy on civil rights which Kennedy was driven to adopt and which Lyndon Johnson carried to fruition in the Civil Rights Act of 1964 and the Voting Rights Act of 1965, but the American dilemma remains as acute as ever. The economic and fiscal problems which preoccupied Kennedy are even more pressing than they were in his time. The office of the presidency, of which he had so articulate a view, is still the centre of American politics and of all debate about American power and purposes. There have been no political assassinations in the United States recently, but America still leads the world in death by private gunshot, and every year almost as many people die in this way as US servicemen died in the whole of the Vietnam War. And the memory of that war, in which Kennedy for a time played so crucial a part, still bedevils the formation and execution of American foreign policy. So if it is ever reasonable to study the past in order to master the present, it is reasonable in this instance. It may not any longer make much sense to take sides about Kennedy's perceptions and decisions, but it is well worth asking why he acted as he did, in order to understand not just America in the 1960s, but also America today.

The scholarly obligation to weigh the extent to which time has changed our concerns with the Kennedy presidency has led me to say as little as possible about the Kennedy myth. It could not be excluded entirely, but it is such a large and potent subject that to do it justice would have required a quite different book, in which the questions of policy and action would have vanished. Jack Kennedy was only intermittently deceived by his own legend (though he was always ready to encourage it when it seemed politically profitable); he would have been appalled by the extent to which it has blotted out concern with the real issues with which he grappled, and his real achievements. It is doubtful if time will ever wholly rescue his reputation: after all, the one thing which everyone knows about Henry VIII, after four hundred years, is that he had six wives. Yet for forty years after Abraham Lincoln's assassination, conspiracy theorists supplied an alarmed and bewildered public with fanciful explanations of the event, but at length the market dried up and no more was heard of them. Byron's sex life eclipsed his poetry in interest for more than a century after his death, but that can largely be explained by the brilliance of the letters in which he chronicled his love affairs, and by the sensational nature of his exploits – everything from incest to homosexuality (Kennedy's sexual adventures seem insipid in comparison). Nowadays, at last, his verse once more commands its proper attention. The history of the Kennedy family, that mixture of saga, tragedy and soap-opera, has served far more often as a distraction from the effort to understand history than as a serious theme. It is like those studies of Napoleon which chiefly concern themselves with Josephine and Marie Walewska. True, the Kennedy legend is an invaluable means for investigating the American consciousness, with particular emphasis on its sentimentality, gullibility and prurience; but the writer of a mere profile can ask to be excused for omitting trivia, even though the market for tittle-tattle and fantasy is unexhausted.

A profile need not be based on fresh archival research, and anyway new information, however much I had uncovered, would be unlikely to make any fundamental difference to understanding Kennedy and his times. We already have more data than we can easily digest. It is the brevity and incompleteness of Kennedy's career which make it baffling, and nothing will alter that. A profile should, however, have a clear theme, and in this instance 'power' is not, I think, the correct term. Rather, this is a profile in leadership. Kennedy was fascinated from his earliest manhood until his death by the problem of leadership in a democracy. He read about it, wrote about it, studied it at first hand, analysed it and practised it until he acquired a deep expertise. Like all politicians, he tended to be impatient and resentful of criticism; he thought himself a better judge than anyone else of what was required of the president, in large matters and small. He played a long game, and by 1963 was confident that it was going to be a winning one: in his last press conference he indicated that he expected all his major legislative proposals – tax reform, civil rights, medical care for the aged – to be enacted in 1964 or, at latest, 1965: 'I am looking forward to the record of this Congress, but . . . this is going to be an 18-month delivery!'[2] His appraisal of his performance in foreign policy was even more buoyant. The final purpose of this book, then, must be to investigate the sources of his self-confidence, to see how his ideas survived the test of practice, and to decide, however tentatively, to what extent his claim to leadership was justified.

.   .   .

NOTES

1. William Manchester, *The Death of a President* (New York: Harper & Row 1967) p. 249.
2. The president's news conference of 14 November 1963; *Public Papers of the Presidents of the United States: John F. Kennedy* (Washington, DC 1962–64) (*PP*) iii p. 849.

Chapter 2

A CANDIDATE FOR OFFICE

Winning the presidency of the United States was John Kennedy's single most difficult achievement, involving three years of labour, calculation and luck. After he had brought it off it was easy to think that his victory had been inevitable, but few thought so before the Democratic party's nominating convention of 1960, and no realist could think so after the narrow electoral win in the autumn. Among the realists was Kennedy himself. When Benjamin Bradlee reminded him that one of his campaign organisers had been described as 'coruscatingly brilliant', the president laughed and said, 'Sometimes these guys forget that fifty thousand votes the other way and they'd all be coruscatingly stupid.'[1] His tiny margin over the Republican candidate, Richard Nixon – 118,574 popular votes, or 0.17 per cent of all those cast – is still the clearest indication of the magnitude of the task that he had set himself.

'Availability' (a term of art in traditional American politics) was the test applied to all public men in 1957, when Kennedy began seriously to plan his candidacy, and by that test he was apparently a hopeless case.[2] By the definitions of Democratic availability (those of the Republican party were somewhat different) he came from the wrong state: Massachusetts cast only fourteen electoral votes and was strongly Democratic anyway. An available Democrat was one who came from a large marginal state – New York, perhaps, or Illinois – which his status as a 'favourite son' would help to carry on election day. Kennedy was too young: 29 May 1957 was only his fortieth birthday (Lyndon Johnson, the formidable leader of the Democrats in the Senate, usually referred to him as 'the boy'). He was a US senator, and neither a distinguished nor a diligent one. By tradition, governors of states were preferred for presidential nominations to members of either House of Congress, both because they usually controlled their state delegations at the conventions, and because their experience as executives was thought to be better training for the presidency than that of a mere legislator, and because senators, by voting on national issues as they had to, made enemies in a way that governors did not. Then, Kennedy was objectionable to the liberal wing of the party because of his equivocal record on the late Senator Joe McCarthy, the Demon King of anti-communism, and because he was the son of a buccaneering billionaire, Joseph P. Kennedy, notorious for his dubious business career and for his illiberal views on both domestic and foreign policy. Finally, to most people, Jack Kennedy's last, worst disqualification was that he was a Catholic (though that good Baptist, former President Harry S. Truman, remarked that it wasn't the candidate's heavenly father but his earthly father that he worried about). Since 1928, when the great Al Smith was overwhelmingly defeated by Herbert Hoover, Democratic leaders had been resolved never again to nominate a Catholic for president.[3]

But times were changing, and Kennedy was smart enough (perhaps because he was young enough) to know it. His father's money, shrewdness and influence were no handicaps, and his own youth might be a precious asset. America was very comfortable under President Eisenhower, but even among those who had twice voted for him, and would have done so again had he not been debarred by the Twenty-Second Amendment to the Constitution from running for a third term, there was a feeling that the country had somehow lost its way under this elderly, prudent rule; was perhaps too comfortable, too somnolent; had lost its sense of purpose and was letting the dreaded Soviet communists overtake it; to meet this anxiety Eisenhower had set up a committee to suggest 'Goals For Americans'. Eisenhower's economic policy might reasonably be judged too timidly conservative: three recessions in eight years were surely too many in an age brimming with Keynesian skills and insights. And even Eisenhower himself felt that in a sense America had passed its peak: the devastation in Europe and Asia caused by the Second World War was now largely a thing of the past, and the unique position of the United States, as the only country to have done well out of that war, was at an end. There was a growing number of effective economic competitors, and the piles of gold stored in Fort Knox were beginning to dwindle. It was time for a change; youthful energy might bring it about. So much was this the general mood that not only Kennedy but also Richard Nixon (aged 48) made it his theme in the 1960 election; and perhaps Nixon's inability to sound as convincing as Kennedy on the point (as Ike's vice-president he had to defend the Eisenhower record) was what denied him victory.

Nor was it really a drawback that Kennedy was a senator; indeed, it was an advantage – so much so that of the five main competitors for the 1960 Democratic nomination four were senators (Kennedy, Johnson, Humphrey, Symington) and the fifth, Adlai Stevenson, got no advantage from having once been Governor of Illinois. The growth of the federal government had given senators new importance in domestic matters, and in the Cold War years foreign policy was invariably the most important campaign issue. It was a matter, literally, of life and death, and no governor could hope to compete with a senator's expertise in that field, unless, like Stevenson and Nelson Rockefeller of New York (a Republican), he had gone to the state house from the State Department. Of the twenty-two major party presidential and vice-presidential candidates nominated between 1960 and 1988, seventeen were, or had been, members of either the Senate or the House of Representatives; three (including Kennedy) had served in both; and five had had significant experience as members of the federal executive. It was the era of Washington insiders, and its waning, when it came, was slow – signalled by the emergence of Jimmy Carter and Ronald Reagan, both former governors, and both outspoken rebels against what they believed to be the corrupt and inefficient government 'inside the Beltway' – the Beltway being the highway built in the 1960s to girdle the District of Columbia and that Greater Washington which had been called into being by the relentless expasion of the federal government and the multiplication of persons wishing to do business with it. The road was a fitting symbol of the age, both at its dawn and at sunset. In 1957, when the age was just beginning and the Beltway was only a plan and confidence in the federal government was still high, it was no drawback to be identified with Washington.

Kennedy's Catholicism could also be turned to his advantage. The Democrats, it might be said, had owned the Catholic vote since the Aliens Act of 1798; certainly since the 1850s, when the

Republicans had inherited the nativist, anti-Catholic vote from the American or 'Know-Nothing' party. The identification in turn of the Catholic vote with the working class of the growing cities had come to be the bedrock of Democratic strength outside the South, and provided the demographic foundation for the huge majorities of the New Deal. But by the 1950s the children of the working class were beginning to describe themselves as middle class, and leaching into the suburbs; Catholics were feeling the attraction of the Republican party. It seemed more reliably anti-communist than the Democratic, the party of Yalta, which had allegedly lost China to the Reds and had failed to achieve anything better than a stalemate in the Korean War. Kennedy, a Catholic of Irish descent, who in 1949 had denounced the Truman administration for its loss of China ('What our young men had saved, our diplomats and our President had frittered away'),[4] could call the Irish and the Catholics back to their traditional allegiance as could no other candidate; although this might not be enough to win him the election (there were too many bigoted Protestants on the other side) it might well, paradoxically, be enough to win him the nomination: his candidacy would have a powerful appeal in the big Democratic cities such as Chicago, Boston and New York where the old machine politics was still alive – or at least not quite dead.

Anyway, the availability tests presupposed a party structure that was in fact collapsing. They were administered by the great bosses and statesmen who, since the Democratic party was first formally organised, had usually directed and controlled it through their hold on the nominating convention. They were not indifferent to principle and policy, but their overriding concern had always been with winning, and the candidates they had chosen (except when, as in 1896, the convention ran away with them, or, as in 1924, when it went on so long that out of mere exhaustion they collapsed at the feet of the last man left standing) had been those who, in their cold judgement, had the best chance of victory, or at least of helping the ticket. The introduction of primary elections in the early years of the twentieth century had apparently made little difference: as late as 1952 President Truman dismissed primaries as 'eyewash'. But within weeks of making that remark Truman had been proved wrong when Senator Estes Kefauver beat him in the New Hampshire primary, thereby not only forcing the president to announce his decision to retire at a moment not of his own choosing, which was bad enough, but also beginning a triumphant sweep through most of the other primaries which nearly culminated in his capture of the party nomination in the teeth of the leadership. Kefauver had been stopped by the superior availability of Governor Adlai Stevenson, which was overwhelming even though Stevenson had not entered a single primary, or in any other way sought the nomination; but in 1956, when it again became necessary to stop Kefauver, Stevenson was obliged to slog it out with him, toe to toe, on the primary trail. Clearly the primaries had acquired a quite new importance, and a candidate who could demonstrate his voter appeal by winning them all, or at any rate all those which he entered, could transcend such drawbacks as the disapproval of Eleanor Roosevelt or coming from a small state. It was a new way of demonstrating availability, and one which Kennedy had to adopt, for it was only thus that he could prove the bosses' doubts to be ill founded. It was just as well that the road looked promising. Kennedy was the sort of candidate who could excite the voters; and thanks to his father's wealth he would have as much money as he needed for his travels to meet them.

These were not the reasons which Kennedy publicly gave for launching his candidacy. Asked if it did not feel strange to be in the race, he replied, 'Yes, until I stop and look around at the other people who are running for the job. And then I think I'm just as qualified as they are.'[5] His campaign slogan, when first running for the Senate in 1952, had been 'He Can Do More For Massachusetts', and now he thought he could do more for the United States, or at least for the Democratic party. He thought that Lyndon Johnson was unelectable because of his identification with the white South and his presumed conservatism on the civil rights issue. Adlai Stevenson had publicly renounced his presidential ambitions after 1956, and by now both Kennedy brothers (especially Bobby, who had worked with the Stevenson election team) had such a poor opinion of Stevenson as a campaigner that they could not believe the party would or should turn to him again. Averell Harriman, Governor of New York and a veteran diplomatist, might have been a dangerous competitor, but he lost his bid for re-election in 1958 at the same time that Kennedy won re-election to the Senate by a huge vote – 73.6 per cent of the total cast. Kennedy had no doubt that he was more than a match for Senators Stuart

Symington and Hubert H. Humphrey. Indeed, his cheerful self-confidence was one of his greatest political assets. None of his rivals could match it.

He had reason. From his first entry into politics, as a candidate for the Eleventh Congressional District in Boston, in 1946, he had shown himself a formidable campaigner. That was the election of which his father had said, 'We're going to sell Jack like soapflakes,' but he might have spared the expense.[6] With his extraordinary charm (which appealed particularly to women), his outstanding record as a war hero, his modesty, his remarkable intelligence and his unflagging determination, 'Jack could have gone to Congress like everyone else for ten cents,' as his cousin Joe Kane remarked (this was the same Joe Kane who said that in politics it takes three things to win: 'the first is money and the second is money and the third is money').[7] His four elections since then had been so many new demonstrations of Kennedy's attractiveness, and of the steady sharpening of his political skills.

Still more convincing proof of Kennedy's potential as a presidential candidate had been given by events at the 1956 Democratic convention in Chicago. Kennedy had gone there as a strong Stevenson backer, hopeful that he would be chosen as the vice-presidential nominee. He had been the narrator of a film made to enliven the opening proceedings, and had given the nominating speech for Stevenson ('by all odds and by all counts our most eloquent, our most forceful, our most appealing figure').[8] Both occasions had demonstrated his enormous appeal to the convention delegates and, at least as important, to the television audience. They had made him a star. Stevenson, for reasons that are still not altogether clear (perhaps he was not clear about them himself), decided to let the convention delegates themselves choose the vice-presidential nominee, instead of doing it for them. This gesture to democracy appalled the professionals, but it livened up the proceedings wonderfully. Kennedy very nearly succeeded in snatching the nomination from Estes Kefauver, runner-up to Stevenson in the primaries; only the last-minute decision of the Tennessee delegation to support their senator saved Kefauver from defeat. The senator from Massachusetts made a gracious concession speech ('What has happened today bears out the good judgement of our Governor Stevenson in deciding that this issue should be taken on the floor of the convention'),[9] but in private he was decidedly, if briefly, cast down by his failure. Kennedys did not like to lose. 'I felt like the Indian who had a lot of arrows stuck in him and, when he was asked how it felt, said, "It only hurts when I laugh." '[10] But he had been notable for his resilient and sunny disposition since babyhood, and he soon realised that the whole affair had done him nothing but good politically. It had made him a national figure and drawn him forcefully to the attention of the kingmakers, while his defeat had saved him from being tied to Stenvenson's losing cause: an important point, because had he been on the Democratic ticket that autumn (a ticket doomed to defeat by Eisenhower's undiminished popularity), many would have blamed his Catholicism for the party's failure, and doubts about his availability would have been reinforced. As it was, Adlai Stevenson was a truer prophet than he wished when he remarked, 'I have a feeling that he was the real hero of the hour and that we shall hear a great deal more from this promising young man.'[11]

Kennedy, therefore, could look ahead to the 1960 contests with high hopes. He was every other Democratic candidate's choice for the vice-presidential nomination (which in itself proved that the Catholic issue was losing its strength); but as he told the journalist Joe Alsop, 'I am completely against vice in all forms.'[12] He had been equally explicit to his friend Dave Powers: 'If we work like hell for the next four years, we will pick up all the marbles.'[13] In this spirit he set out to redefine availability.

As all the world knows, he succeeded; but it is not nearly so self-evident that by other tests he was fit to be president. Availability has very little to do with merit or experience. It is hardly surprising that to many older heads in the party Kennedy seemed unready for the job. The presidency was then at the historic peak of its prestige. Three outstanding men had filled it in turn, the Democrats Roosevelt and Truman and the Republican Eisenhower. The great successive challenges of the Depression, the Second World War and the Cold War had been met triumphantly, and the country had enjoyed almost uninterrupted prosperity since 1945. The potential of American strength had at last been realised, and just as the country towered over the other nations of the word, so the president, as its embodiment, loomed larger than any other statesman. His responsibilities were as enormous as his power, and it did not seem unreasonable to require that whoever took on the job after Eisenhower's retirement should be of proved ability and experience at least equal to Ike's. The only snag was that this requirement was impossible. Of all the probable candidates only Adlai Stevenson came anywhere near the specification, and there was little reason to believe that having lost two bids for the presidency he could be more successful third time round.

The framers of the US Constitution, for all their cult of ancient history, had not thought to establish a *cursus honorum* like that which had reserved the office of consul in republican Rome for those who had previously served in lesser posts. An informal *cursus* had emerged during the first fifty years of constitutional government, in which time no one except George Washington was elected to the presidency without having previously served as vice-president, Secretary of State or US senator: Martin Van Buren had been all three. But the 1840s had brought the triumph of availability, and ever since then the main political parties had cared for nothing about a candidate except whether he could win: this test was certainly not going to be abandoned for the election of 1960. And even in the nineteenth century, when James Bryce wrote his classical exposition of Why Great Men Are Not Chosen Presidents, the system had not, on the whole, served the United States badly.[14] If it had occasionally inflicted a Buchanan or a Grant on the republic, it had also delivered a Polk, a Cleveland and, above all, a Lincoln (whose career up to 1860 gave little discernible evidence that he was fit for the job). Instead of erecting some abstract and unrealistic test of fitness by which to measure Kennedy (and his competitors) it made more sense to ask what qualities he would actually bring to the presidency, if elected. As the 1950s wore to their end many experienced politicians and journalists began to answer the question enthusiastically.

Kennedy was an American aristocrat, though the snobs of Boston and Philadelphia might hate to admit it. His family was parvenu, though scarcely more so than that of Lord Melbourne, the English Whig prime minister whom he admired so much and in many ways so much resembled. Both his grandfathers had been leaders of the Democratic party in Boston: his maternal grandfather, John 'Honeyboy' Fitzgerald (most commonly known as 'Honey Fitz') had been the first Irish-American mayor of the city. His father had been an early backer of Franklin Roosevelt and subsequently served the New Deal as Chairman

13

of the Securities and Exchange Commission (a perfect instance of poacher turned gamekeeper) and as head of the Maritime Commission. Between 1938 and 1940 he served as US ambassador to Britain, at first successfully, then disastrously: he stuck to the policy of peace at any price even after his friend Neville Chamberlain had abandoned it, and became widely detested, both in Britain and in his own country. He was manoeuvred into supporting Roosevelt's bid for a third term, but after that his political career was finished, and he had to find satisfaction in bringing forward his sons (his daughters were firmly consigned to supporting roles). He had seen to it that the boys received a helpful, i.e. not very Catholic, education, attending gentlemanly Protestant boarding schools, Harvard College and distinguished graduate academies (his eldest son, Joe Jr, went to the London School of Economics). Jack, number two, took full advantage of his chances, in every sense: J.K. Galbraith remembers looking with some irony, some wistfulness, at his luxurious undergraduate antics, when Galbraith himself was just an indigent junior Harvard teacher, an outsider from the farm provinces of Canada. The irony lay in the fact that Kennedy always regarded himself as one of the underdogs, one of the oppressed Irish who had been trampled on first in Ireland by the English, and then in Massachusetts by the Proper Bostonians. The attitude was common among the Boston Irish, however rich, and was one day to be an important bond between Congressman Kennedy and his constituents. It was fantasy all the same.

Young Jack seized other opportunities at Harvard than those for dating fast women and driving fast cars. During his junior year he began to take his academic work seriously, and enjoyed some rather special educational experiences that marked him for life. At the suggestion of Felix Frankfurter, Ambassador Kennedy used his two elder sons in turn as private secretaries, following the example of the Adams family, three successive generations of which had furnished US ministers to London. Jack had already made his mark as a wildly popular young beau on the London social scene, but his stint as secretary (February to September 1939) was such a training as no future president has enjoyed so young since John Quincy Adams. The training was not thrown away: Jack acquired a fascination with foreign affairs and military policy that was never to leave him.

The travelling was the least of it, though he roved as far

as Moscow and Jerusalem, and visited both Nazi Berlin and Fascist Rome (where the Kennedys represented their country at the coronation of an old acquaintance, Cardinal Pacelli, as Pope Pius XII). He assisted his father with some of the routine work of the embassy, and performed similar services for the US ambassador in Paris, William Bullitt, who, like Ambassador Kennedy, would shortly be falling out with President Roosevelt. When, in the first hours of the Second World War, the Germans torpedoed a liner full of Americans, Jack was sent to Glasgow to comfort and assist some of the survivors, and acquitted himself well. But the real significance of these months lay elsewhere. Thanks to the friends he made and the life he led, he became a firm Anglophile: the style and values which he met in the governing class of Britain became his own, and were the standards by which, as a public man, he would always try to shape his conduct (his sentimental attachment to Old Ireland never seriously modified this attitude). And he suddenly completed the transition to manhood, under the stress of those days when Hitler was rushing Europe and the world into war.

For all his rakishness, none of those who knew him well had ever mistaken Jack Kennedy for a mere playboy. His parents (especially his mother) brought up all their children to an ideal of public service and insisted on their taking an intelligent interest in politics. Now Ambassador Kennedy was playing a leading part in the greatest crisis of the twentieth century. It is scarcely surprising that after his return to Harvard in the autumn of 1939 Jack decided to exploit his experience at the ringside by writing a thesis for his senior year on Britain's failure to rearm effectively in the 1930s. Awarded a grudging *cum laude* grade in April 1940 (the spelling and syntax were deplorable, as Kennedy, in typical student fashion, had not left himself enough time to tidy them up) the thesis was immediately revised for publication, and came out as a small book in July, under the title *Why England Slept*. It was a bestseller; President Roosevelt sent the author a letter of congratulation (as well he might, seeing how stoutly the book supported his leadership). At the age of 23 John F. Kennedy had the beginnings of a national reputation.

Why England Slept is well constructed, well documented, and written with the utmost clarity. Perhaps it drives home its simple points a little too repetitiously. Not all its arguments carry conviction today: in particular, its interpretation of the Munich crisis is dubious. But it will always have an honourable place in the small library which the controversy about British policy under Baldwin and Chamberlain has called into being. It belongs with *The Gathering Storm, Guilty Men*, and *Is Innocence Enough?*[15] Like these other works, it was not just a contribution to historical understanding: it was a political intervention. Hence its great success: it was an effective version of a message that the American people were hearing from many other quarters. It was young Kennedy's contribution to the great task of rousing them to the dangers and duties which, in 1940, lay immediately before them. It was his plea and warning that America could not afford to continue in the belief that it need fear and do nothing, that its ocean barriers would protect it from all attack, and that therefore it did not need an army, and hardly a navy. Sixteen months before Pearl Harbor Kennedy urged the United States to profit from Britain's bad example and rearm in time. Reading between the lines it is clear that Kennedy expected war, but he knew better than to say so. Rather he tried to make unarguable the point that armaments did not of themselves cause wars, that pacifism was an insane response to such a threat as Nazi Germany, and that the people must recognise both their peril and their responsibility, for otherwise their leaders could not serve them successfully. He deserved a hearing. But today the chief interest and importance of *Why England Slept* lie in what it tells us of the author, for as Nigel Hamilton has remarked (erring, if at all, only on the side of understatement), 'Nothing else Jack would write in his life would so speak the man.'[16] It lacks only any trace of his characteristic humour. Had any curious Democrats read it in 1960 they might well have concluded that here indeed was someone of presidential calibre.

The book speaks the man, but not in the least because it is designedly self-revelatory. Kennedy conforms to academic requirements by being scrupulously impersonal, in tone and material, throughout. But the cool scepticism which would one day become familiar to the world colours every page. The only note of passion to be heard is in Kennedy's plea to his fellow-citizens to face facts:

> Now that the world is ablaze, America has awakened to the problems facing it. But in the past, we have repeatedly refused to appropriate money for defense. We can't escape the fact that democracy

in America, like democracy in England, has been asleep at the switch. If we had not been surrounded by oceans three and five thousand miles wide, we ourselves might be caving in at some Munich of the Western World.[17]

The book announces his political emancipation from his father. The ambassador was an ardent appeaser and isolationist; he believed that the United States should never fight a war unless it was attacked first, and he was deeply disturbed at the prospect of risking his sons' lives in battle. In 1938 his views were representative of the conservative business class to which he belonged, and in Neville Chamberlain he found a man after his own heart. Jack was more attracted by Winston Churchill, but at the time of his return to Harvard he was (or thought he was) still of his father's views otherwise. Events, the influence of his Harvard teachers, and the hard work of preparing his book changed all that. The father's influence was never going to be negligible (until his stroke in 1961) and Jack incorporated some of his views, indeed some of his very words, in *Why England Slept*, but here, at the threshold of his career, the son proved that if necessary he could ignore it. A new consensus was forming as to America's place in the world. Isolationism was fast becoming a creed only for the middle-aged or elderly. But it would take the attack on Pearl Harbor to complete the conversion of the young: until then Joe Jr, for one, stuck to the traditional creed. Jack thus showed real independence of character, not to mention intelligence, in the course he took, though in itself it was not particularly surprising that a sharp young American, with first-hand knowledge of Hitler's Europe, should abandon the old complacent faith and declare his support for the British cause: should become, in the jargon of the time, an interventionist.

He was at ease in the actual world. In his book he refuses both the smug self-deceptions of the conservative and the moralistic delusions of the progressive.[18] Events were reinforcing the bias of his temperament: like everyone else in the 1930s, he had been forced to reflect on the comparative strengths and weaknesses of dictatorship and democracy, and his conclusions were not wholly favourable to democracy. He saw its justice, and its long-term strength, but he saw also that its short-term incompetence had brought the West to the brink of destruction. He was never to give up his view that public opinion in a democracy (or at any rate in Britain and America) seldom wakes up before it is too late: only a great shock can be relied on to rouse it (no doubt he saw Pearl Harbor and its sequel as proof that he was right). A little inconsistently he seems also to have believed that it is nevertheless worthwhile for prescient statesmen to agitate and orate and publish: that was why he so much admired Winston Churchill. He particularly loved to quote Churchill's remark that democracy was the worst form of government, except for all the others. As president he was delighted to award Churchill an honorary US citizenship, saying, 'In the dark days and darker nights when England stood alone . . . he mobilized the English language and sent it into battle.'[19] It is impossible not to suspect that in this warnings of an impending crisis and about the missile gap, and his general alarmism during his first year in office – not to mention his constant striving to be eloquent – he consciously aspired to be the Churchill of his generation. The older man's influence was evident in the very title of *Why England Slept*, which was a deliberate allusion to a Churchillian volume, *While England Slept*. Ironically, Kennedy's position as president, wrestling with priorities, would be much closer to that of Chamberlain than to that of the defiant, single-minded leader to victory.

In spite of his pessimism about public opinion, Kennedy was and remained strongly of the view that in the end human beings were rational and made sensible choices: the business of the leader was to educate them so that these choices were as well informed as possible. Thus, in *Why England Slept*, even while deploring the panic in Britain about bombing ('the bomber will always get through,' said Stanley Baldwin) which so grievously distorted policy in 1937–38, Kennedy could comment, 'as though to prove that man is essentially, over a long period of time, reasonable, during the year after Munich this [panic] was to burn itself out.'[20] This faith in rationality was neither so unusual nor so naïve as it may appear; and it served Kennedy well as a guide until his death.

Above all, *Why England Slept*, no doubt reflecting the influence of the Harvard political science department, is a case-study of the problems of democratic leadership. Kennedy is clearly fascinated, not just by the problems of foreign policy, but by the dilemmas of democratic politicians: even if they see what is required of them (not that Kennedy thinks that Baldwin and Chamberlain did so) they may be unable to act if their constituents disagree with them; or if they do act, they may destroy themselves politically (as Churchill nearly did). It was a theme which recurred years later, in *Profiles in Courage,* and a problem with which Kennedy was still struggling at his life's end. He was not yet a candidate for any office, but no reader (especially if aware of this Harvard undergraduate's earlier study of a congressman) could doubt that here was a potential politician. Still less can any reader today, noting how the 23 year old states what was to be his country's central concern in defence and foreign policy for the rest of the century: 'We must always keep our armaments equal to our commitments. Munich should teach us that; we must realize that any bluff will be called.'[21] This seems to be the Kennedy of the Berlin crisis, and undoubtedly the emphasis on the need to awaken and educate the people ('England needed a man who was able to look beyond the immediate situation and form some just estimate of changing conditions and eventualities in the future')[22] anticipates the 1960 presidential campaign. Even the theme of the inaugural address seems to be foreshadowed in the observation about Britain in the 1930s, that 'there was a great lack of young progressive and able leaders. Those who should have been taking over were members of the war generation, so large a portion of whom rested in Flanders fields.'[23] Read today, Kennedy's future seems implicit in every line.

Next, he was off to war himself. Even before Pearl Harbor he enlisted in the US Navy, and after an intelligence hitch in Washington (chiefly notable for a scrape he got into because of his love-affair with a suspect Danish journalist, Inge Arvad, who had at one time been close to the Nazi German leadership) he found himself in command of a patrol torpedo (PT) boat in the South Pacific. His ship was one of a type which seems to have combined a need for great courage and skill in the handling with near-total naval uselessness.[24] The boats were not fast enough, they were made of unarmed plywood, and their torpedoes were obsolete. Yet they appeared to give opportunities for derring-do, they had been glamorised by the press and were semi-independent in operation; altogether their appeal to a reckless, naturally insubordinate young blade like Jack Kennedy is understandable. But the contribution to victory of his PT boats (*109*, and then, after the first was sunk, *PT 59*) was negligible: probably Kennedy's most useful deed was his part in rescuing a company of encircled Marines from their position on Choiseul island in the Solomons.[25] Kennedy soon saw that if the PT boats had a future, it could be only as gunboats, but it was their very vulnerability and inadequacy that turned him into a hero. On 1 August 1943, during a hopelessly bungled operation (a flotilla of PT boats had been sent out, on a pitch-black night, to intercept four Japanese destroyers taking reinforcements to their base on New Georgia island: only a few of the boats carried radar, and *PT 109* was not one of them), Kennedy's ship was rammed and sliced in half by the enemy destroyer *Amagiri*, with the loss of two men. Kennedy managed to keep his crew together, clinging to the wreckage, and next day led them in a swim to a desert island ten miles off: he towed a badly injured sailor all the way himself, by means of a leather strap held between his teeth. The commander who had sent them out on the mission in the first place failed to organise a proper air search for survivors, and it was pure good fortune that after a few days Kennedy and his men were discovered by two friendly natives in a dug-out canoe. After that, rescue was not long in coming. In due course Kennedy and his second-in-command received well-earned medals for their conduct in saving their men's lives, maintaining their morale, and helping to bring about their rescue. Without Kennedy's exertions the crew of *PT 109* would have vanished without trace, adding to the endless roll of lives needlessly lost in war by the incompetence of the high command.

This adventure had a profound effect on Jack Kennedy. It was long before he forgave himself (if he ever did) for losing two of his men. Once, during a political parade, a cheeky young admirer yelled at him, 'How did you get to be a hero?' 'I lost my ship,' said the candidate, and there is no reason to suppose that he saw more to it than that. He had done his duty as an officer should, and would have thought meanly of himself for ever if he had not. His considered opinion seems to have been that had the flotilla been properly handled the whole episode would not have happened, and in due course his burgeoning distrust of the top brass was to have important historical consequences. He was glad that he had overcome pain, fear and exhaustion and kept faith with his crew; his bond with them was one of the strongest that he ever formed. As president-elect he invited them to his inaugural parade, and he later found jobs for several of them with the federal government. (They in turn supported him loyally.)

But Kennedy was neither a fool nor a sentimentalist. After 1945 the United States was full of returned heroes trying to parlay their war records into political careers, often on the flimsiest grounds. Richard Nixon had passed his naval career playing poker. Lyndon Johnson was handed a Silver Star by General MacArthur as a public relations gesture (Johnson's notable deed had been to fly as a passenger on a single bombing mission, but he was a congressman and MacArthur knew how to deal with such people). Joe McCarthy, like Kennedy, was awarded a Purple Heart for wounds received in combat, only in his case it was for a broken leg, injured when he fell downstairs at a party (no doubt drunk). He bullied the Pentagon into awarding him a Distinguished Flying Cross for flying twenty-five combat missions or more: he had been on none.[26] Given such behaviour, Kennedy would have thought it madness not to make the most of *PT 109*, and with his father's help he did so spectacularly. The writer John Hersey, a family friend, wrote an article about the adventure for the *New Yorker*; it was reprinted in *Reader's Digest* and then, as Kennedy said, 'in every campaign I ever ran in we had millions of copies of the Hersey article scattered around.'[27] In this way it was made plain to the American people that he was not just a rich kid: he had grit; he stuck by his friends.

Kennedy did not mind being a hero; it boosted his already notable self-assurance; but he was no boaster, and he was surprised, even amused, when in 1961 Robert J. Donovan decided to write a book on *PT 109*. However, he saw how useful the project could be to him, and was entirely co-operative. Later he took a leading hand in bringing about the movie based on Donovan's book, supervising the script and the casting, and making sure that it did not damage the Kennedy administration (but he over-reached himself, and the movie flopped).[28] It was a typical piece of Kennedy image-building. Similarly, in spite of his wife's genuine, and his own affected, love of privacy, he made sure that he got every squeezable drop of publicity out of his marriage and his children, even to the degree of taking a press photographer on his honeymoon in 1953. His promiscuous sex life, on the other hand, though an open secret in Washington, was kept out of the news with amazing success. The revelations of later years have done more than anything else to damage his reputation, but in the short run the legend of John F. Kennedy the devoted family man was put over as efficiently as that of the naval hero, and served its turn by increasing his availability.

There was also the legend of Kennedy the athlete: the yachts-man, the touch footballer, the swimming star, the football star who got his letter at Harvard. The truth was that his sport-ing triumphs, yachting apart, were at best minor (he had to miss the swimming match against Yale because of ill-health and seems to have got his 'minor H' at football solely because of the casual kindness of the coach – rather as LBJ got his Silver Star).[29] His health made anything better impossible. He seems to have been born with an asymmetrical frame: he was longer on one side of his skeleton than on the other, and this mal-proportion, aggravated by his reckless attitude to his body and his determination to excel physically, soon led to chronic, and eventually to life-threatening, back problems. Still worse was his Addison's Disease, a deficiency of the adrenal glands which seems to have been congenital (his sister Eunice is reported to have the same condition). This disease is no doubt the expla-nation of Kennedy's sickliness as a child: Addison's weakens the immune system, and young Jack contracted every ailment that was going. As a result he spent weeks and months of his youth alone in a sick-room, which frustrated him horribly but also made him an obsessive reader and writer (which would be of enormous value to him in politics). His service in the Navy, when he spared his body nothing, was ruinous both to his back and to his glands: he was invalided out in 1945, and for the next ten years fought what at times seemed a hopeless battle against his debility, which was not even diagnosed as Addison's until 1947. Fortunately cortisone was just being introduced, and when, during the 1950s, an oral form of this drug became available, the disease ceased to be a major problem: cortisone could not cure it, but could mitigate most of its effects. The back was another matter: neither surgery, nor drugs, nor the famous rocking-chair could regenerate Kennedy's spine; not until he became president and came into the care of Army doctors was there any significant improvement. By 1963 a strict regime of massage and swimming had given Kennedy some-thing much nearer the health normal to a man of his age than seemed likely at any earlier point of his political career. Bobby Kennedy had every reason to remark, after Jack's death, that 'At least one half of the days that he spent on this earth were days of intense physical pain,'[30] but just before he went to

Dallas Kennedy remarked that he felt better than he had for years.

He had to protect his back by always wearing a supportive corset; he had to wear a shoe with a built-up sole so that he could walk easily and not strain his muscles by going lop-sided; he needed daily doses of cortisone and could not undertake a dozen simple physical actions. He remarked of his little son that 'he's going to carry me before I carry him,'[31] and in 1961 was not able to plant a ceremonial tree without putting out his back and plunging himself into acute agony which lasted for months. There was thus enormous irony in the circumstance that in 1960 he 'won' the first of his four televised debates with Richard Nixon because Nixon, convalescent from a minor injury to his knee, looked a wreck, while Kennedy seemed to be bursting with health and vigour.

The vigour, at least, was real enough. Like all the Kennedys, Jack was naturally a fountain of energy and appetite for life. It was lucky for him that he also possessed the sunny temperament of his grandfather Honey Fitz: it enabled him to bear his various trials with astonishing serenity (though it seems to have been wearing thin in the mid-1950s, when his back was at its worst: he became so irritable that his devoted secretary, Evelyn Lincoln, thought about leaving him). He had no intention of surrendering to his ailments: rather, he fought them with the same iron-hard will that had seen him through the war in the Pacific. He seems to have entertained political dreams, if not precise and settled ambitions, as early as 1942.[32] It was natural enough. Both his parents believed in the merits of public life, and though the ambassador was above all a businessman, politics was his real love. He would have liked to be president himself, but having spoiled his chances (never good), he came to centre all his ambitions on his eldest son. When young Joe died in combat in the last year of the war, to his father's overwhelming grief, it seemed only proper that Jack should step into his place. Jack was quite willing. He was still youthfully shy and introverted; at his best in small groups, disliking the effusiveness of democratic politics; but all his training, as student, amateur diplomatic officer, author, sailor and journalist (he had worked briefly for the Hearst papers after being invalided out of the Navy), had been equipping him, designedly or not, for a political career. His competitive instinct – strong in all the Kennedys – was aroused: he had again been challenged to prove himself. So he ran for Congress even though he knew he was threatened with a life of, at best, semi-invalidism; and he never admitted that he might not survive to complete the course. He became a fatalist, if naval service had not made him one already; he seems to have been convinced that he would die young; he grabbed his fun where he could find it; he was indifferent to physical risk (was not his whole life a gamble?) and showed it by his terrifyingly reckless driving; and he never let prudence stop him when he wanted something. It was imprudent to challenge Henry Cabot Lodge Jr for the Senate in 1952; older heads, including his father, thought him unwise to try for the vice-presidential nomination in 1956; and there was a measure of effrontery in so young a man reaching for the presidency in 1960. Kennedy ignored all such considerations. He was not sure how much time he had; for him, imprudence was the only sensible thing.

This attitude was, no doubt, part of his charm, but, had it been brought home to the American people, might well have frustrated his presidential candidacy. Only a nation of hypochondriacs could have considered Kennedy's ill-health a definitive disqualification for office; he was less of an invalid than Franklin Roosevelt, who had not done badly in his time. Even had all the facts been known either in 1944 or in 1960 it might still have made sense to elect the Roosevelt–Truman and Kennedy–Johnson tickets, rather than Dewey–Bricker or Nixon–Lodge. But it is easy to frighten the American public about medical matters, and in both years the truth was carefully concealed. This was especially prudent in 1960, for FDR had been a known quantity with a formidable record. Kennedy was still being discovered, and it would have been reasonable to ask if it would be wise to elect a man with so casual an attitude to speed limits. The Republicans would have asked it at the top of their voices.

The curious thing is that the recklessness was only part of the story, and seems to have affected Kennedy solely in what concerned himself alone. During the late 1950s those who cared to enquire got to know a man whose essential political attitude was one of careful deliberation. As the Eisenhower years sleepily multiplied he became convinced that it was time, as his famous slogan would have it, to get America moving again. But the movement which he had in mind would have nothing of the doctrinaire, impulsive quality which (for example) was to characterise Margaret Thatcher's innovations during her premiership. Kennedy, except in *Why England Slept*, was slow to acknowledge the influence of Franklin Roosevelt, his father's patron and enemy; but no politician of his generation could escape that influence, and it taught him not only that there was much great work for government to do, but also that it could best be achieved by the cool and skilful application of the political arts. Inspiring public leadership was one thing: he valued it very highly, and became one of its supreme exponents; but his instinct told him that opportunities for bold advance came infrequently. In the day-to-day work of politics caution was the watchword, for improvements could come only piecemeal and on a small scale, one step at a time, and even they could be jeopardised by carelessness. No doubt he knew *Roosevelt: the lion and the fox*, by his own first biographer, James MacGregor Burns. Kennedy's career would also be an illustration of Machiavelli's maxim that as events require, the prince must be the one and then the other.

It is impossible to say when Kennedy first looked ahead to the day when he might become the prince. In 1947, having entered Congress, his immediate concern was to consolidate his hold on the Eleventh District in Boston. Like all good American politicians, he set to work to build a record. He did so efficiently, but without distinction. He scrupulously obeyed Sam Rayburn's celebrated advice, and voted his district, with the result that he compiled a solid liberal – that is, New Deal – voting score on matters such as veterans' housing and labour issues (he was one of the devoted handful voting to sustain President Truman's unsuccessful veto of the Taft–Hartley Act), while vociferating heartily the anti-communist, anti-subversion rhetoric of those years. North Boston would see no contradiction in these attitudes, though Cambridge (also part of his district), the seat of Harvard, might. There is no reason to think that Kennedy was merely opportunistic. When he first began to think about his political career he read up the labour question assiduously, and as to anti-communism, it was gospel to almost all American Catholics at that time (with the hierarchy taking the lead) and emphatically so to Ambassador Kennedy. Through Eunice Kennedy, Joe McCarthy became a friend of the family, including Jack. But these early allegiances now look less significant (a man can change his opinions, and this one was to do so) than the congressman's frequent absenteeism. He was a phenomenally quick study, who could easily get up a subject when necessary, and he knew how to make the headlines too; but he soon became bored with the House of Representatives, in part because its individual members had so little power ('we were just worms,' he said some years later),[33] and in part because he was as yet little interested in domestic issues. He was frequently missing, both from roll call votes and from committee hearings, being away after pleasure or to receive medical treatment, and on one occasion gave Congressman John McCormack, the head of the rival Boston political clan, the chance to score:

> he sat down with a group of congressmen considering housing legislation, looked around elaborately for the absent Kennedy, held aloft a Boston newspaper headlining a Kennedy demand for more housing, and asked, 'Where's Johnny? Where's Johnny?'[34]

Only once did Kennedy take a markedly individual line, when McCormack asked him to sign a petition to get James Michael Curley out of jail. Curley (who continued to act as Mayor of Boston from his cell) had long ago ended the effective political career of Kennedy's grandfather, Honey Fitz, by threatening to make public his adultery; Honey Fitz's grandson probably thought it would be carrying magnanimity to unnecessary lengths to help spring the old reprobate (Curley had been sentenced for fraudulent use of the mails). But Curley was still immensely popular in Boston; he had been Kennedy's immediate predecessor in the Eleventh District, and Ambassador Kennedy had subscribed to his mayoralty campaign, which got him out of the House and cleared the way for Jack. So it took some courage to refuse McCormack. More important, the action announced that Kennedy was going to be a new kind of Irish-American politician. The old tribal loyalties had given him his start in politics, and he would continue to exploit them to the end; he was on excellent terms with the professional politicians of Boston, but he was determined not to be mistaken for one of them, even in small things. In his youth he had enjoyed collecting headgear of all kinds, but when once he had discovered that every Irish-American politician in Boston was known by his hat, he abandoned the things, and became famous instead for the dashing way in which he always went hatless, even in blizzards.

Foreign affairs were still his first love and the field of his greatest expertise. As a journalist, he had covered the opening session of the United Nations at San Francisco in 1945, and the British general election of that year; James Forrestal, the secretary of the Navy, had taken him to the Potsdam conference; in 1951 he had travelled to Europe and the Far East (including Vietnam), which had helped to modify the stridency of his views on Truman's foreign policy (but the most important legacy of the Far Eastern journey was that it brought him really close, for the first time, to his brother Bobby, who was one of his travelling companions). There was not much scope in foreign affairs for a junior congressman; but then Kennedy never contemplated making a career in the House. To be happy in that chamber you have to have something of a small-town temperament, of which Kennedy had no trace. He very soon decided to run for statewide office, and while waiting for the right opportunity pioneered what became his central political technique, of accepting every invitation from anywhere in Massachusetts to speak to any group about anything. 'I'll bet he talked to at least a million people and shook hands with seven hundred and fifty thousand,' said one of the family retainers. James MacGregor Burns accepts the claim as not much exaggerated.[35]

Building on this foundation, he ran successfully for the US Senate in 1952, and was elected with a majority of 70,000 votes (51.5 per cent of those cast for senator). It was a notable if narrow victory: 1952 was the worst year for Democrats since 1928. They lost the presidency and their majority in both Houses of Congress; in Massachusetts they also lost the governorship. So Kennedy had reason to be pleased with himself. He seems to have owed his triumph to an accumulation of favourable local factors: he had, as it were, a hand full of small trumps. But they would have gone for nothing without the unremitting efforts of the candidate and his family. Defying his back pain, which was getting worse than ever, Kennedy announced his candidacy in early April, and thereafter never let up until election night. His opponent, the incumbent senator Henry Cabot Lodge Jr, by contrast started late and never really hit his stride.[36] As in 1946, Kennedy unleashed his mother and his siblings. Rose Kennedy was particularly effective, speaking about her wonderful son to dozens of tea-parties and coffee-mornings, which were all the more successful when the wonderful son himself turned up to bask (willingly, no doubt) in female adoration. And young Bobby (aged 27) proved to be a superb campaign manager: he was as energetic as his brother, and under no compulsion to be nice to anyone who got in the way of the campaign.

Perhaps that was why Bobby was brought in: he was the only person who could stand up to his father.[37] Nevertheless the 1952 campaign was Joseph Kennedy's masterpiece. He called in all his political debts; he mobilised his numerous right-wing, Republican friends in Massachusetts; he kept a close eye on all decisions, strategic or tactical, and engineered the dismissal of at least one of Jack's closest advisers; and nobody knows how much he spent, or how he did it (the official cost of the Kennedy campaign was reported at approximately $350,000, but no one believed that was the whole story). He was by now a Democrat only in name (he had contributed money to the re-election campaigns of both Robert A. Taft and Joe McCarthy; though also to the presidential campaign of Adlai Stevenson) and would have liked his son to run as an avowedly anti-Truman, isolationist candidate, since Lodge, in defiance of his own family traditions, was a notable internationalist. Jack dared not offend the many Massachusetts liberals by adopting any such posture; anyway it can have had no appeal to the author of *Why England Slept.*

Equally he could not prudently annoy his Irish and Catholic constituents, his natural base, by taking an explicitly anti-McCarthyite position. Nor did he want to do so: although he recognised that McCarthy's denunciations were unnecessary, he may not have recognised that they were nothing but lies, and he certainly did not yet accept that they were a threat to American democracy. He liked McCarthy personally, and soon after the election angrily denounced a speaker at a Harvard function who drew a parallel between Alger Hiss and McCarthy: 'How dare you couple the name of a great American patriot with that of a traitor!'[38] Young Mr Kennedy still had a lot to learn: he was still very much his father's son and the congressman from Boston; but both to win the senatorial election and to stay elected he had to move to loftier ground. Probably the best service the ambassador rendered was to use his contacts to keep Joe McCarthy out of Massachusetts during the campaign. The great demagogue was at the height of his popularity; Jack Kennedy could not afford to be either attacked or supported by him, and so long as he did not appear in the state, neither would happen.

Yet as was shown by the emergence of Bobby, and various other straws in the wind, a genuine change was at hand. From 1952 onwards Joe Kennedy's influence grew less and less weighty, as the senator became more and more his own man. The needs and wishes of his constituents, now enlarged to include all the citizens of Massachusetts, necessarily began to shape much of his political course; he had to study the state's grave economic problems closely, in order to make plausible his campaign claim that he could do more for Massachusetts, and having been elected his studies had to continue. He found also that Massachusetts was so much part of the wider region of New England that to make any progress he would need to take on board the problems of Connecticut, Rhode Island, Maine, New Hampshire and Vermont as well as those of his own state. And he also quickly realised that to be the Senator from New England, to extend his support throughout the Yankee states, was not only good senatorial politics: it was good presidential politics too. His studies went on successfully, and though he never felt at home with agricultural issues he was otherwise a master of domestic policy by 1960, and positively relished the challenge of economics. The whole process steered him steadily away from his father's wishes, his father's opinions, and his father's men.

Until 1953 he had been content to work with a team that was largely chosen by Ambassador Kennedy, and was almost wholly drawn from the ranks of streetwise Irish Bostonians. Kennedy got on very well with all of them, but he was quite ruthless in judging which would still be valuable to him now that he was in the Senate, and which would not. Of the original team only David Powers stayed with him to the end, as a sort of court jester; the rest of the famous 'Irish Mafia' – Larry O'Brien, Kenneth O'Donnell, Ralph Dungan and others – were recruited separately, either for the 1952 campaign or in the years immediately following; they were the senator's men, not the ambassador's. It was another necessary assertion of independence, and one that Jack was glad to make. He had never liked the knowledge that some of the people round him were spying on all his actions and reporting back to his father.

Larry O'Brien was an immensely valuable recruit, a man of vast political skill, as his career during and after Kennedy's presidency was to demonstrate; but in 1953 an even more important associate came on board. Theodore Sorensen is usually described as Kennedy's speechwriter, but from the first he was much more than that. He was hired to help the senator think as well as to help him speak. It was his business to master all the information and issues of the day and so enable Kennedy to take up and defend political positions. His relationship to his employer was something like that of an English solicitor to a barrister: he briefed Kennedy for appearances in court, or at any rate on the stage of politics. He was also Kennedy's ghost, drafting most of the articles with which the senator kept his name before the public as a thoughtful and well-informed young statesman. It was a common enough practice (and has become more common since) and probably did little harm. The intimate collaboration which it entailed between the two men educated both of them. Sorensen was a Mid-Western progressive of the most authentic strain (his Republican father had been close to Senator George Norris, the patron of the Tennessee Valley Authority); even younger than Robert Kennedy (he was 24), he was deeply committed, in the New Deal tradition, to using government to help the unfortunate, if necessary by structural political and economic reform. Kennedy, as befitted a Bostonian, had always voted correctly, from Sorensen's point of view, in the House of Representatives; it was not hard to enlarge his vision and encourage him to take still bolder steps. It was agreeable work to help widen the gap opening between Senator Kennedy and Senator McCarthy.[39] In return Kennedy taught Sorensen the rules and requirements of practical politics.

The election to the Senate was part of a general stock-taking and tidying up in Kennedy's life. In September 1953, he married Jacqueline Bouvier, which brought about a new stability, even if it did not end his ragamuffin philandering. Husband and wife were to take their secrets to the grave where they lie together, but it seems safe to say that although the marriage was often stormy, it was of the greatest importance to both of them, and for Jack, after the arrival of his two children, something that was ever more valuable. Mrs Kennedy was not the normal politician's wife, and never learned to like the campaign trail; but her very waywardness (from the Capitol Hill point of view) set her apart, and, like her beauty and her elegance, proved that Jack Kennedy had married no ordinary woman. In the eyes of the American public, the Kennedys had 'class'. Jack tried to fortify the impression by giving up the casual, indeed scruffy garments of his bachelorhood and became instead something of a dandy. He also tried to do something radical about his back trouble – something that would liberate him, if not from pain, at least from crutches. He underwent two dangerous and agonising spinal operations. It was no good: the improvement was minimal. But while recuperating he read incessantly, as so often before, and the idea of a book began to germinate.

The biographers regularly remark that Kennedy was not really an intellectual, just as his Bostonian cronies insist that he was not really a liberal; but it might just as usefully be said that he was not really a politician. If he could be outstandingly genial and exuberant, a person of infectious warmth whom all his associates remember fondly, he could also be notably withdrawn if he found himself in a false position. Indeed, Larry O'Brien thought that at this time he was still not a natural politician: 'he was too reserved, too private. To stand at a factory gate and shake hands was never easy.'[40] But shaking hands was an art that could be and had to be and was learned. Kennedy saw more spontaneously the need of establishing his credentials as a thinking man if he was to get beyond the Senate (and, from the first, he meant to). He had a marked academic strain. He called in J.K. Galbraith to teach him economics, at which he proved a quick study; and now from his sick-bed he summoned Sorensen to help him with his next major self-defining achievement.

Profiles in Courage is a larger but thinner work than *Why England Slept*, and reads all too much like the series of magazine articles that it might well have been. It consists mainly of eight essays on as many politicians, all of them members of the US Senate in the nineteenth and twentieth centuries, who had to struggle with the problem which Kennedy had first put to himself in *Why England Slept*: what must a democratic statesman do when his party and his constituents want something which his judgement insists is dangerously wrong? The senators discussed all did the right thing, or what they thought was the right thing, by following their own judgements; history has not always vindicated them (Robert A. Taft's protest against the Nuremberg tribunal does not seem particularly wise). Many of them paid a heavy political price. It was an interesting idea for a book. Unfortunately neither Kennedy nor Sorensen (the acknowledged 'research associate' and unacknowledged co-author) was sufficiently master of historical scholarship to get beneath the surface of the stories, which as a result are little more than compilations of entertaining anecdotes. The book is of importance today only because, like its predecessor, it is strongly autobiographical; but that is enough. Read as a document about John F. Kennedy, *Profiles in Courage* is nothing less than fascinating.

It is a scissors-and-paste job, which for pages at a time might as well have no author at all. But Kennedy's introductory essay, 'Courage and Politics', is another matter: it is much more avowedly personal than *Why England Slept*, and wonderfully candid. Whatever Sorensen's hand in it, it is the voice of Jack Kennedy speaking. In places it has the easy humour of his youthful letters to his friend LeMoyne Billings:

> If we tell our constituents frankly that we can do nothing, they feel we are unsympathetic or inadequate. If we try and fail – usually meeting a counteraction from other Senators representing other interests – they say we are like all the rest of the politicians. All we can do is retreat into the Cloakroom and weep on the shoulder of a sympathetic colleague – or go home and snarl at our wives.[41]

But it reveals most in its argument. Professedly the introduction to a series of essays praising political courage, it is in substance an apologia for the arts of political compromise. Better a half-good bill, or even a poor bill, than no bill at all, says the author at one point.[42] The hero of this chapter is not one of the intransigent giants of politics – not John Quincy Adams – but the Great Compromiser, Henry Clay. Here Kennedy speaks from deep political and personal conviction, which went back a long way. It had not received full expression in *Why England Slept* because it would have looked too much like an attempt to exonerate Baldwin and Chamberlain. In *Profiles*, Kennedy was free to make his points: that the pressures brought to bear on a democratic statesman are mostly legitimate; they are, anyway, very strong; it makes no sense to fight them incessantly, for that way you only condemn yourself to premature retirement. Politics is a matter of riding the storm, and of securing the best result you can. On the other hand, Kennedy genuinely respects courage and integrity. As is shown in Chapter 2, which he also had the largest hand in writing, he is fascinated by John Adams and John Quincy Adams, since in so many respects they could be seen as forerunners of Joseph P. and John F. Kennedy; like the English Whigs, they set a standard to which the senator

aspired. But no one less like the wheeler-dealer Kennedys than
the granite Puritans of Braintree can well be imagined. So Jack
Kennedy sees the integrity of the younger Adam's career, genuinely respects it, commends it to his readers, but remains puzzled by it; even, if he had let himself admit it, unconvinced.
Nor was he wrong: it is hard to feel that Adams's support for
Jefferson's embargo, which cost him his Senate seat, was any
use either to America or to Massachusetts; but it relaunched
John Quincy's diplomatic career.

This was the choice between the lion and the fox again, and
if Kennedy had not resolved it, at least he was facing it intellectually as well as politically. What this meant is perhaps seen
most clearly in the chapter on Edmund G. Ross and the other
Republican senators whose votes saved President Andrew
Johnson at his impeachment in 1868. Kennedy does not doubt
that the impeachment was a mischievous and dangerous intrigue, tending to undermine the Constitution; but the point
he insists on is that Ross, Fessenden and the others were determined to see that Johnson got a fair trial: 'I wish all my friends
and constituents to understand that I, and not they, am sitting
in judgment upon the President. I, not they, have sworn to do
impartial justice. I, not they, am responsible to God and man
for my action and its consequence.'[43] This is surely Fessenden
making a point for Kennedy, offering an explanation of why in
1954 that gentleman had not voted to censure Joe McCarthy.
He was too ill to appear in person (the vote took place just
after his first operation, which had been such a near thing
that he had received Extreme Unction) but his failure even to
arrange a pair, so that he could be recorded, was to cost him
dear; he wrote about Ross by way of indirect apologia. It was
not, perhaps, a very convincing apologia. Certainly McCarthy
should only have been debated and judged constitutionally
and legally; his fellow senators were under an absolute obligation to respect those decencies which he himself so repeatedly
flouted; and as Kennedy later put it to Arthur Schlesinger Jr,
'If somebody is not there, why should they be allowed a judgement on it?'[44] But the real reasons which compelled Kennedy
to do as little as he possibly could against McCarthy were his
family's close ties with the man, especially his father's; the strong
support for McCarthy in Massachusetts (the Boston *Post* accused
all the New England senators who voted against McCarthy of
having done just what 'the Kremlin' wanted),[45] and, above all,

Kennedy's own ambiguities and misperceptions. He was not much wiser than many other Americans of the time, and seems really to have believed (as he stated on many occasions) that communist subversion in the United States was a serious danger. He therefore approved of the witch-hunters' goal, and was not, apparently, much upset by their methods. Some years later he conceded, 'Perhaps we were not as sensitive as some and should have acted sooner.'[46] It was not much of a concession, and referred only to the Senate's sluggishness in handling McCarthy; it somewhat recalls Richard Nixon's belated and grudging admission of sin in the matter of the Watergate affair. And as to Senators Ross and Fessenden, they defied their constituents, while Kennedy surrendered to some of his. All in all, the entire business sufficiently explains why Kennedy had to work so hard to win the confidence of the liberal Democrats when he discovered, as he soon did, that he needed them, and was indeed compelled to take up most of their positions.

Not that *Profiles in Courage* shows any sign of this movement. It was not put together without careful political calculation, and Kennedy was well aware that no Democrat was likely to win his party's presidential nomination without support from the South, let alone the presidential election. So none of the heroes celebrated in the book was a northern Democrat, and Kennedy found it all too possible to say unkind things about the abolitionists and kind things about John C. Calhoun (he was unaware of the revolution in the historiography of slavery, the Civil War and Reconstruction that was gathering pace even as he wrote, and was going to make his view of that era untenable). He is notably charitable towards Robert A. Taft, but there may have been some self-identification at work: 'I recall,' he says, '. . . my strong impression of a surprising and unusual personal charm, and a disarming simplicity of manner. It was these qualities, combined with an unflinching courage which he exhibited throughout his entire life and most especially in his last days, that bound his adherents to him with unbreakable ties.'[47] He included a photography of the indomitable Taft using the crutches that carried him into the Senate chamber in those last days: they were like the pair which Kennedy often had to use himself. Kennedy was bidding, throughout the book, for the approval of the Centre and the moderate Right; of the South and the Mid-West. In the central Eisenhower years he did not foresee that the Left would before long regain the initiative; and indeed he was to win the presidential nomination in part because, to the leaders of the southern Democrats, he seemed the least radical of the northerners. *Profiles in Courage* apparently proved it.

But the abiding impression left by the book is very different. Whether speaking up for courage or compromise or both (the acts of courage which he praises tend to be the deeds of moderates resisting extremists) the senator is ceaselessly reflecting on the nature and skill of political leadership, and his conclusion is the sound if banal one that at the end of the day the highest law is the good of the nation: when that is at stake the statesman must be prepared to defy all pressures, even if defiance entails temporary or permanent political defeat. This was Kennedy's creed, and in the years to come he tried consistently to live up to it. It was his central act of self-definition, and expressed his strong desire to lead for America. It was – it could only be – the stance of an aspirant to the presidency, and demonstrates forcibly how far he had come since he had almost lackadaisically agreed to run for Congress, ten years previously. The fierce competitive drive which his parents had instilled in all their children was now completely engaged – not surprisingly, when we consider that politics had been Kennedy's world for most of his adult life.

Few of the reviewers, if any, noticed the bestseller's subtext: works of popular history seldom get the serious analysis that they may deserve. Instead, Kennedy found that the book's success had tumbled him into another scrape.

He had used Sorensen to draft the profiles as he used him to write his speeches and articles, and parts of the book reflected the speechwriter's interests as well as the senator's. It had not occurred to Kennedy that he might be acting unethically. Everyone on Capitol Hill knew that *Crime in America*, a recent bestseller by Senator Kefauver, had largely been written for Kefauver by his staff, though his name alone had appeared on the title page. The practice might be hard on unworldly readers, but it made sound commercial sense: *Profiles* would have had much less market appeal had it sailed as a collaboration by Kennedy and Sorensen rather than as the work (however assisted) of a young war-hero-scholar-senator writing on his own. Similarly, in the nineteenth century, one of the most famous of all novels, *The Three Musketeers*, passed as the exclusive work of Alexandre Dumas, since his collaborator and research assistant was too

obscure and dull a writer to merit full, or indeed any, acknowledgement. Besides, Sorensen was not paid to make his own
literary reputation. The difficulty came when the book won the
Pulitzer Prize for biography. Kennedy had not sought it (though
there are dark rumours that his father nobbled the jury) but
he did not refuse it: winning the Pulitzer was one of the proudest
moments of his life. Even if the notion of a refusal had crossed
his mind, it would have had to be instantly rejected, for the only
grounds for such a gesture would be that he was not the sole
author of the book: he would have accused himself of fraudu-
lence, with hideous damage to his reputation, even though in
most senses he *was* the author (and if the labours of the literary deconstructionists have done nothing else of value, they
have at least shown just how tricky a concept 'authorship' is):
to accuse himself would be to accuse an innocent man. After
all, even the chapter on George Norris, which is the most indu-
bitably Sorensenian, emphasises the Protestant senator's virtue
in supporting Al Smith, a Catholic, for the presidency in 1928:
a Kennedy touch. The moral dilemma, then, was posed not by
the deed itself but, as so often in American life since, by the
cover-up which followed when journalists began to ask sharp
questions. Drew Pearson actually asserted that Sorensen was
the real author. Kennedy had no choice. As he remarked to
Sorensen, who counselled caution, 'This challenges my ability
to write the book, my honesty in signing it, and my integrity in
accepting the Pulitzer Prize.'[48] He might have said, as Dumas
did, 'I have collaborators the way Napoleon had generals,' but
on such matters it is unsafe to jest with the high-minded American press. So he felt that he had to fight, he had to lie, and
having won his case (Drew Pearson allowed himself to be persuaded that he had been wrong) he and Sorensen were committed for the rest of their lives to the pretence that there was
nothing in the least problematic about the authorship of the
book. It is all very comprehensible, but it throws an ironic light
on the phrase 'profiles in courage'. At least this senator had
the courage to brazen out an emergency.

He spent most of his time after 1957 in chasing the presidency. He secured his home base by firmly asserting control of
the Democratic party in Massachusetts, and set out to make
himself known to Democrats throughout America, partly by
continuing his blizzard of newspaper and magazine articles, and
partly by adapting his Massachusetts technique to an even larger

stage, and accepting as many speaking invitations as possible. It meant being a largely absentee senator, but that consideration never stopped him from taking to the road – or rather, to the air. In later years Ted Sorensen (who was usually at his side) had fond memories of Kennedy working the windscreen wipers of small planes by hand while the rain pelted down, or peering down from the co-pilot's seat looking for a landing-strip, or of himself holding a defective door shut all the way from Phoenix to Denver. According to Sorensen they were in real danger only once, when on a flight to Reno their plane nearly turned turtle as they came in to land at an airstrip in the Rockies. They completed that journey by moonlight in another single-engine plane, the pilot assuring them all the way that one engine was quite as safe as two. They landed at one end of Reno airport

> just as the Democratic dignitaries and brass band awaiting us marched out to meet a more dignified twin-engine plane at the other end of the field bearing two surprised industrialists.[49]

It was a relief to Sorensen when in 1959 Joseph Kennedy gave his son a plane of his own, named *Caroline* after Jack's young daughter; and the senator came to find it so convenient that during the 1960 primaries he wondered condescendingly how the unaffluent Hubert Humphrey could manage without one.

This ceaseless journeying (James MacGregor Burns estimates that in 1957 alone Kennedy gave at least 150 talks 'throughout the country', and in 1958 'probably two hundred more')[50] gave him a wide if superficial knowledge of the United States, but its purpose was less to get to know America than to enable America to get to know him. By his willingness to turn out for Democratic candidates anywhere, anytime, he proved himself to be an organisation stalwart (Richard Nixon was making the same point to Republicans about himself throughout the 1950s); by his charm and his Sorensen-assisted eloquence he convinced many doubters that here indeed was a possible president. He did not confine his attention to the rank-and-file. 'I've learned that you don't get far in politics until you become a total politician. That means you've got to deal with the party leaders as well as with the voters. From now on, I'm going to be a total politician.'[51] He had reached the Senate by building a separate Kennedy organisation; in faction-ridden Massachusetts he had

had no choice; but to win the presidency would require less of a Lone Ranger approach.[52] He struck oil when the great Catholic leaders began to come over. They had been among the most resolute doubters, believing that anti-Catholic bigotry, if roused by Kennedy at the head of the ticket, would injure Catholic candidates for lesser offices, but gradually they began to realise that Kennedy was a quite different type from Al Smith. They were particularly impressed by his overwhelming re-election victory in 1958. After that John Bailey of Connecticut knew that Kennedy would carry New England, and Dick Daley of Chicago thought he might carry Illinois. Daley had been a close associate of Adlai Stevenson, but now Stevenson assured him that he was not in the race. Daley felt free to back Kennedy, and became active in persuading other Catholic and urban bosses to do the same. He was assisted by Kennedy's excellent record in the eyes of organised labour, a fount of funds and campaign workers: Kennedy had been extremely effective in watering down the Landrum–Griffin bill, an anti-union measure that became law in 1959 thanks to the congressional coalition between Republicans and southern Democrats.

The 1960 race was in many respects determined by the transition that was under way from one political system to another, and Kennedy was the beneficiary. Bosses were no longer omnipotent, if they ever had been, but they still carried great weight, and Kennedy was prudent to cultivate them. But there were also the primaries, and only they could demonstrate that he could overcome the religious handicap (of which boss support was if anything a reminder) by proving that he had greater appeal to the voters than any other Democrat. Fortunately, in this transition period, he did not need to enter more than a sample of the primaries: they were not the only means of accumulating convention delegates. Still, it would not do to win only those primaries where he had token opposition or none. He needed a fight, and a victory, and thanks to Hubert Humphrey he was given both.

As creative a politician as he was ebullient, perceptive, decent and slightly naive, Humphrey was in some respects the best of the Democrats competing in 1960. But it was not his year, though for long he refused to accept the fact. Coming from Minnesota, where he was impregnable, he believed that he stood a good chance of carrying the primary in the next-door state of Wisconsin. Kennedy agreed, and would have given much to stay out of that particular race, but there was no avoiding the challenge. Wisconsin Democrats were mostly rural, liberal and Protestant; they all knew and liked Humphrey, and they had voted against that other Catholic-Irish senator, the recently deceased Joe McCarthy. For these very reasons Kennedy had to go in. If he could do respectably in Wisconsin he would indeed have demonstrated his availability: the candidate who could win in Wisconsin, a state as representative of 'Middle America' as any in the Union, could win anywhere between the Hudson and the Rockies. Kennedy did indeed win, but not by very much: perhaps because of anti-Catholic prejudice, perhaps because he was too much the rich, urban easterner, perhaps because of Humphrey's popularity. The victory was inconclusive, and might have done little for Kennedy's campaign except that its very narrowness kept Humphrey's hopes alive, so that he gave his rival what he needed. He entered the West Virginian primary.

West Virginia was one of the most Protestant and most corrupt of all the states. For that reason it gave Kennedy a wonderful chance. If he could win against Humphrey there he would have laid the religious bogey to rest; and win he did. Both sides resorted to dirty tricks which they were afterwards sorry for, but when all was over there could be no doubt about the meaning of the result. Kennedy took 61 per cent of the vote; he carried all but seven counties; he won among the farmers, the miners and the blacks. And above all he won because the Democrats of West Virginia were anxious to prove that they were no bigots.

After that the nomination was just about guaranteed. Neither Lyndon Johnson nor Senator Stuart Symington – a colourless politician who might have been the party's candidate if Kennedy and Johnson had eliminated each other – had tried to beat Kennedy in the primaries, though they too needed to demonstrate their availability, Johnson because he was widely known as a Washington wheeler-dealer, not very trustworthy, and because he was so much a Southerner, and Symington because he was without a national following. They had allowed themselves to believe that the convention would be controlled by their friends, the power-brokers, whereas Kennedy had been coldly realistic from the start. Nothing in his life had taught him to take comfort in illusions (he would have detested the Camelot myth had it developed in his lifetime) and he was perhaps a little surprised at the soft-headedness of his competitors.

Symington and Johnson had not got down to the hard work of counting delegates: he had. Adlai Stevenson had shown, again and again, touches of vanity, irresolution and aloofness that made it hard to believe that he would make an effective candidate in a tight year; besides, he had been beaten twice already. Who else was left? The party could turn only to Kennedy, now that he had his small but sufficient majority of delegates, won in the primaries and in hard negotiation with the bosses. True, if the party leaders knew his rivals' weaknesses they also knew Kennedy's; but then, so did he. Unlike the other hopefuls, he judged himself as coolly and dispassionately as he did his competition, and his years on the campaign trail had been undertaken expressly to correct his drawbacks. It is a striking feature of the 1960 election that no other Democrat made a similar effort until it was far too late.

So Kennedy went to the convention in San Francisco with enough votes to be nominated on the first ballot, which was just as well, for he could not count on all his delegates standing firm in a second or third. A last-minute attempt to stampede the convention for Stevenson was a complete failure. The leaders of the party began the traditional process of binding up its wounds, a process in which the nominee enthusiastically joined.

His chief contribution came with what turned out to be one of the two or three most important decisions of his career (not that he knew it). He gave the vice-presidential nomination to Lyndon Johnson, in spite of having assured his brother Bobby and anyone else who asked that he would not do so. Like Stevenson's very different decision in 1956, this act is still somewhat mysterious, but the obvious explanation is probably the correct one: Kennedy had made his usual cool calculations, and knew that Johnson would benefit the ticket more than any other candidate. It was essential for the Democrats to maximise their strength in Texas and the rest of the South (where Eisenhower and Nixon had done dangerously well in 1956) and only Johnson could guarantee that. Whether Kennedy assumed that Johnson would accept the offer is another matter, but LBJ had done his own figuring. His extraordinary performance as master of the Senate under an acquiescent Republican president could not be repeated under a Democrat, or even under Richard Nixon; it was time to move on, and the vice-presidency, a national institution, would give him the chance to shed his purely regional identity and re-establish his liberal credentials (this was the man who, within twenty-four hours of Kennedy's death, would remark, 'as a matter of fact, to tell the truth, John F. Kennedy was a little too conservative for my taste').[53] So he grabbed Kennedy's offer, which the nominee then had to justify to his supporters. There were plenty of good arguments besides the electoral one. Johnson was clearly of presidential stature, probably the Democrat best qualified to take over if anything should happen to Kennedy; the choice pleased Sam Rayburn, the powerful Speaker of the House of Representatives (once he had come to see it as the best way of keeping Nixon out of the White House), Harry Truman and the rest of the old guard; and it would eliminate Johnson as a possible troublemaker in the Senate. The liberals, who had nowhere else to go, learned to live with the choice. Robert Kennedy did not. He and Johnson were born to dislike each other; from this moment onwards their mutual detestation steadily deepened, perhaps helped along on Bobby's side by a realisation that in this important matter Jack had not taken him fully into his confidence, indeed had manipulated him. The consequences were to be far-reaching, but still more important was the fact, which nobody could have foreseen, that by this choice Jack Kennedy had secured the eventual triumph of his domestic programme and had also compromised his own historical reputation: for if Johnson, as president, was to push through a progressive agenda with a speed and completeness that Kennedy might never have managed, he was also to plunge the United States into a disastrous war which Kennedy might have avoided. But no such idea crossed anyone's mind as the bargain was sealed and the convention scrambled to complete its business. There was an election to be fought.

Kennedy could not believe that, left to themselves, a majority of the American people would prefer Richard Nixon to him. But they would not be left to themselves. Nixon, too, was a strenuous politician. He was much the better known of the candidates. Democrats might detest him ('Would you buy a used car from this man?' was their favourite joke) but notoriety keeps a politician's name before the public, and for eight years the vice-president had been using his position to strengthen his hold on the Republican party and win the respect of the uncommitted. He was also the heir of the immensely popular Eisenhower. It would be a tough election.

Kennedy dared not attack Ike directly, but he saw his task as that of running against the Eisenhower years at least as hard as against Nixon. For unless he could persuade the voters that a change from Eisenhower's policy and Eisenhower's team was necessary he would almost certainly lose the election, since Eisenhower was still a mighty force, as was shown in the last days of the campaign, when the president took to the stump. According to the opinion polls Kennedy, previously, had been solidly in the lead; now there was what Arthur M. Schlesinger Jr calls 'a strange, imperceptible ebbing away'; at the time Kennedy himself remarked, 'Last week Nixon hit the panic button and started Ike speaking, and with every word he utters I can feel the votes leaving me.'[54] There was little he could do to counter Ike's magic (which, fortunately for Kennedy, was invoked too late); but he could, and did, attack his record. So a lot was made of alleged sins of omission and commission:

> beneath today's surface gloss of peace and prosperity are increasingly dangerous, unsolved, long postponed problems that will inevitably explode to the surface during the next four years of the next administration – the growing missile gap, the rise of Communist China, the despair of the underdeveloped nations, the explosive situations in Berlin and in the Formosa Straits, the deterioration of NATO, the lack of an arms control agreement, and all the domestic problems of our farms, cities, and schools.[55]

These themes, and others, were emphasised throughout the campaign; they do not seem very convincing today, especially not the allegations about a missile gap. On this point, in fairness to Kennedy, it must be said that the existence of this gap was an article of faith among all Democrats, and even among many independent experts: the success of the Soviet Union in launching *Sputnik*, the first space satellite, in 1957, had been a gross shock to American self-confidence, and led to an equally gross overestimation of the achievements and capability of Soviet military technology. Somehow the reassurances of former General Dwight D. Eisenhower, President of the United States and sometime commander of NATO (North Atlantic Treaty Organisation) and the Allied Expeditionary Force in Western Europe, failed to strike home, though they were well founded. Kennedy's speeches on these matters, both before and during the 1960 campaign, with their emphasis on a clear and present danger, read oddly now. In a speech in the Senate in August 1958, he explicitly compared the 1950s in America to the 1930s in Britain, using Stanley Baldwin's phrase, 'the years which the locusts have eaten' (which he subsequently reattributed to Winston Churchill).[56] Next year he likened 1959 to 1939.[57] Today all this seems hopelessly overdrawn.

We need to remind ourselves that we know what Kennedy did not: that there was not going to be a war between the Soviet Union and the United States, and that the Soviet economy was going to collapse totally because of its chronic and incurable inefficiency. All the same, the inconsistencies and contradictions in Kennedy's utterances are obvious; the fact that they were hidden from the speaker and his audiences is now perhaps the most interesting thing about them. Americans were full of both anxiety and self-confidence: they attacked the Eisenhower administration for doing both too little and too much; they were afraid of nuclear ruin, economic collapse and the loss of national independence, but like their young orator they believed that modern American capitalism

> may, from time to time, pause or show weakness. But it is still capable of greater heights than any Mr. Khrushchev has ever seen or imagined. It is still capable of building all the defenses we need *and* all the schools and homes and industries, too – and at the same time helping to build situations of strength and stability throughout the non-Communist world.[58]

Another contradiction, more apparent than real, but also more dangerous, lay in Kennedy's attempt to use his warnings of national danger and weakness as a reason for insisting on the need for negotiation with the Soviet Union. His point was actually a simple one, that nuclear war was so terrible a thing that both sides had an overriding interest in peace, and therefore in diplomacy; he had no intention of negotiating from a position of weakness; but it would be easy for Americans, and others, to misread him; to see him as a Chamberlain rather than a Churchill.

For the time being the speeches served their turn: if Kennedy did not succeed in frightening the American people into believing that they stood on the brink of one of the most dangerous eras in their history, at least he seems to have convinced himself. His urgency could strike nobody as factitious. Yet the judgement must be that if the election had actually turned on these specific issues, he would have deserved to lose (which is not the same as saying that Nixon would have deserved to win).

But Kennedy had three forces working for him which fed each other and in combination gave the victory of 1960 its significance. First was the general feeling of dissatisfaction and anxiety, fed by the recession of 1957–58 and the crisis in Soviet–American relations illustrated by the breakdown of the 1960 summit meeting in Paris over the U2 incident (the Soviet Union had managed to shoot down a U2 spy-plane over its territory, and could not forbear to make the most of this priceless opportunity for propaganda). Americans, perhaps, found it impossible to believe that their peace and prosperity would last; perhaps, in Puritan mode, they wanted to punish themselves for their good luck; anyway Nixon was not half so reassuring a figure as Eisenhower. These anxieties certainly helped the Democrats (and Kennedy, as we see, tried to make them more specific and powerful), but they were not of themselves decisive. However, the effect of anxiety was reinforced by a generational challenge. Ever since the GIs came back from the war in 1945 there had been an anti-establishment current in American politics, which Kennedy had exploited with brilliant success in his Massachusetts contests. Now he made his appeal on a national scale, thereby turning his comparative youth from an electoral weakness into an asset. 'This is still a young country,' he cried on 4 July, 'founded by young men 184 years ago today and it is still young in heart, youthful in spirit, and blessed with new young leaders in both parties, in both houses of Congress, and in governors' chairs throughout the country. The strength and health and vigour of these young men is equally needed in the White House'[59] (and Richard Nixon was not the man to supply them, because though, 'of course' also a young man, 'His approach is as old as McKinley').[60]

These references to strength and vigour were decidedly impudent: audiences would remember Eisenhower's age, his heart attack and his bout of ilietis, and did not know about Kennedy's own health problems. The tactic seems to have worked triumphantly. Kennedy's candidacy gave an opening to all young, high-hearted idealists, many of whom had been inspired by the campaigns of Adlai Stevenson. In the last week of the campaign he launched his proposal for a Peace Corps. The response was immediate and immense; the press approved, Richard Nixon did not ('a program which looks good on the surface – but which is inherently dangerous').[61] It was a defining moment: more than any other in the campaign, perhaps, it expressed what the Kennedy candidacy was about. But Kennedy also attracted into his following a vast number of less altruistic rebels against brass hats and high hats; against all those cautious, conservative politicians born in the nineteenth century who had allowed Joe McCarthy to run wild for so long, and who had left the management of the economy entirely to Wall Street and its allies ('What's good for General Motors is good for America' was an utterance all too clearly recollected) and stood by when the white South fought to preserve white supremacy and racial segregation, and seemed unable to understand or come to grips with the new international problems of the day. It was a feeling rather than a reasoned critique, and Kennedy was excellently placed to exploit it. Not only could he present himself as the successor to Adlai Stevenson; it also did not hurt that he had not been the original choice of the veteran party leadership. The Democrats had their establishment as well as the Republicans; Kennedy could pose as the challenger to both sets, even though he, most unlike Nixon, had been born in the very lap of the American Establishment. And by accepting the strongly liberal party platform, largely drafted by followers of Hubert Humphrey, Kennedy won to himself all that was most idealistic, innovative and energetic in American politics. He even, at last, secured the blessing of Eleanor Roosevelt.

But the deepest drama of 1960 was that of the religious issue. It is perhaps easier in the 1990s, when other religious issues are so urgent, between and within nations, and the politics of multiculturalism is so hotly debated, to understand what was at stake than it was for many at the time or in the years between. In a year when American politics was so strongly shaped by questions of race, class and foreign policy it was hard for many observers and participants to see in the passions raised by 'the religious issue' anything but atavism and obsolescence. Today, when we are so perennially reminded of the power of religion as a way to individual and social identity, we can recognise the immense importance of Kennedy's candidacy and victory, both as a means of understanding the United States in 1960, and as an instrument by which a small measure of genuine social progress was solidly achieved.

Senator Eugene McCarthy, a slightly sour and decidedly

devout observer of the Kennedys, remarked that it was unfortunate that the Catholic candidate was such a bad Catholic. This was unfair. Except possibly with his sister Kathleen, who married outside her country and her faith, Jack was exceedingly reticent about his religious opinions, and if his private life was not exemplary by the standards of any Christian denomination, he scrupulously kept up the observances of the faith, saying his prayers and going regularly to Mass, and he enjoyed good sermons.[62] He refused to describe himself as 'the Catholic candidate', saying that he was not sure he would vote for such a person himself, but against much advice he was prepared explicitly to defend the right of a Catholic to run for the presidency. He would meet the issue head-on, and answer seriously all questions on the matter, even the silliest. It turned out to be good politics, and it was another exercise in self-definition. Whether he liked it or not, he *was* the Catholic candidate, and had to respond to the responsibilities of that role. Not that he was really reluctant to do so: his disavowal of sectarian politics was sincere, but meant primarily for Protestant ears. It did not cover all the circumstances. His sense of himself as a member of a persecuted religious minority was very strong; he was of no mind to betray his people by finessing the religious issue, even if it had been possible, which it was not.

The Protestants of the United States had last asserted themselves effectively in the 1920s, when they had imposed their idea of America on the republic by passing the restrictive Immigration Acts of 1921 and 1924 and by defeating Al Smith. Since then they had gradually lost ground: Franklin Roosevelt had repealed prohibition and brought Jews and Catholics into the heart of the federal government, and since 1945 both groups, but especially the Catholics, had made enormous advances in electoral politics: even Philadelphia had gone Democratic. The time was at hand when the white Protestants would discover that they were just another ethnic group, instead of being, as once, synonymous with 'Americans'. Some rise of social tension, or even violence, might have been expected; but the law of unintended consequences was at work. Thanks to the Immigration Acts (one of Kennedy's lesser commitments was to get them amended or repealed) the proportion of foreign-born people in the American population had shrunk from 13 per cent in 1920 to 5.6 per cent in 1960, while the actual population had grown from 106 million to 179 million. In terms of ethnic and religious divisions it had thus been a period of ever-increasing stability; two generations of Americans had grown used to each other, and in the New Deal and the great war for democracy they had learned to be ashamed of bigotry, as the primary in West Virginia demonstrated. In short, Kennedy was to some extent pushing at an open door, but that did not diminish the political courage it required, nor render the enterprise free of risk. Historians debate the matter now, as journalists and political scientists did then; but it seems likeliest that his religion almost cost Kennedy his election. It is certain that his candidacy was a bold and necessary challenge to one of the oldest, most powerful and least tolerable of American prejudices.

The finest moment of the campaign came in September when Kennedy confronted a meeting of Protestant ministers in Houston, Texas. 'They're tired of being called bigots for opposing a Catholic,' said Pierre Salinger, Kennedy's press assistant, but their questions showed them up as being, at best, remarkably unworldly: one enquired if the candidate would ask Cardinal Cushing, 'Mr Kennedy's own hierarchical superior in Boston', to get Vatican approval for the doctrine of the separation of church and state. Kennedy did not allow this sort of thing to ruffle him ('I am the one that is running for the office of the Presidency and not Cardinal Cushing').[63] He performed with dignity and courtesy, and his speech was perhaps the most effective statement of the case for religious freedom and equality ever made by an American politician (it was certainly read or heard by more Americans than any other).

I believe in an America where religious intolerance will some day end – where all men and churches are treated as equal – where every man has the right to attend or not attend the church of his choice – where there is no Catholic vote, no anti-Catholic vote, no bloc voting of any kind – and where Catholics, Protestants, and Jews, at both the lay and the pastoral level, will refrain from those attitudes of disdain and division which have so often marred their works in the past, and promote instead the American ideal of brotherhood. . . . This is the kind of America I believe in – and this is the kind I fought for in the South Pacific and the kind my brother died for in Europe. No one suggested then that we might have a 'divided loyalty,' that we did 'not believe in liberty,' or that we belonged to a disloyal group that threatened the 'freedoms for which our forefathers died.'[64]

47

Kennedy and his election team were sure that this speech would make or break his campaign. It was probably more effective in giving heart to Catholics, Jews, unbelievers and liberals than in reassuring no-popery zealots, who continued to agitate the religious question until election day. But Kennedy gained in stature by his stand, and his eventual victory, however narrow, and the eloquent, intelligent and convincing way in which he asserted his right, and the right of all non-Protestant citizens, to claim their country and aspire to the presidency, killed the issue for good. It was a not unimportant triumph in the perpetual struggle to get traditional America to accept modernity.

But if a Catholic's right to run for national office had to be defended, it was still more important to convince a majority of the voters that this particular Catholic was the man for that office, that year. In spite of the crowds that adored him, the task might have defeated Kennedy but for Nixon's agreement to appear with him in four televised debates. These ritual tourneys are now so much part of presidential politics that it is hard to understand why the proposal to stage them seemed radical in 1960; yet so it was, and Nixon could safely have declined the contest. But he disregarded advice that he would only be giving Kennedy valuable publicity. He thought he could discredit the Democrat by out-arguing him. It was a complete miscalculation.

The details of the debates hardly matter nowadays. Both candidates were on their best behaviour, or what they supposed to be such. Nixon repressed his instinct for low blows (not quite successfully). Kennedy carefully hid his sense of humour (though at one point he did laugh engagingly); it was as if he had resolved *not* to charm his way into the presidency. Nixon was equally determined to show himself a responsible statesman. As a result the two of them exuded for most of the time an air of ponderous insincerity. In the third session, one of the journalists (the 'debates' were really no more than joint press conferences on camera) asked the candidates to comment on some characteristically earthy language which Harry Truman had just been pouring out against the Republicans. Nixon, whose own dreary profanity was to become public knowledge during the Watergate affair, mouthed pious nothings about the importance of using presidentially dignified language on all occasions; Kennedy, who also used a good many four-letter words in private, replied candidly that it wasn't his business to tell Mr Truman what language to use, but he did not laugh at the question, at any rate on-camera. Both candidates gave hostages to fortune which the winner, whoever he was, would have reason to regret. Above all Kennedy insisted on the importance of doing something about the recently installed tyranny of Fidel Castro in Cuba, if necessary by supporting the anti-Castro exiles if they attempted a counter-revolution. He may or may not have known that the Eisenhower administration was adopting just such a policy: either way, the words would soon come back to embarrass him.

From the electioneering point of view, all this was unimportant. The four debates showed Kennedy and Nixon arguing as equals, and from then on Kennedy, so much the more attractive candidate, emerged as the front-runner. Eisenhower's last-minute intervention was damaging, but the president was not well enough to campaign as hard as was necessary, though it was probably his intervention which made Kennedy's margin of victory so narrow. Ike was still the most popular and trusted man in the United States.

The Democrats had made the right nominations: probably no other team could have overcome Nixon's advantage as the candidate of a popular administration in a time of peace and prosperity. Johnson worked the South in his own inimitable fashion while Kennedy tried to nail down the rest of the country. Mistakes were made (the campaign in California was chaotic, so that Nixon was able to take that state by 36,000 votes) but none was fatal, and at critical moments Kennedy showed that he could act intuitively as well as from calculation. On 19 October Martin Luther King Jr was arrested in Atlanta in the course of a civil rights demonstration (he had been sitting-in at a segregated restaurant). A few days later he was jailed for four months, which was monstrous in itself and exposed him to a real risk of being lynched. Kennedy's brother-in-law, Sargent Shriver, suggested to Kennedy that he might telephone Mrs Coretta King to offer help, and Kennedy instantly did so. Mrs King was immensely pleased, and the news at once got out. Even more impulsively Bobby Kennedy telephoned the judge in the case to protest at the abuse of a defendant's rights, and the next day King was released. The black community was hugely impressed, and voted overwhelmingly for Kennedy on election day. It looked like smart politics, but the two brothers seem to have acted solely from natural indignation and good feeling, and without consulting each other: 'the finest strategies are usually the result of accidents,' said Jack Kennedy a few weeks later.[65] His comment on the reaction of Martin Luther King Sr to the incident was equally characteristic. While the son still maintained neutrality in the election, the father said, 'I'll take a Catholic or the Devil himself if he'll wipe the tears from my daughter-in-law's eyes. I've got a suitcase full of votes – my whole church – for . . . Senator Kennedy.' Hearing this, the senator remarked, 'That was a hell of a bigoted statement, wasn't it? Imagine Martin Luther King having a bigot for a father. Well,' (smiling) 'we all have fathers, don't we?'[66]

Reading such anecdotes it is hard not to feel that Kennedy deserved to win, but he would not have done so with charm alone, even if assisted by Bobby's redoubtable skills as a campaign manager. Lyndon Johnson and the other southern Democrats reclaimed Louisiana, West Virginia and, crucially, Texas from the Republican column. In the North the ancient arts of machine politics proved decisive, for the last time. Legend has it that Mayor Daley of Chicago stole the election in Illinois for Kennedy, and thereby the presidency. Legend is wrong, for Kennedy's victory did not depend on carrying Illinois, but the state's twenty-seven electoral votes made a handsome addition to the Democratic majority. Kennedy would not have got them but for the Chicago machine's exertions: the election was Richard J. Daley's finest hour, and it is not surprising that he and his family were Kennedy's first overnight visitors in the White House. Kennedy's first action as president was to acknowledge another political debt by issuing an executive order doubling the amount of food given by the federal government to America's 4 million needy. This was his response to the acute misery he had seen in the mining communities of West Virginia. He had been deeply shocked by this encounter with poverty of a kind he had apparently never seen before; running for the presidency is an educational experience. And West Virginia had played as large a part as Chicago in making him president.

All the efforts paid off on 8 November 1960 when Kennedy won his narrow plurality over Richard Nixon and the candidates of the minor parties (Socialist Labor, Prohibition, National States Rights, and so on). It was a cliffhanger election: the *New York Times*, which gave the victory to Kennedy in its early editions, stopped the presses at 4.45 in the morning, and it was not until after 7 a.m. that an extra edition finally announced

KENNEDY IS APPARENT VICTOR. When in due course James Reston told Kennedy what an awful night it had been he replied, 'If you were scared at the *Times*, you should have seen me.'[67] Nixon could count as well as anyone in the United States, and did not admit defeat until 10 a.m. (Kennedy's men had been furious that he had not conceded when he appeared on televison at 3 a.m., but Kennedy himself just remarked, 'Why should he concede? I wouldn't').[68] If the margin of victory had been so doubtful, the turnout was impressive: 64.5 per cent of the electorate had voted, 11 per cent up on 1956 and unapproached since. Kennedy might not have got America moving again, but he had certainly stirred it up; only, as so often happens, when stirred, half the voters proved to belong to the other side. As Theodore H. White pointed out long ago, the result was something in the nature of a fluke: had a few thousand votes gone the other way in Illinois and Texas, Nixon would have won, with a majority of two in the electoral college and fewer popular votes than Kennedy overall.[69] What was no fluke at all was the enormous increase in the Democratic presidential vote. The Republicans lost more than 1 million of the votes they had received in 1956, but still did better than they had in Ike's first landslide year, 1952. The Democrats gained nearly 8 million votes, for a grand total of over 34 million. In only two states (Oklahoma and – a warning – Mississippi) did their vote go down. Even allowing for the natural growth in the size of the electorate, it was an extraordinary achievement.

But what exactly did it mean? Reviewing the results, Kennedy might well conclude that the country, or at least that part of it which had voted for him, had accepted that there was a need to get America moving again; it had turned to the party of activism, and to the candidate who had proclaimed a New Frontier:

> Franklin Roosevelt's New Deal promised security and succor to those in need. But the New Frontier of which I speak is not a set of promises – it is a set of challenges. It sums up not what I intend to offer the American people, but what I intend to ask of them. It appeals to their pride, not to their pocketbook – it holds out the promise of more sacrifice instead of more security.[70]

He was president-elect now; the citizens who had elected him could not say that they had not been warned. He had a mandate for action.

What he did not have was a mandate for any specific action. Much would depend on what he could get through Congress, and here the outlook was far from rosy. The Democratic vote for Congress was on the whole a rising tide between 1952 and 1964, but between each large gain it tended to fall back a trifle, and in 1960 the party lost altogether twenty seats in the House and two in the Senate. Add to that the fact that most southern Democrats were conservatively inclined, and all too ready to co-operate with conservative Republicans, and Kennedy faced formidable difficulties in getting his programme through. There was the further point that almost as many Americans had voted for Nixon as had for Kennedy. To be sure of re-election in 1964, and to consolidate his authority in the meantime, he would have to win over as many former Nixon supporters as possible; and since on the whole they were supporters of the status quo, this necessity clashed with his radical instincts. Not that his instincts were so very radical. Most of the New Frontier shopping-list consisted of Democratic proposals that had been lying around for years – in some instances, since the second Roosevelt administration. However, new exigencies would produce new proposals, as the years immediately ahead would amply demonstrate; but how could conservatives be won over to support them, and him, and give him both an increased personal majority and a co-operative Congress in four years' time? On the day of his victory Kennedy could have been pardoned for feeling that to solve one problem was merely to create another: that having won the election of 1960 he had instantly to start running for the next.

In every other sense, he was a candidate for office no longer. He spent the two months between November and January in putting together his administration and in preparing his inaugural address; an encouraging sign was the mounting interest and enthusiasm that, if journalists and opinion polls were to be believed, attended his every activity. It seemed that already many of those who had not voted for the New Frontier were wishing that they had. On 20 January 1961, a day of brilliant sunshine and bitter cold (a blizzard had blanketed Washington the night before), he took the oath of office and delivered his most famous speech. It was as usual a collaborative effort: Sorensen had prepared a draft based on the president's wishes and various other people's suggestions, then he and Kennedy had smoothed it into its final shape. Years of practice had turned the once-awkward Kennedy into an effective, if not yet a great, orator: now his harsh voice hammered out a message which no one who heard it was ever to forget. It was his most ambitious statement of his purposes so far. It was determined, in almost every sentence, by the pressure of the Cold War as Kennedy saw it, and was not free from the curse of over-lofty rhetoric which has been the American style since the Declaration of Independence. Even after thirty years and more it retains a certain power:

> In the long history of the world, only a few generations have been granted the role of defending freedom in its hour of maximum danger. I do not shrink from this responsibility – I welcome it. I do not believe that any of us would exchange places with any other people or any other generation. The energy, the faith, the devotion which we bring to this endeavour will light our country and all who serve it – and the glow from that fire can truly light the world.
>
> And so, my fellow Americans: ask not what your country can do for you – ask what you can do for your country.
>
> My fellow citizens of the world: ask not what America will do for you, but what together we can do for the freedom of man.
>
> Finally, whether you are citizens of America or citizens of the world, ask of us here the same high standards of strength and sacrifice which we ask of you.

The speech was deservedly a huge success; but some noticed that it was concerned only with America's place in the world. It said nothing about the domestic problems of the United States or about Kennedy's plans for tackling them. This exclusion came about partly because Kennedy did not want to mar the elegance of his address with the debris of the Democratic party platform; but he also wanted to avoid the risk of arousing congressional opposition before he had to. The presidency was already imposing its compromises upon him.

. . .

NOTES

1. Benjamin C. Bradlee, *Conversations with Kennedy* (London: Quartet 1976) p. 234.
2. The classic analysis of availability is that of D.W. Brogan, *An Introduction to American Politics* (London: Hamish Hamilton 1954) pp. 196–202.

3. It will be seen that except for the liberals, those incurable ideologues, availability had very little to do with a candidate's opinions on the great issues of the day. A Democrat, it was assumed, would maintain the legacy of the New Deal and stand up to the Russians as necessary. The rest was negligible.
4. Quoted in James MacGregor Burns, *John Kennedy: a political profile* (New York: Avon 1960) p. 89.
5. Bradlee, *Conversations*, p. 16.
6. Nigel Hamilton, *J.F.K.: Reckless Youth* (London: Century 1992) p. 753.
7. Ibid., p. 758.
8. John F. Kennedy, '*Let the Word Go Forth*': *the speeches, statements, and writings of John F. Kennedy, 1947 to 1963*, edited by Theodore Sorensen (New York: Delacorte 1988) (*LTW*) p. 85.
9. Ibid., p. 87.
10. Herbert S. Parmet, *Jack: the struggles of John F. Kennedy* (New York: Dial Press 1980) p. 380.
11. Ibid., p. 382.
12. Joseph Alsop, *I've Seen the Best of It* (New York: Norton 1992) p. 406.
13. Kennedy Memorial Library, Oral Histories (KOH): Dave Powers.
14. James Bryce, *The American Commonwealth*, pt I, ch. 8 (London 1888).
15. Winston S. Churchill, *The Gathering Storm* (London: Cassell 1948); 'Cato' [Michael Foot, Peter Howard and Frank Owen], *Guilty Men* (London: Gollancz 1940); D.W. Brogan, *Is Innocence Enough?* (London: Hamish Hamilton 1941).
16. Hamilton, *J.F.K.*, p. 317.
17. John F. Kennedy, *Why England Slept* (London: Sidgwick & Jackson 1962 edn) (*WES*) p. 180.
18. Which is probably why Harold Laski disliked the book so unreasonably.
19. *PP* iii p. 315.
20. *WES* p. 127.
21. Ibid., p. 180.
22. Ibid., p. 171.
23. Ibid., pp. 171–2.
24. Hamilton, *J.F.K.*, pp. 500–2.
25. Robert J. Donovan, *PT 109: John F. Kennedy in World War II* (New York: Warner edn 1989) pp. 199–210.
26. Richard H. Rovere, *Senator Joe McCarthy* (Cleveland and New York: Meridian edn n.d.) p. 95.
27. Donovan, *PT 109*, p. 7.
28. Pierre Salinger, *With Kennedy* (London: Cape 1967) pp. 102–5.
29. Hamilton, *J.F.K.*, p. 210.

30. Parmet, *Jack*, p. 15.
31. Bradlee, *Conversations*, p. 159.
32. Hamilton, *J.F.K.*, pp. 472–3.
33. Burns, *John Kennedy*, p. 100.
34. Ibid., p. 99.
35. Ibid., p. 106.
36. He did no better in 1960, when he was the Republicans' notably unenergetic vice-presidential candidate.
37. Parmet, *Jack*, p. 238.
38. Ibid., p. 245.
39. Theodore C. Sorensen, *Kennedy* (New York: Harper & Row Perennial edn 1988) pp. 45–9.
40. Lawrence F. O'Brien, *No Final Victories* (New York: Ballantine 1974) p. 32.
41. John F. Kennedy, *Profiles in Courage* (New York: Pocket edn 1961) (*PC*) p. 9.
42. Ibid., p. 5.
43. Ibid., p. 124.
44. Parmet, *Jack*, p. 310. The answer to Kennedy's question must be that McCarthy was not on trial; that his conduct was a matter of universal public knowledge; and that Kennedy himself had gone carefully over all the evidence in the previous year. He knew how he would have voted; but for the politics of it, there was no reason why he shouldn't tell the world. In his memoir Sorensen loyally takes the blame (*Kennedy*, p. 49) but he would have done better to tell the truth, as he later did to Herbert S. Parmet.
45. Parmet, *Jack*, p. 311.
46. Sorensen, *Kennedy*, p. 47.
47. *PC* p. 182.
48. Sorensen, *Kennedy*, p. 69.
49. Ibid., p. 101.
50. Burns, *John Kennedy*, p. 199.
51. Kenneth P. O'Donnell and David F. Powers, with Joe McCarthy, '*Johnny, We Hardly Knew Ye*': *memories of John Fitzgerald Kennedy* (Boston: Little, Brown 1972) p. 126.
52. Ibid.
53. James N. Giglio, *The Presidency of John F. Kennedy* (Lawrence, KS: University Press of Kansas, 1991) p. 120.
54. Arthur M. Schlesinger Jr, *A Thousand Days: John F. Kennedy in the White House* (New York: Fawcett Premier edn 1971) (Schlesinger, *TD*), p. 76; Paul B. Fay, Jr., *The Pleasure of his Company* (New York: Harper & Row 1966) p. 59.
55. *LTW* p. 18, speech at National Press Club, 14 January 1960.
56. 14 August 1958; reprinted in John F. Kennedy, *The Strategy of Peace*, edited by Allan Nevins (New York: Harper 1960) (*SP*)

pp. 33–45. This revised version does not contain the explicit parallel with 1930s England to be found in Burns's account of the speech (Burns, *John Kennedy*, pp. 190–1). The Baldwin reference is, of course, a throwback to *WES*.

57. 1 October 1959; *SP* pp. 19, 13–14.
58. Ibid., p. 13.
59. 4 July 1960; *LTW* p. 93.
60. Acceptance of presidential nomination speech, 15 July 1960; ibid., p. 100.
61. Gerard T. Rice, *The Bold Experiment: JFK's Peace Corps* (Notre Dame, IN: University of Notre Dame Press 1985) p. 16.
62. Private information.
63. 12 September 1960; *LTW* pp. 135–6.
64. Ibid., pp. 131–2.
65. J.K. Galbraith, *Ambassador's Journal: a personal account of the Kennedy years* (Boston: Houghton Mifflin 1969) p. 6.
66. Arthur M. Schlesinger Jr, *Robert Kennedy and his Times* (London: André Deutsch 1978), p. 218.
67. James Reston, *Deadline: a memoir* (New York: Times Books edn 1992) p. 297.
68. Theodore H. White, *The Making of the President* (London: Cape paperback edn 1964) p. 25.
69. Ibid., pp. 350–1.
70. 15 July 1960; *LTW* p. 101.

Chapter 3

ALARMS AND EXCURSIONS

Foreign affairs are almost always the most pressing concern of national governments. Certainly nothing seemed more urgent in Washington in 1961. No sooner had Kennedy taken his oath of office than he was confronted with a series of overlapping foreign crises which did not end until long after his death. It is only appropriate to consider how well prepared he was to manage these emergencies.

From his youth in London until his appointment to the Senate Foreign Relations Committee in 1957, and still more thereafter, he had regarded himself as something of a specialist in foreign policy. He lacked executive experience, a shortcoming that was to have painful results during his first year in office (such was the price of availability). But for the rest, he had travelled, he had conferred, he had studied, he had made speeches and published articles, the more important of which owed as much to him as to Sorensen. These activities had deepened his impatience with the older generation, the men of the 1940s and 1950s, now beginning to pass from the scene. It seemed to him, for instance, that there was nothing to be gained from respecting the plans and interests of the decaying European empires. His journey to Indo-China had left him with nothing but contempt for French imperialism, the British were winding down their empire with commendable speed, he did not value Portugal as an ally enough to compromise over issues concerning its colonies, and Belgium stood openly disgraced as a brutally incompetent imperial power which had left behind an insoluble problem when it scuttled from the Congo. On issues of this kind Kennedy was positively radical (far too radical for such old-stagers as Dean Acheson, formerly Truman's Secretary of State). America's interests, he believed, lay in cultivating the post-imperial states of Africa and Asia, and he wanted as much as possible to shake off the quasi-imperialist past of the United States itself in Latin America. All these attitudes made sense in 1961; they were becoming increasingly fashionable and they stand the test of hindsight, for it is impossible to see any rational alternative to them. Kennedy's special contribution was that he was prepared to turn them into energetic and detailed policies, as he showed in 1957, when he made his most notorious pre-presidential speech, urging the United States to support the cause of Algerian independence against its ally, France.[1] In such ways he demonstrated that a fresh young mind could indeed give a distinctive new direction to US foreign policy, and his short presidency was to launch many initiatives that, to the misfortune of America and the world, have not been sustained subsequently. Kennedy believed that the former colonies wanted to Americanise themselves; that is, that they were in search of national independence, democracy and prosperity, and as an inheritor of the revolution of 1776 he was eager to help them. There was a large measure of naïvé in this approach, as events were to show; but events were to show that there was much wisdom in it too.

Unfortunately these perceptions and aspirations were inextricably tangled with quite different concerns. Like almost all policy-makers and opinion-formers of his time, Kennedy was convinced that the central problem facing America and the world was a global competition, not just between the United States and the Soviet Union for influence, but between Western democracy and Eastern communism. No doubt he desired for its own sake the friendship of such new states as Ghana and the Republic of India; but he was also mortally concerned lest American inactivity open the door for Soviet expansionism. All his speeches on what would later be called the Third World (and will soon have to be called something else) couched their argument in terms of the international communist menace. Kennedy did not make the mistake of Eisenhower's Secretary of State, John Foster Dulles, in supposing that every state which tried to be neutral in the Cold War was really an enemy, or crypto-communist; but in his analysis he tended to fall all too easily into another fallacy to which Dulles was prone: he saw all developments in foreign countries solely in terms of the Soviet–American competition, he assumed that the rival great powers had more influence within nations such as Egypt and Indonesia than in fact they had, and he came near to assuming that the governments of such countries could never act autonomously, and shared either American or Russian priorities. Where the New World was concerned, he assumed that the United States had an overriding interest in making sure that no American state went communist or, if it did, stayed communist.

These opinions show only that Kennedy had not succeeded in breaking free of all the commonplaces of his generation. The Monroe Doctrine, loosely interpreted to mean that the United States had a hegemonic responsibility throughout the Americas (regardless of the fact that Lima is further from Washington than London, Rio de Janeiro is further than Berlin, and Buenos Aires further than Moscow), was a permanent ju-ju of American politics, and no candidate for office would dare say that it mattered very little to the United States what system of government was adopted by states to the south of the Rio Grande, and not much what were their relations with the Soviet Union. As late as the 1980s Ronald Reagan could suggest, apparently seriously, that if El Salvador were allowed to 'go communist' the next thing would be a Red march on Texas. He was widely ridiculed for this, but it did him no harm with most of the voters. And as for Kennedy, he couched all his foreign policy proposals in Cold War terms. So did everybody else. For more than forty years the Americans allowed themselves only the simplest dichotomy for interpreting world affairs; and now that it has collapsed they find themselves at a loss. Whatever Kennedy's private views were, he had no alternative to accepting and using Cold War categories when seeking support for his foreign policy. At best he could only educate Americans in the ambiguities and nuances of diplomacy, which, to his honour, he increasingly attempted.

For one thing, the competition with the Soviet Union, whatever its causes and nature, was a reality, and potentially the most dangerous of all realities. Given the facts, and his experience of the struggle against Hitler, it is not surprising that Kennedy, on coming into the White House, saw his central duty as that of managing the Cold War more effectively than had Eisenhower. All his statements (including the inagural address) show that he thought the situation required greater effort, greater intelligence, greater sacrifice (which in practice would mean greater defence expenditure). He thought that Eisenhower had depended too much on the nuclear deterrent: the armed forces should have a greater diversity of weapons and tactics at their disposal. He thought that the Soviet Union had got into the way of supposing that the United States was a declining force which could be bullied: it must learn better. He also thought that reason and patience could reduce Cold War tensions and resolve some of the disagreements which divided East and West. This last attitude struck the old guard as weak and contradictory; but it may have been simply common sense.

Kennedy's real weakness lay in the difficult area where grand designs have to be turned into concrete policies. He had no direct experience of it: it is one of the faults of a system of separated powers, as opposed to a parliamentary one, that a politician can reach the presidency without having had any ministerial training. A strong Secretary of State might have made good this deficiency, and the right man was at hand, Adlai Stevenson; unfortunately Kennedy had by now conceived a personal antipathy to Stevenson that not only was going to lead him into several unworthy (and uncharacteristic) deeds of spite in the time ahead, but also would have made collaboration in Washington impossible. So Stevenson was sent off to New York as ambassador to the United Nations, where he was to serve so well as to prove what an excellent Secretary he could have been. Chester Bowles, almost as well qualified, could not be confirmed without a major battle in the Senate (Richard Nixon had warned Kennedy that he would publicly oppose Bowles's nomination). Senator William Fulbright, whom Kennedy would have liked best in the post, was impossible because of his support for white supremacy in the South, and because he was uniquely useful as Chairman of the Foreign Relations Committee. So Kennedy fell back on Dean Rusk, a former Undersecretary and Assistant Secretary of State, who was strongly recommended by Dean Acheson and others. Kennedy had never met him, but he was doubtless attracted by the assurances he received that Rusk was the perfect second-in-command: Kennedy meant to be his own Secretary of State, although, as Rusk himself was to comment years later, nowadays the job is so large that even a Secretary of State cannot be his own Secretary of State.[2] Rusk did indeed turn out to be the perfect messenger-boy; both Kennedy and, in due course, Lyndon Johnson came to appreciate warmly his professionalism, self-effacement, loyalty and integrity. Unfortunately that was not exactly what the American system required. The history of the State Department shows unequivocally that it functions best when the Secretary is his own man, capable of standing up to his president, challenging his views when necessary; capable also of devising and executing his own foreign policy (with the president's approval and co-operation); a man capable of leading a united and effective diplomatic team. Such had been George Marshall, Dean Acheson and (for all his faults) John Foster Dulles; such was to be Henry Kissinger. Such was not Dean Rusk, and there were far too many unfortunate, even disastrous, consequences.

To all public appearances, Kennedy's chief preoccupation in the first days of his presidency was not foreign policy so much as the economy and related matters. Messages went to Congress proposing legislation on social welfare, taxation, public expenditure, the minimum wage, and so on; and Kennedy seemed to be trying as a first priority to overcome the mild recession which he had inherited from Eisenhower. In this honeymoon period, with his popularity continuing to soar (according to the opinion polls), Congress showed itself reasonably co-operative, but its lengthy procedures meant that it was not going to produce many results in a hurry, and meanwhile, behind the scenes, foreign affairs had inevitably established first claim on the president's attention. He had two immediate problems on his hands, and a third coming up: Laos, Cuba and Berlin. He could not know it, but they incarnated the main issues with which he was to grapple throughout his presidency, and which dominate posterity's view of him.

In the last decade of the twentieth century the tragedy of Indo-China[3] looks to be something in which the United States should never have involved itself. It now seems clear that once the French empire had collapsed there was bound to be a bitter contest to fill the vacuum thus created: superficially, a contest involving the old Buddhist order, or what remained of it, the newer, westernising elite, and the communists; at a deeper level, a competition between the Vietnamese, both the weaker nations of Laos and Cambodia, and a gigantic China which throughout history had pursued its own imperial designs in South-East Asia. The United States could affect this struggle only marginally, as events were to prove: in Marxist jargon, the balance of force was against it. But American policy-makers in the 1950s did not, and probably could not, see matters so clearly. At least some of them saw that Laos was essentially unimportant to America. It had to make a new place for itself in the changed world; small, landlocked and surrounded by predatory neighbours, the utmost it could realistically hope for was to find its new niche, whatever it was, peaceably. The hope was to be cheated, and American errors were in part to blame for the decades of agony that it was to undergo. In the last analysis these errors were begotten by the Cold War and the mentality which it bred, and Kennedy was not immune to them. But in 1961, at the very beginning of his stewardship, Kennedy handled the problem of Laos rather well.

Two questions faced the Americans. The first was what would happen if the United States turned away? It had been bluntly answered, many times, by President Eisenhower; as he was to say in his memoirs:

> Despite its remoteness, we were determined to preserve the independence of Laos against a takeover by its neighbors to the north – Communist China and North Vietnam. For the fall of Laos to Communism could mean the subsequent fall – like a tumbling row of dominoes – of its still-free neighbors, Cambodia and South Vietnam and, in all probability, Thailand and Burma. Such a chain of events would open the way to Communist seizure of all South-east Asia.[4]

This 'domino theory' found widespread acceptance at the time. History has not been kind to it: the eventual communist victory in Indo-China had many appalling consequences, but international destabilisation on the scale predicted has not been among them. The best that can be said for the US campaigns in Indo-China is that they may have bought time for Malaysia and Singapore; but even that is very doubtful, and less bloody means might have been found for that end.

Kennedy, however, on coming into office, was faced not just with the domino theory but also, in large part because of Eisenhower's activities, with the second question: what would happen if the United States continued to intervene in Laos? To this question also Eisenhower had an explicit answer, which he laid before Kennedy at their pre-inaugural meetings. The Russians were pouring supplies into the country, to aid the communist rebels, backed increasingly by the communist government in North Vietnam and its hardened army. The United States must continue to supply the anti-communist forces, and if necessary send in its own troops. Ike was no doubt demob-happy: Kennedy could not understand how he could be so relaxed about these appalling recommendations.[5] He was more appalled when he discovered that the joint chiefs were prepared, if necessary, to use nuclear weapons in Indo-China, confident that this would not precipitate the Third World War. It was a confidence he could not share.[6] Indeed, all these briefings (he complained later that he had spent more time on Laos than on anything else during the first months of his presidency) seem to have had a counter-productive effect. Nuclear war was not something he was prepared to contemplate for such a matter; another policy would have to be found; and the more that he and his advisers debated, the clearer became the alternative (it was one to which even the Eisenhower administration had been moving in its final days).[7] Bismarck remarked that the Eastern Question was not worth the healthy bones of one Pomeranian musketeer. Kennedy decided that Laos was not worth any American bones. Nor was it worthwhile to destroy his administration either by continuing the intervention or by overt disengagement. The Laotian commitment must nevertheless be liquidated. A 'neutralist' government must be set up by international agreement: it might even establish itself successfully. The Soviet–American competition for influence could be pursued elsewhere. This decision had its costs. From the point of view of Laotians struggling to avoid the thraldom of communism it was criminally dishonourable. From the point of view of anti-communist Vietnamese it was extremely dangerous, opening up what became the Ho Chi Minh Trail, down which supplies went from North Vietnam to the insurgents in the South. It certainly did not solve all problems of American policy in the area. But from the point of view of the President of the United States it was the least bad alternative, and therefore the one which he had to choose.

To make the new policy succeed would be tedious and time-consuming work: it was mainly entrusted to Averill Harriman, ambassador at large and soon to be Assistant Secretary for the Far East. But Kennedy did not swerve. He had seen the two central points: Laos was of no real strategic value either to Moscow or to Washington, and so long as the superpowers could save themselves from pinning their prestige to what happened there the dispute should be negotiable; second, the American people hardly knew where Laos was, and certainly did not care. So long as they were not induced to believe that the Kennedy administration was 'losing' Laos (as the Truman administration had allegedly 'lost' China) they would happily ignore its problems. It followed that Kennedy should try for some agreement with the Soviet Union which would at least appear to solve the Laotian question and so get it off the front pages of the newspapers and off the television news bulletins. That achieved, the Republicans would find it difficult, probably impossible, to get it back on again. These calculations, like the others, were ignoble; but Kennedy was right to make them. His younger self, the author of *Why England Slept*, might have remembered Neville Chamberlain's deplorable remark about Czechoslovakia ('a far-away country of which we know nothing') and accused him of conniving in another Munich: certainly communist bad faith, in subverting the agreement negotiated by Harriman at Geneva in 1962, was to be as pronounced as Hitler's had been. But such criticisms miss the essential point: Munich was a futile attempt to avert a war which was inevitable; Geneva at least helped to avert a war which it was in everyone's interests (even the Laotians') to avoid.

Kennedy's other problem was Cuba, and there he did not see the issues so clearly. Like most of his fellow-citizens he was the victim of too many unexamined assumptions about the subject. He disliked vulgar clichés, but in effect he believed, along with every Rotarian in the Mid-West, that the Caribbean, indeed perhaps the whole of Latin America, was the 'backyard' of the United States, and therefore should be treated proprietorially (here any non-American may detect the pernicious effect of the Monroe Doctrine). He had been uneasy about US support for the corrupt and feeble Cuban dictatorship of Fulgencio Batista, and like many other Americans had welcomed the romantic insurgency of Fidel Castro, which overthrew Batista in 1959. Unfortunately Castro was bigotedly hostile to the United States. He expropriated vast amounts of American property. This was bad enough, but the Cold War mentality made it inevitable that official Washington would also smell a plot by the Soviet Union to extend its influence in a manner highly dangerous to US security. Accordingly the Eisenhower administration enlisted many of the refugees now pouring out of Cuba;

by the winter of 1960–61 the Central Intelligence Agency (CIA) brought together an insurrectionary force of 1,500 men which it began to train in Guatemala for a counter-revolutionary invasion of the island.

In some respects the Cuban and Laotian problems were alike. Two weak nations were struggling to achieve effective independence, each being overshadowed by a mighty neighbour (Laos, pitiably, was overshadowed by two – Vietnam as well as China). Their difficulties were made worse by the Cold War. Superpower meddling was not to do much good in either instance. The difference between the two was that Cuba was far more visible from the United States than Laos, and had been a US satellite since 1898. Americans had a sincere dislike for the dictatorship which Castro was establishing; American government agencies grossly underestimated the difficulty of toppling the new regime. Kennedy shared these attitudes (so did Eisenhower, so did Nixon, so did most of the country's wise men), and may in addition have felt some personal competitiveness with Castro, who was another young politician on the make.

So far so comprehensible. Less understandable are the steps which Kennedy took with regard to Cuba in the first months of his administration. He saw that the proposed expedition against Castro was a matter of the highest importance. When the National Security Council could spare time from Laos, it debated Cuba. Kennedy sought assurances from the CIA and the Pentagon. He got them: Admiral Burke, the chief of naval operations, told him that 'As far as we have been able to check it out, this is fine. The plan is good.'[8] Alan Dulles, the head of the CIA, told Kennedy that he was much more confident about the Cuban plan than he had been about the successful coup which the agency had mounted some years before in Guatemala.[9] Several intelligent and weighty voices were raised against the scheme, but had no effect, probably because Kennedy, overborne by the experts, was stifling his own doubts. Still, the British government protested that the adventure was illegal, by those standards of international law which the United States is supposed to support; it predicted failure. Dean Acheson characteristically said to the president that he did not think it was necessary to call in Price Waterhouse to discover that 1,500 Cubans were not as good as 25,000.[10] Fulbright said that the invasion would be a disaster, whether it succeeded in its aims or failed, and denounced the obssession with Castro: 'the Castro regime is a thorn in the flesh; but it is not a dagger in our heart.'[11] Arthur Schlesinger, working in the White House, forcefully argued that even if the invaders established themselves in Cuba, a long civil war would almost certainly follow, creating a quagmire which would suck in the United States, and Kennedy's burgeoning international reputation as a man of 'intelligence, reasonableness and honest firmness' would be sacrificed.[12] Dean Rusk had his own doubts, but as he sadly admits in his memoirs he did not express them effectively:

> Having been both a colonel of infantry and chief of war plans in the China–Burma–Indian theater in World War II, I knew that this thin brigade of Cuban exiles did not stand a snowball's chance in hell of success. I didn't relay this military judgement to President Kennedy because I was no longer in the military.[13]

It might have made no difference if he had. Kennedy was fatally allured by the notion of overthrowing Castro at little cost. Here was a scheme whose success was guaranteed by the CIA, then at the height of its ill-deserved prestige. The chiefs of staff, to whom he might have listened had they demurred, were acquiescent or supportive (according to Rusk, 'They figured that since the whole show was a CIA operation, they would just approve it and wash their hands of it').[14] Gary Wills has made the point that Richard Bissell, the CIA man in charge of the affair, had taught several of the New Frontiersmen at Yale, including McGeorge Bundy, the National Security adviser, so that they tended to defer to him; and he might well feel confident of the president's approval because the whole scheme was a paradigmatic New Frontier adventure, romantic, unorthodox, improvised, bold; the kind of thing that James Bond would have done (Kennedy was much too fond of Ian Fleming's thrillers).[15] No doubt Kennedy also felt that, in his position, Eisenhower or Nixon would have gone ahead, so he could too; and he probably remembered a rash promise to support Cuban 'freedom fighters' made in the election campaign.[16] On 14 April he gave the word, and the operation began.

The invasion was a tragic fiasco. Secrecy had leaked away beforehand; so much so that the president had been confronted with some awkward questions at his press conference on 12 April (his answers were ingeniously misleading without quite being lies). Forewarned being forearmed, Castro had no difficulty in crushing the invaders as they struggled to establish a beach-head at a place called the Bay of Pigs. There was no general rising in Cuba in support of the liberators. For some days afterwards Kennedy hoped and believed that survivors of the battle had escaped into the mountains to launch a guerrilla campaign (according to his brother Robert, it was only because he believed that such an escape was possible that he had authorised the enterprise),[17] but he was deceived: when planning for the Bay of Pigs the CIA had failed to notice that there were no mountains nearby, only a swamp where it was easy for the Castro forces to pick the fugitives out, off or up. The only crumb of comfort was that the whole thing was finished so rapidly (in less than a week). There was nothing left for the United States to build on, no temptation to throw in more resources, endlessly, fruitlessly, as Schlesinger had feared.

Undoubtedly the Bay of Pigs episode was the lowest point of the Kennedy administration. It exposed a wide range of American weaknesses, from the incompetence of the CIA (an agency that regularly causes the US government more trouble than it is worth) to the complacency of the joint chiefs and the limitations of Dean Rusk's conception of his duty. It showed up the hollowness of some of Uncle Sam's pretensions: he simply could not resist meddling illegally and violently in the Caribbean, even though he had sworn off the foolish habit many times. But to President Kennedy the heart of the matter was his own role in the disaster. He made no bones about accepting the blame, and did so in all sincerity (unlike President Reagan, who in similar circumstances was to admit that things had gone wrong 'on my watch' only as a prelude to passing the buck). Others might try to rewrite the record: as he told a news conference on 21 April, 'there's an old saying that victory has a hundred fathers and defeat is an orphan.' He himself would accept the obvious: 'I'm the responsible officer of the Government.'[18] But his was responsibility of a peculiar kind. He had let himself be talked into something which his instincts had vainly warned him against; he had jeopardised the interests of the United States by failing to make sure that the CIA's proposals had been adequately analysed; by his mistakes he had allowed some brave Cuban exiles to go to fruitless deaths, and hundreds more to fall captive to Fidel Castro. He felt this last point acutely, for it reminded him of the loss of *PT 109*, when he had redeemed himself in his own eyes only by his success-ful efforts to save her crew. Now he had failed again, and once more men for whom he felt responsible were paying the price. 'How could I have been so far off base? All my life I've known better than to depend on the experts. How could I have been so stupid, to let them go ahead?'[19] He brooded, indeed he grieved over his failure. Bobby Kennedy later said that 'he was more upset at this time than he was at any other,' and noticed that during one of the post-mortems on the affair 'he kept shaking his head and rubbing his hands over his eyes.'[20] He also let some of his distress appear when, at his request, ex-President Eisenhower visited him at the presidential mountain retreat, Camp David, on 22 April (Kennedy did not want the Repub-licans to start making uninformed attacks on his failure: he had also called in Richard Nixon). Ike found him 'very frank but also very subdued and more than a little bewildered'.

KENNEDY: No one knows how tough this job is until after he has been in it a few months.
EISENHOWER: Mr. President, if you will forgive me, I think I men-tioned that to you three months ago.
KENNEDY: I certainly have learned a lot since.[21]

That was the nub. Kennedy had discovered that the presid-ency was an endless education. It was to change him radically, and the Bay of Pigs was his hardest, sharpest lesson. The good effects of it were felt almost at once, when the joint chiefs (who do not seem to have learned any lessons at all) began to advoc-ate the dispatch of US troops to Laos. Some sharp questioning by the president (of the kind he had not put to the Bay of Pigs planners) laid bare the fact that if the troops were landed they would immediately be overwhelmed by larger forces, in which case, the chiefs advised, atomic weapons would have to be used.[22] The troops were not sent.

Though the president accepted his responsibility for the Cuban disaster, he could not punish himself, he could not resign (not that he wanted to): he had to carry on with the job to which he had been elected. But there was no reason to over-look the blunders of the subordinates who had so dismally let him down, the less so as, in his heart of hearts, he blamed them even more than they deserved. He did his best to forestall a destructive bout of recrimination within the administration by stopping public discussion of the affair (the press let him get away with a bland refusal to discuss it at his news conferences) but he also took steps to replace the men who had lost his confidence. It was easy enough with the joint chiefs: they were nearing retirement anyway, and could be ushered offstage with medals presented in the rose garden in the White House. (Admiral Burke was apparently offered a further term as chief of naval operations, but had the good sense to refuse it, as he was expected to do.)[23] The chairman of the joint chiefs, General Lemnitzer, was allowed to finish his term, but meanwhile Kennedy installed his favourite general, Maxwell Taylor, in the White House as his military adviser, to the annoyance of the Pentagon; in due course Taylor succeeded Lemnitzer as chairman. In November Allen Dulles, whom Kennedy had confirmed in office the day after his election victory, got his medal and resigned. Bissell was replaced by Richard Helms as head of covert operations. After all this shuffling of the chessmen the president hoped that the bureaucracy had got the message.

But to make sure that he never lost control again he also made some decisive changes in the way he ran the government. They amounted to this, that a greatly strengthened White House staff would from now on actively supervise all governmental activities. McGeorge Bundy was given the task of reviewing and co-ordinating all defence and foreign policy recommendations that came to the president. Maxwell Taylor's appointment has already been recorded. The president told Ted Sorensen, who had hitherto been involved chiefly in domestic policy, that he must start giving some time to foreign affairs.[24] And Bobby Kennedy (who, like Sorensen, had not been brought into the planning for the Bay of Pigs: he had been settling in as Attorney-General) was determined that never again would obtuse subordinates be allowed to do so much damage to his brother. It was his mission to see to it, and with his sharp mind, boundless loyalty to Jack, and readiness to make enemies, he was well qualified. In this way his bond with the president constantly strengthened, leading the vice-president to remark sourly, 'don't kid anybody about who is the top adviser . . . Bobby is first in, and last out, and Bobby is the boy he listens to.'[25] When taking office, Jack had decided not to appoint a chief of staff like Eisenhower's Sherman Adams; but now he had got one.

Bobby Kennedy said in 1964 that 'the Bay of Pigs might have been the best thing that happened to the administration,'[26] meaning that it taught many invaluable lessons. A successful president may be defined as one who makes his big mistakes early. The experience keeps him humble and alert until he steps down. Presidents who triumph regularly in their first years get complacent or arrogant, and disaster follows. This happened even to Franklin Roosevelt, who would have left office with a much diminished reputation in 1941 had he not been rescued by the Second World War. Or a president, by failing to blunder in good time, may have no room to learn from his mistakes, or correct them. That happened to Jimmy Carter.

What is not possible is to avoid making serious mistakes. Even Eisenhower, who pursued as steady a course as any modern president, handled the Joe McCarthy problem abominably, botched the civil rights question, and by his stubborn conservatism over the economy created the conditions which made Kennedy's victory possible (which Ike certainly regarded as a disaster). Presidents are human, the presidency is an intensely personal office, and no one has ever devised machinery which can infallibly protect an incumbent against himself. Eisenhower's elaborate National Security Council system did not save him from the U2 mess, Kennedy's informal procedures did not avert the Bay of Pigs, and Lyndon Johnson's still more informal ones did not save him or his country from the dispatch of an American army to South Vietnam. It is hardly surprising: in each case the president had set up a system with which he was comfortable, a system which would, he believed, enable him to govern most effectively and shape the policy of the United States government most to his liking. It liberated his virtues; inevitably, being so personally adjusted, it liberated his vices too. In practice only the president can recognise his errors and correct them. It is therefore important that he be a quick learner, and also that he have something to learn from.

If all this is true, then the Bay of Pigs catastrophe was indeed the best thing that ever happened to President Kennedy. It was his own particular balls-up, he could not evade the knowledge that it was so, and in all future crises the determination not to repeat his mistakes (of which he thought his failure to ask enough questions was the worst) was one of his prime considerations. There were some important things that he did not learn, such as the point, which now seems tolerably obvious, that it was both wrong and inviting a second failure to continue to attempt to overthrow the Castro government. Nor did he altogether succeed in his attempt to improve his decision-making procedures. But on the whole Bobby Kennedy's aphorism may stand.

The incident did surprisingly little harm to the president's standing with his fellow-citizens: if anything it made him more popular than ever, which he found incomprehensible and slightly alarming. Shown a poll result putting his support at 82 per cent, he said contemptuously, 'It's just like Eisenhower. The worse I do, the more popular I get.'[27] The Left demonstrated against him at home and abroad. But America's allied governments, relieved that the episode was over so swiftly, rallied to his support. Only in one quarter did it do serious damage – in Moscow. Unfortunately, as Arthur Schlesinger Jr has remarked, that was where the supreme test lay – 'in Kennedy's capacity to deal not with Fidel Castro but with N.S. Khrushchev'.[28]

To the degree that there was validity in Kennedy's constant assertion that in 1961 the United States faced great danger, it lay in the state of Russo-American relations. The Soviet Union had demonstrated its technological prowess by developing both an atomic and a hydrogen bomb, and by sending up *Sputnik* (in the spring of 1961 it also sent up Cosmonaut Gagarin, the first human traveller in space). It had brutally but successfully repressed risings in Berlin and Hungary in the years immediately following Stalin's death: its hegemony in Eastern Europe was reaffirmed. Its official statistics showed that its rate of economic growth was greater than that of the United States: few realised the worthlessness of its official statistics. Khrushchev, who had only slowly emerged as Stalin's successor, had finally consolidated his ascendancy in 1957. He immediately showed that the Soviet Union had become a more self-confident, more venturesome power by challenging the West over the status of Berlin and East Germany. In 1958 he threatened to sign a unilateral peace treaty with the German Democratic Republic, as it was called, and thereby (he claimed) liquidate the right of the Western allies to maintain their presence in Berlin and guarantee the freedom of the West Berliners. The West had stood firm, and Khrushchev had not carried out his threats, but the crisis over Berlin was still smouldering when Eisenhower handed over to Kennedy, and threatened to burst into flames at any moment. Khrushchev had begun making contingency plans before the Bay of Pigs happened. That débâcle, when it occurred, gave him reason to think he might be facing a weakling, and he was not the man to ignore the opening which this gave him.   *Russian dictator*

In some respects Khrushchev and Kennedy were caught in the same dilemma. Kennedy, in order to get elected, and Khrushchev, in order to stay in power, had alike to demonstrate their devotion to building up their countries' international strength; neither wanted foreign adventures which would distract them from their pressing domestic programmes. But it would take time for this common ground to become perceptible. Khrushchev was a highly individual, explosive compound. His loudly affirmed faith in the achievements and promise of the communist system, which had deeply alarmed American opinion, was perfectly genuine, but was combined with an acute awareness of actual Soviet weakness in both military and economic performance. His bombast was largely an attempt to conceal this weakness from the world, when it was not designed to keep his opposition in the Soviet Union quiet. He hoped for a détente with the West, partly for its own sake, partly because relations with Maoist China were becoming more and more difficult; but he could not pursue it with too many of the amenities of conventional diplomacy, for fear lest his Stalinist old guard, in the communist leadership and elsewhere, should think that he was weakening towards the capitalist world. He could display a human charm which many Westerners found endearing; but he could also act as a hard, loud bully. He could be disarmingly frank, but he was also on occasion a liar without scruple. He found it difficult to understand the West, of which he had exceedingly limited experience: a mixture of provincialism and dogmatic ideology blinded him to many capitalist realities. To his dying day he never believed that the model kitchen in which he and Richard Nixon held their once-celebrated debate was anything other than a utopian fiction: the idea that such kitchens might actually be commonplace in the United States was beyond his imaginative reach.

Kennedy was ill prepared for dealing with such a man, and in a way realised it: like Eisenhower, he did not believe in summit conferences as forums for settling substantive issues and had been willing to recruit Dean Rusk in part because Rusk was on record as being of the same mind. But he could see no harm in a private, getting-to-know-you meeting with the Soviet leader; as Charles Bohlen remarked (he was a former ambassador to Moscow), Kennedy, like almost every person that I ran into during the course of my specialization in that field, really felt he had to find out for himself. The issues and consequences of mistakes of a serious nature in dealing with the Soviet Union are so great that no man of any character or intelligence will really wholeheartedly accept the views of anybody else.[29]

But this is an oblique admission of the president's inexperience; a further difficulty was Kennedy's well-advertised defence policy. The United States, he said, could not meet the communist threat solely by relying on nuclear superiority. He accepted the doctrine of 'flexible response' put forward by Maxwell Taylor, and appointed the outstandingly able Robert S. McNamara to apply it, as Secretary of Defense. The new policy meant, among other things, increased expenditure on arms: the author of *Why England Slept* was unalarmed. He remembered how military weakness had forced Chamberlain to Munich, and was determined not to go the same way. 'Let us never negotiate out of fear.'[30] Rearming out of fear, on the other hand, was only common sense. So during the first months of his presidency he constantly reiterated that the United States was facing a grave historical emergency. That got his defence requests through Congress, but it alarmed the Russians, just as Khrushchev's rhodomontade alarmed Kennedy. They could not make Kennedy out: they had expected him to be much less bellicose than Nixon. Then came the Bay of Pigs. This seems to have decided Khrushchev to accept an invitation to a meeting which Kennedy had sent him in February but which had previously gone unanswered. Since Kennedy would be visiting France in early June, it was agreed that it would be convenient for him to extend his journey to Vienna, where Khrushchev would be waiting for him.

In 1961 Berlin was the Russians' chief preoccupation. A flood of emigrants was pouring from East to West Germany through the open sluice of the old capital. This emigration threatened to destroy the East German economy (since on the whole it was the most intelligent and the best trained who left) and it was as clear in 1961 as it would be thirty years later that the collapse of East Germany would carry down the whole Soviet empire with it. But whereas in 1989 Gorbachev felt impotent to resist events, Khrushchev did not. It was necessary only to settle exactly what was to be done, and when. Khrushchev regarded the Vienna meeting as his chance to find out what the Americans would tolerate. Then there was the question of nuclear testing. Concern about its fall-out, and the politically destabilising consequences of the tests, was widespread in the West; indeed, the thirty years or so after Hiroshima might be called the Age of Nuclear Anxiety, and Kennedy, as a child of that age, had a heartfelt wish for a test ban treaty; but the Soviet commanders needed well-advertised nuclear weapons for the intimidation of the Chinese, and Khrushchev needed them to appease his generals. He indicated that the Soviet tests would shortly be resumed, in spite of the voluntary moratorium which the US and the USSR had observed for the past three years; but as he expected the Americans to be the first to abandon the moratorium he thought it worth waiting until they did; let them be the ones to suffer the condemnation of world opinion. In this respect, Vienna would be a chance to lull the Americans into a false sense of security.

The president and Mrs Kennedy left New York for Paris on the night of 30 May and were welcomed next day at Orly airport by General de Gaulle. There followed a dizzy three days which were extremely good for Kennedy's morale. It suddenly became clear that Europeans could be as enthusiastic about him as any Americans; the French seem to have been particularly entranced by Jacqueline Kennedy's beauty, elegance, intelligence and excellent French. When Kennedy held a news conference he began by remarking, 'I am the man who accompanied Jacqueline Kennedy to Paris, and I have enjoyed it.'[31] Everywhere they went there were vast, enthusiastic crowds; all the magnificence which the French state had at its disposal, in the tradition of its kings, from golden bathtubs in Paris to a glittering banquet at Versailles, was lavished on the Kennedys. The two presidents had five meetings, and treated each other with distinguished consideration, though each harboured some private reservations. The old General, with his peculiar insight, gave his young guest what he needed most. He supported the policy of neutralising Laos, as to which he was truly prophetic, if his memoirs are to believed:

> The more you become involved out there against communism, the more the Communists will appear as the champions of national independence, and the more support they will receive, if only from despair. . . . You will sink step by step into a bottomless milit-

ary and political quagmire, however much you spend in men and money.[32]

He told Kennedy that a statesman must have confidence in his own judgement; and he insisted that it was possible and prudent to stand up to the Russians in the matter of Berlin. Khrushchev was bluffing; he had been making threats for two and a half years which had come to nothing; he would never go to war over Berlin.[33] Thus fortified, Kennedy went on to Vienna on 3 June.

Cheering crowds turned out in that city too, but Kennedy had not come just to see and be seen by Austrians, and his two days of meeting with Khrushchev were a painful contrast to his sessions with De Gaulle. He had not expected to undertake any substantive diplomacy, but he had hoped that sufficient common ground might be discovered to make progress possible in negotiations elsewhere. Khrushchev had no such illusions. He had come to Vienna to test Kennedy and if possible to intimidate him, anyway to throw him off balance. As Kennedy quickly discovered, this rendered him impervious to charm, frankness, reason, courtesy or anything else. Instead he pushed, pushed and pushed at his adversary, trying to establish how far he could go – what he could get away with. Kennedy was appalled by such behaviour: after the first day's meeting he asked Llewellyn Thompson, the US ambassador to Moscow, 'Is it always like this?' 'Par for the course,' replied the ambassador.[34]

Anything less like the cameraderie of the US Senate would be hard to imagine. Try as he might, Kennedy could find no real common ground with Khrushchev, so that the cool discussion, leavened with humour, at which he was best, was impossible. Khrushchev began by brushing aside his nagging concern that a nuclear war might break out by miscalculation on one side or the other: 'Miscalculation! All I ever hear from your people and your news correspondents and your friends in Europe and everyplace else is that damned word miscalculation. . . . We don't make mistakes. We will not make war by mistake.'[35] He had nothing useful to say on nuclear testing: 'we will never be the first to break the moratorium. You will break it, and that will force us to resume testing.'[36] The subject of Berlin roused him to heights of bombast and assumed fury. He made few threats that he had not made before, insisting that it was time a peace treaty was signed recognising East Germany as a legitimate state and giving it control over East Berlin (West Berlin could be a 'free city'), but now he was making them face to face with the President of the United States, slapping the table and glaring as he cried, 'I want peace. But if you want war, that is your problem.' Unless the United States made some sort of concession, the Soviet Union would sign a peace treaty with East Germany in December. 'If that is true,' said Kennedy, 'it's going to be a cold winter.'[37]

He left Vienna sunk in gloom, irritation and anxiety, but the situation was less grave than he supposed. He had kept his temper, made no concessions to Khrushchev, and held his own under fire: it was not his fault that the Russians had not learned that he was not a man to be bullied. He could not know it, but Khrushchev, while not abating an ounce of his pressure, had apparently taken a liking to him. He had extracted one concession from the Soviet leader which, while of little importance to Khrushchev, meant a good deal to Kennedy: Laos, they had agreed, was too unimportant to be a subject of overt dispute between the superpowers. This convergence of views would do little for the Laotians, but it meant that there was one fewer possible flashpoint for war between the United States and the USSR, and one less stick for the Republicans to beat the president with. And he had learned, he felt, all he needed to know about Khrushchev's personality: he never agreed to meet him again. As his natural high spirits reasserted themselves he might have reflected that the conference, after all, had changed nothing: the Western allies were still in Berlin, NATO was still solid. De Gaulle might well be right: to judge by Khrushchev's deeds rather than his words, the actual danger of war was slight. He did not delude himself that the Berlin crisis had been averted, but he refused to talk it up. On his return to the United States he gave one of his cool, lucid television broadcasts by way of report to the American people, in which he was (by British standards) amazingly frank, but he did not lay any stress on the Berlin difficulty. Instead he suggested that East–West rivalry was going to be conducted chiefly in the Third World for the next decade, and used the idea to justify his foreign aid programme, which was just then under consideration in Congress. After that he went to ground: he did not hold a press conference for three weeks; when he did meet the press, he made a long, strong statement on the Berlin question: 'There is peace in Germany and in Berlin. If it is disturbed, it will be a direct Soviet responsibility.'[38] However, he did not yet have any policy to announce, and the journalists seemed, on the whole, to be interested in other matters. But behind the scenes the president was feverishly studying the crisis in all its aspects.

It was a pity that, distracted by Cuba and Laos, he had not done so sooner, for the Russians held the initiative, and they did not lose their opportunity. On 10 June they publicly renewed their threat to sign a separate peace treaty with East Germany, though Kennedy had made it clear that such an action would lead to a major crisis in East–West relations. Perhaps they thought that he was bluffing. If so they were much mistaken. In late July documents began to pour out of Washington making the allied case, and on 25 July Kennedy gave a television address *ad urbem et orbem*. He had largely allowed others to make the running since he assumed the presidency; now he tried to seize command.

Taking a line agreed by all the allies, Kennedy insisted that if there were a threat to peace, it was solely of Soviet making. 'The world knows that there is no reason for a crisis over Berlin today – and that if one develops it will be caused by the Soviet Government's attempt to invade the rights of others and manufacture tension.'[39] He tried to make it as plain as possible that the Western allies, and the United States in particular, meant to defend those rights. A programme was sent to Congress requesting over $3 billion in extra defence spending, and an extra $207 million for civil defence. More soldiers and sailors were to be recruited, reserve units were to be called up, individual service personnel were to have their hitches lengthened, ships and planes due for retirement would be kept in service, and there would be a vast additional procurement of non-nuclear weapons, ammunition and equipment.[40] The message could hardly be more explicit. Kennedy was standing by the three essentials laid down by the Eisenhower administration: access to air and ground in Berlin, continued Western military presence there, and the continued freedom of West Berlin.[41] This was NATO's sticking-point, and in the outcome it was asserted successfully; but something was omitted. W.W. Rostow noticed it at once: 'Kennedy was prepared to risk war to defend West Berlin but not to maintain access between the Soviet and Western Sectors,'[42] although such access was quite as much one of the West's legal rights as the other three matters.

Kennedy mentioned West Berlin fourteen times in his television speech, as if the rest of the city was of no concern to him.

In this he was being frank with the American people, but he was also, perhaps unintentionally, showing his hand to the Russians.[43] When he was told of the three essentials in May, Egon Bahr, one of the associates of Willy Brandt, then Mayor of Berlin, protested uselessly: 'This is almost an invitation for the Soviets to do what they want with the Eastern Sector.'[44] The West Berliners were not the only ones to think so. It seemed clear to the Soviet government that NATO was ready to leave East Berlin to its fate. So at midnight on 12 August 1961 the communists began to build what became the notorious Berlin Wall. In this way the Russians secured their own sticking-point.

The building of the Berlin Wall sent a shock of fear and outrage through the West. Instantly it became a sinister symbol of communist tyranny, and so it remained until the downfall of the East German regime nearly thirty years later. Its evil reputation was enhanced by the fate of so many of the rash souls who tried to get across it: killed, wounded, or merely seized by the border guards under the very eyes of the West, their fate perpetually reaffirmed West Berlin's identification with freedom and East Germany's hatefulness and incompetence. Khrushchev did not help matters by shrugging his shoulders: 'Such unpleasantness had to be expected,' and speaking of the Wall only as 'border controls'.[45] In the long run the Wall consolidated Western opinion, denied East Germany all legitimacy, and contributed to the de-romanticisation of the Soviet Union in Western eyes (thereby clearing the way for romanticism about Mao's China and Castro's Cuba). But none of these considerations justify Kennedy's acquiescence in the building of the Wall.

Yet it is hard to see what else he could have done. It is true that the 1945 agreements which legitimised the British, French and American presence in West Berlin also envisaged the unitary government of Berlin: the Iron Curtain was not supposed to run in front of the Brandenburg Gate. But in practice the Western powers had conceded the Eastern sector to the communists, both Russian and German, ever since the Berlin Rising of 1953, in which the West had conspicuously refused to interfere, as it had refused to help Hungary in 1956. The West might in theory refuse to admit the existence of the German Democratic Republic (GDR), but in practice had to accept it. The Berlin Wall simply put the fact of this acquiescence into barbed wire and concrete. Kennedy did not believe that the right of free movement between the sectors was worth a war, or the risk of a war; and it is noteworthy that none of his advisers, not even the headstrong Dean Acheson, ever suggested otherwise. All of them understood that Soviet prestige and power were deeply bound up with the permanence of the Ulbricht regime, and accepted that Khrushchev would have to take decisive action if it ever became necessary. And when, during July, the flow of refugees from East to West reached the rate of 10,000 a week, it was hard to deny that the time had come.

The Germans, in fact, held the key to the situation. No doubt alarm about the crisis, a determination to escape while the going was good, somewhat increased the flow of emigrants, but there is no reason to believe that the migration would have died away if Khrushchev had done nothing, nor had it been started by the crisis: rather, the crisis had been pushed into an intense phase by the migration. Kennedy and Khrushchev had been treading on each other's corns ever since January, but it was Ulbricht's insistence that something had to be done which brought about the Wall, and Khrushchev could not forever resist that insistence without imperilling his own political position. It is not even clear that a continuation of Eisenhower's stalling tactics, which had more or less defused the first phase of the Berlin crisis, would have worked; anyway, the 1960 election had brought the Democrats into power, and all of them, from Acheson to Adlai Stevenson, disapproved of Eisenhower's conduct of foreign policy. They did not believe in obfuscation, and Khrushchev must have been greatly relieved when the lines were so clearly drawn. At the same time, the essential caution of Soviet diplomacy was made clear: building the Wall was quite the least aggressive course it could have pursued. It consolidated the status quo, which Kennedy was always swearing to defend. In the short term it weakened neither side, and it postponed the day when the whole German question would have to be settled. As one historian has pointed out,[46] the ghost of the Grand Alliance still walked the stage. Neither East nor West really wanted German reunification just then; even the federal government in Bonn did not want it; and no one wanted a nuclear war either to bring about German reunification or to rescue Berlin. These facts lay just below the surface of events, undeniable but unmentionable, and largely explain what occurred. The ignoble resolution of the Berlin crisis (for as the year went on it gradually faded from the headlines, and was never revived) suited everyone very well, except the indignant Berliners.

Nevertheless, since they were so much the losers, it must be asked if any other outcome was possible; the reply seems to be No. Veterans of the Berlin Blockade, such as Acheson, were always inclined to believe that the Russians would climb down every time if treated stonily enough, but Acheson's bluster, as we have seen, did not exactly match his recommendations to the president. The European allies were unhelpful: as Sorensen says, 'the French were against all negotiations; the British were against risking war without negotiations; and the Germans, as their autumn elections drew nearer, were against both of these positions and seemingly everything else.'[47] Bobby Kennedy, reminiscing after his brother's death, remembered the French as being particularly uncooperative:

> The French were making speeches about it and refusing to talk to Khrushchev. On fundamental questions – what you would do if a plane was shot down from the ground . . . would you attack that ground installation with what kind of bombs; if planes came out to attack you as you were attacking the ground installation, would you send fighters up; how many fighters would you send; if a plane was shot down by another plane, what would you do – on all those fundamental questions, the individuals who wanted to take strong action in case the Russians or the Communists took action against us were always opposed by the French. The French were making public pronouncements about standing up on Berlin and not giving an inch. But when it finally got to the really unpleasant part of it, they were not going to stand fast.[48]

The Bay of Pigs affair had given both Kennedys a deep distaste for incompletely thought-out romantic schemes, and nothing they heard during the Berlin summer, except the course they actually chose, could stand up to prudent questioning. The new air force chief of staff, Curtis Le May, had only one answer to any problem: 'Bomb the hell out of 'em.'[49] This merely confirmed Jack Kennedy's doubts about his generals.

For one burden lay on him that no one could share, not even Bobby, and was never far from his mind. Being, by the Constitution, the US Commander-in-Chief, he, and he alone, of all Americans, could by making a mistake launch a world-destroying nuclear exchange. It was all very well for Acheson to look back fondly to the days of the Berlin airlift: the Soviet Union had not then possessed a nuclear arsenal. It was all very well for General de Gaulle, newly master of a *force de frappe*, to talk of defying Russia because, even if he could not destroy it, he could at least inflict unacceptable damage on it. It was noteworthy that the three veteran nuclear powers, the United States, Britain and the Soviet Union, were all in their different ways the most cautious during the dispute. Kennedy was certainly convinced that he should err on the side of caution, and brought round both McNamara and Rusk to his view.[50] Kennedy believed that the heart of the crisis lay in Khrushchev's perceptions of the United States. If he thought the American attitude a weak one, he might blunder into war one way – 'If Khrushchev wants to rub my nose in the dirt, it's all over.' If the Soviet leader thought that Kennedy was trying to bully him, he might react with equally fatal defiance. Somehow Khrushchev had to be taught to see sense, but 'That son of a bitch won't pay any attention to words. He has to see you move.'[51] This was for Kennedy the most educational aspect of the Berlin affair, and was to have invaluable consequences a year later. As to the Berliners, Kennedy was sorry for them, and prepared, within reason, to do his utmost for them; but he regarded the whole Berlin situation as an unfortunate historical anomaly, the unforeseen and unwanted consequence of the Second World War, and certainly not a fit cause of the Third World War. He was inclined to blame the West Germans for the melodrama surrounding Berlin: 'Well, if they think we are rushing into a war over Berlin, except as a last desperate move to save the NATO alliance, they've got another think coming.'[52]

In retrospect, the long Berlin crisis can be seen as one of the two dramatic episodes – the other being the Cuban missile crisis – which opened the second phase of the Cold War: what might be called the Kissinger phase, after the statesman who emerged as its leading theorist and practitioner. The Cold War had already become an institution of state, West and East, and had endlessly ramifying effects on the life of the world's peoples. It was Kennedy's fate to be part of the generation of statesmen who had to accomplish the transition from the first phase: the Acheson phase. They themselves had first to unlearn certain lessons. It was not many years since John Foster Dulles had talked of rolling back communism; whenever Western statesmen met in high conclave the question of German reunification was discussed as if it might be an immediate prospect; Kennedy did not believe this,[53] but on one notorious occasion he was to talk of a 'free Cuba' as if it might soon be attained.[54] Slowly the truth dawned, that the Cold War was no longer one of movement, if it ever had been, but one of attrition. NATO and the Warsaw Pact were permanent features of the landscape; communism would not advance westward to the Rhine, let alone to the Channel; Western democracy would not roll back Bolshevism to the borders of the Soviet Union. In the Kissinger period both sides would accept that neither expected, or sought, more than marginal, incremental gains, and that the nuclear threat made some degree of co-operation between the superpowers essential. It was on the whole a Western, even an American, logic; and it was the Kennedy administration which first imposed it on the East. It remained in operation until the economic and political weakness of the Soviet Union induced the third and final phase of the Cold War, the Gorbachev phase.

But how far the Soviet Union was from accepting this outlook was shown not only by Khrushchev's loudly trumpeted view of the Berlin affair: he saw it as a clear victory for Soviet policy; but by the news which reached Kennedy on 28 August, that the Soviet Union was about to resume nuclear tests in the atmosphere. 'Fucked again!' said the President of the United States.[55] He was furious: more furious, his advisers thought, at this betrayal than at any other piece of Soviet skulduggery during his presidency. He had stuck to the moratorium at no little political risk (most of his fellow-citizens thought that he should have resumed testing long since); he had believed Khrushchev's pledge not to be the first to resume; he was deeply committed to reducing the threat of nuclear weapons and nuclear fall-out; and now Khrushchev had shown that he preferred the development of Soviet weaponry, the appeasement of his military men, and the demonstration to the world of Soviet might (perhaps as compensation for having got so little out of the Berlin affair) to co-operation with the West.[56] Kennedy recalled the US delegate from a now pointless disarmament conference at Geneva. On 4 September, after three enormous Soviet atmospheric tests, he authorised the resumption of US tests underground. To pin the blame on the right chest, he and the British prime minister, Harold Macmillan, jointly proposed that the nuclear powers agree to forswear atmospheric tests in the future; predictably Khrushchev rejected the suggestion out of hand. Even now Kennedy was reluctant to resume atmospheric testing. When he appeared before the United Nations general assembly on 25 September he made his disarmament proposals the centrepiece of his address, but it was no good. On 30 October the Soviet Union, ignoring a last-minute plea from Kennedy, tested a 50 megaton bomb; so Kennedy that same day ordered preparations for the resumption of US atmospheric testing. American security seemed to require it, and if it did not, the American public did.

Superficially, Kennedy's first year in command of American foreign policy could hardly be rated a success. The Bay of Pigs had been a pure disaster, and his other initiatives had not been triumphs. The most he could claim was that he had kept the peace and maintained the Western alliance, while launching a new defence programme that would vastly strengthen the United States. It was not exactly what the inaugural address had promised. But below the surface much had been achieved. Kennedy had learned the rules of the complicated game in which he was now a player, and strengthened his hand for the future. Khrushchev might think him a greenhorn, but men had underestimated John F. Kennedy in the past, and paid for it later. Above all, the constant crises had strengthened Kennedy's hold on American opinion. Americans might or might not be safer in January 1962 than they had been in January 1961, but they felt that they were in good hands. Kennedy had convinced them, and much of the world, that while he was determined not to be outgunned or outmanoeuvred by the Soviet Union, he was genuinely anxious to negotiate, to work by peaceful means towards a reasonable settlement of outstanding disputes. This personal authority was to grow steadily for the next two years, and to prove itself an asset that Khrushchev could not, in the end, equal or resist. It is doubtful if Kennedy would have attained such a position so quickly if he had not inflicted so many lessons on himself in 1961.

. . .

NOTES

1. See *SP* pp. 65–81.
2. KOH: Dean Rusk. 'The mass of business is such that not even a Secretary of State can be his own Secretary of State.'
3. I use this term because it is geographically unambiguous and

finite, as the alternative, 'South-East Asia' (which, when appropriate, I also use), is not. 'Indo-China' means Vietnam, Cambodia and Laos; 'South-East Asia' can mean anything between the Philippines and the Bay of Bengal.

4. Dwight D. Eisenhower, *Waging the Peace*. Quoted in Jane Hamilton-Merritt, *Tragic Mountains: the Hmong, the Americans, and the secret war for Laos, 1942–1992* (Indiana 1993) p. 69.

5. Herbert S. Parmet, *JFK* (New York: Dial Press 1983) p. 81; Theodore C. Sorensen, *Kennedy* (New York: Harper & Row Perennial edn 1988) p. 640.

6. Sorensen, *Kennedy*, p. 645.

7. See Arthur J. Dommen, *Conflict in Laos: the politics of neutralization* (London: Pall Mall Press 1964) pp. 175–7.

8. KOH: Jack Bell.

9. Schlesinger, *TD*, p. 234.

10. KOH: Dean Acheson.

11. Schlesinger, *TD*, pp. 235–6.

12. At about this time Schlesinger took D.W. Brogan to have lunch at the White House with the president, who with characteristic indiscretion asked the distinguished foreign visitor what he thought of the scheme. Brogan said he was against it.

13. Dean Rusk, *As I Saw It* (New York: Norton 1990) p. 210.

14. Ibid., p. 209.

15. Gary Wills, *The Kennedy Imprisonment* (Boston: Little, Brown 1982) pp. 219, 222.

16. Schlesinger, *TD*, pp. 212–13.

17. Edwin O. Guthman and Jeffrey Shulman (eds) *Robert Kennedy in his Own Words* (New York: Bantam 1988) (RK, *Words*) pp. 240, 254.

18. *PP* i pp. 312–13.

19. Sorensen, *Kennedy*, p. 309.

20. Arthur M. Schlesinger Jr, *Robert Kennedy and his Times* (London: André Deutsch 1978) (Schlesinger, *RK*) p. 446.

21. Stephen M. Ambrose, *Eisenhower the President* (London: Allen & Unwin 1984) p. 638.

22. RK, *Words*, pp. 247–8.

23. When in 1962 Burke took to publicly criticising the administration, Kennedy cried impatiently, 'God, 31-Knot Burke! To think I used to admire these people!' (Richard Reeves, *President Kennedy: profile of power*, London: Papermac 1994, p. 307).

24. Sorensen, *Kennedy*, p. 295.

25. James N. Giglio, *The Presidency of John F. Kennedy* (Lawrence, KS: University of Kansas Press, 1991) pp. 40–1.

26. RK, *Words*, p. 246.

27. Schlesinger, *TD*, p. 273.

28. Ibid., p. 279.

29. Ibid., p. 285.

30. *PP* i p. 2, inaugural address.
31. Ibid., p. 429, press luncheon in Paris.
32. Michael R. Beschloss, *Kennedy v. Khrushchev: the crisis years 1960–63* (London: Faber 1991) pp. 184–5.
33. Ibid., pp. 183–6. On the main point De Gaulle was certainly right, as Khrushchev's memoirs show. Whether he knew how far Khrushchev was ready to carry his bluff, or what he was in actuality prepared to do about it, are different matters.
34. Ibid., p. 205.
35. Ibid., p. 196.
36. Ibid., p. 221.
37. Ibid., pp. 223–4.
38. *PP* i p. 477, president's news conference, 28 June 1961.
39. Ibid., p. 514, president's news conference, 19 July 1961.
40. Ibid., pp. 535–6, radio and television report to the American people on the Berlin crisis, 25 July 1961. Here and elsewhere 'billion' means the US billion – one thousand million.
41. Beschloss, *Kennedy v. Khrushchev*, p. 149.
42. Douglas Brinkley, *Dean Acheson: the Cold War years, 1953–71* (New Haven, CT: Yale University Press 1992) p. 145. Brinkley's discussion makes it plain that this was the attitude of the whole US team, including Acheson.
43. It is unlikely that he was confusing 'Berlin' with 'West Berlin', but cf. the American habit, in the 1960s, of saying 'Vietnam' when 'South Viet Nam' was meant.
44. Beschloss, *Kennedy v. Khrushchev*, p. 243n. Beschloss quotes Bahr as mentioning 'the Western Sector', but since this reduces the remark to nonsense I have ventured to emend it.
45. Nikita Khrushchev, *Khrushchev Remembers* (London: Book Club Associates 1971) p. 456.
46. Most regrettably, I cannot remember who.
47. Sorensen, *Kennedy*, pp. 590–1.
48. RK, *Words*, p. 274.
49. Ibid.
50. Sorensen, *Kennedy*, p. 590. Ann Tusa tells me that in fairness to Acheson it should be pointed out that he was trying to instil the precept that only brinkmanship could ever deter the Russians. Kennedy was to discover the truth in this when the missile crisis occurred.
51. Schlesinger, *TD*, p. 363.
52. Kenneth P. O'Donnell and David F. Powers, with Joe McCarthy, '*Johnny, We Hardly Knew Ye*' (Boston: Little, Brown 1972) p. 300.
53. Ibid., p. 299.
54. See p. 146.
55. Beschloss, *Kennedy v. Khrushchev*, p. 291.
56. Ibid., pp. 293–5, for all this.

Chapter 4

THE VIEW FROM
THE WHITE HOUSE

Foreign policy was the weightiest of the responsibilities laid by the US Constitution on the president's shoulders; but it was by no means the only one, and was only intermittently the chief concern of American politicians and the American people, even during the Cold War. According to the Constitution, the president is vested with the executive power of the government; with less dignity but equal accuracy he might as well have been described as the national housekeeper. Before everything else his duty is to make sure that nothing goes wrong; he takes an oath to 'preserve, protect and defend' the Constitution. Law-making is supposedly reserved to Congress, but practical necessity has eroded these distinctions. Not only does the president nowadays, of necessity, have a legislative programme, but also Congress has to be brought into the business of executive government. The president is to a large extent judged by the laws he gets through Congress, fails to get through Congress, or vetoes; senators and congressmen suffer or are benefited at election time in part according to their relationship with the president. The great task of national housekeeping is in fact, and has always been, a shared one. No one can be a successful president who does not take it seriously and is not prepared to devote at least half his time to it, and usually more.

Such was the reality which Kennedy faced, and knew he faced. He welcomed the challenge; he liked the idea of being Chief Legislator (in Harry Truman's phrase) and exercising the power which had eluded him in his days on Capitol Hill. But he hardly needed Richard Neustadt's warning that his power was severely limited;[1] he had been reflecting on the fact since he began to write his senior thesis. He knew quite well that next to democracy itself, no principle is more firmly rooted in the American public mind than that of the separation of powers. Both in its vertical form – the separation of the legislative, executive and judicial functions – and in its horizontal – the division between federal, state and local governments – it shapes the entire political structure, and is perhaps sufficient of itself to explain the proliferation of lawyers that is so marked a feature of American society. It is certainly sufficient to explain why the life of a president is a constant struggle, against the odds, to get things done; but he must also wrestle with another constraint, which may almost be called a third separation of powers. If the corporations, media, churches, labour unions, single-interest lobbies and so on are not constituted bodies that Montesquieu would have recognised, they do function as a permanent system of interlocking elites which all politicians have to take account of, the president most of all; their influence is acknowledged in numerous semi-official bodies in which they and officials both participate. So a president like Kennedy, with a large and challenging political programme to realise, will find himself facing a system that was originally designed precisely to impede bold action of any kind, and has, since its creation, developed a highly effective back-up.

The obstacles are formidable, and though they may vary slightly in detail from generation to generation, they are in essence always the same. To overcome them the president is supposed to have the aid of one of the two great political parties, but in reality the parties have created an additional layer of obstruction, since the forces which maintain the Republicans and Democrats frequently insulate their state and congressional leaders from any marked need to co-operate with the titular heads of their parties. This is above all true of presidential candidates who lose: the party headship, for them, becomes purely nominal the moment that the count of votes is complete. A president is in a much stronger position, but loyalty and discipline are rewards that he has to earn, and keep on earning. As between their voters and their president, party politicians have no difficulty in seeing where the greater power lies, and behave accordingly.

These constraints merely define the problem, they do not show that it is insoluble. Surveying the record of his three immediate predecessors, Kennedy had no particular reason to feel discouraged. Roosevelt, Truman and Eisenhower had each endured serious defeats at the hands of Congress, or the people, or sections of the people, but each had scored some remarkable victories too, and changed the course of American history. From the day of his election onwards, it was Kennedy's business to develop a strategy and tactics which would enable him to do at least as well, and for choice, better; a strategy that would re-elect him, and as many Democrats as possible, in 1964. He intended to succeed. He accepted that there would be many bumps in the road.

The first jolted him immediately after the inauguration, and thrust him into a battle which, had he lost it, would have been a catastrophe in domestic politics equivalent to the Bay of Pigs – and deriving, like that affair, from the new administration's inexperience. The Kennedy forces in the House of Representatives very nearly lost the vote on enlarging the Committee on Rules.

After the 1960 election the Democrats still controlled both chambers of Congress, but they had lost twenty seats in the House. This might not have mattered if the party had been united on matters of policy, but that was far from being the case. Although 'the Solid South' was beginning to break up under the strains of the civil rights revolution almost all senators and congressmen from Dixie were still nominally Democrats, and many of them were not only staunch supporters of white supremacy but also firmly conservative on everything else. By virtue of the seniority system gentlemen from the South headed most of the important congressional committees, from the Senate Foreign Relations to the House Ways and Means, and were thus excellently placed to influence presidential proposals and determine what would, or would not, pass through Congress. What is more, these reactionary Democrats had worked in informal coalition with the Republicans since 1938, when they had deserted Franklin Roosevelt. Their dominance explained why Congress had passed comparatively little liberal legislation in the two decades before 1960.

The Committee on Rules had originally been set up simply to streamline and expedite the House's business. Its job was to decide on the timetable of debate and decision, and it had been no part of its mandate to determine matters of policy. But over the years the committee had in effect usurped part of the legislative power. Its chairman was 'Judge' Howard Smith of Virginia, a rock-hard reactionary, who with the support of fellow southern Democrats on the committee and the Republican minority had taken it upon himself to kill almost every progressive proposal that came before him: he would not release any from his committee to the House floor for a vote. Procedures existed for prising a bill from his jaws, but they were cumbersome, time-consuming and uncertain. Kennedy could be sure that Smith, left to himself, would smother most of the presidential programme, which was bad enough; but that the Rules Committee, a body with little or no democratic authority, created solely for the convenience of the representatives, should have in effect turned itself into a third chamber of Congress was intolerable. If the Founding Fathers had wanted such a body they would have created it; but they had deemed the Senate and the House sufficient.

Kennedy was far from alone in his opposition to the committee's usurpation. The House liberals had been struggling against it for years, and would certainly back the president if he made a fight. More important, the venerated Speaker had come to the conclusion that there was nothing for it but to have a showdown. Mr Rayburn, whose governing maxim for congressmen was 'if you want to get along, go along', had tolerated Smith's behaviour for years, so long as the chairman was prepared to go along when the Speaker told him it was really necessary. The two veterans had known each other all their political lives, and Rayburn remembered that it was he who had put Smith on the committee in the first place. But Smith, arrogant with the growing certainty of his invincibility, chose to forget this, and during the 1950s, especially after the rise of the civil rights movement, proved less and less co-operative with the majority of what was supposed to be his own party. Even before Jack Kennedy won the presidential nomination, Mr Rayburn had made up his mind that something would have to be done.

Frontal assault of any kind was out of the question. Given the institutional conservatism of the House and its members' devoted respect for the seniority principle, it would be useless to attempt to remove Judge Smith from his chairmanship or his supporters from the committee. The Speaker decided that he would try to add three new members to the twelve-member committee: one Republican and two trustworthy Democrats. In this way he would give the president's supporters a majority of one. Mr Rayburn had been deeply impressed by Kennedy's campaign and by his inaugural address, and as he got to know him better he liked him more and more. If anyone could defeat Judge Smith, he could, and his heart was in the business. So Kennedy was content to leave the battle to the veteran commander. But though the Speaker had warned him it would be tough, Kennedy was not expecting to be told, on the day before the vote was scheduled, that he was going to lose.

As Larry O'Brien was to put it later, the new White House team had barely taken off the tuxedos they had donned for the inauguration Balls,[2] but they swung into action immediately. The vote was postponed until the day after the State of the Union message, and O'Brien, with some trusted assistants, hurried up to the Hill. Every ounce of presidential influence was used: it was one of the three occasions during his presidency when Kennedy staked everything, all his power and prestige, on an unambiguous test.[3] He had little choice. In public he said that it was all a congressional matter, from which he, as president, was and ought to be standing aloof. He told a press conference that while he supported Rayburn, 'the responsibility rests with the Members of the House, and I would not attempt to infringe upon that responsibility. I merely give my views as an interested citizen,'[4] but everybody laughed cynically, as no doubt he meant them to. Everyone knew that the success of the Kennedy administration largely depended on victory in this battle. On the day of the final vote in the House there was high drama: Mr Rayburn came down from the Speaker's chair, as he very seldom did, and made as strong a plea as he knew how for the proposal to be passed – and so it was, 217 to 212. His biographers give Rayburn all the credit, but without the intervention of the White House there would have been no victory to celebrate.

Victory; but as Kennedy remarked to Sorensen, 'with all that going for us, with Rayburn's own reputation at stake, with all of the pressures and appeals a new President could make, we won by five votes. That shows you what we're up against.'[5] The moral was obvious: legislative leadership could not be delegated to the Democrats in Congress. Rather to his surprise, Larry O'Brien was given the permanent job of organising liaison with both chambers, and his *ad-hoc* group became a fixture. This turned out to be one of Kennedy's most successful dispositions. His leadership of Congress has been unfairly denigrated over the years by comparisons with his successor, Lyndon

Johnson, who was one of the most successful managers of Congress in history; possibly the most successful. LBJ was certainly a genius at bending Congress to his will, but even geniuses need favourable circumstances in which to operate at their best, even geniuses need collaborators, and Kennedy had furnished his successor with both. The body which Johnson inherited was already much more manageable than it had been in 1961, and Johnson kept O'Brien – Kennedy's man – in the job which he did so well. Contrary to myth, Kennedy himself was a fine congressional manager; the fact is usually overlooked because, throughout his years, he had such a narrow margin of support in Congress, and partly because his style was so different from Johnson's. O'Brien had two maxims, neither of which had much appeal to LBJ, but both of which were pure Kennedy. He scrupulously respected the separation of powers, as he had to: there had never been a permanent White House congressional liaison team before, and it would have been all too easy to convince touchy legislators that it was an intrusion and a usurpation. Second, O'Brien never asked a senator or representative to commit political suicide for the president. 'We really, really need your vote; do this for Jack' was the farthest he would go.[6] Kennedy himself took the same line in the Oval Office: if a congressman or senator indicated that it was politically impossible for him to help the president, Kennedy quietly accepted the assertion. To the Johnsonian school, all this was mere weakness; but as usual Kennedy was taking a long view. He never forgot how little Congress owed to him, how small was his majority in 1960; he saw his job as that of gradually building up respect and loyalty, accumulating a capital fund on which he could later draw. O'Brien cultivated Congress full time; when he was not actively negotiating, ahead of some crucial vote, he was entertaining legislators to brunch, or to trips on the presidential yacht, *Sequoia*. Before long he was on excellent terms with everyone in Congress except the notoriously intransigent Representative Otto Passman, of Louisiana, whose mission in life was to sabotage the foreign aid programme. There was nothing to be done about Passman, who had been as unbearable to President Eisenhower as he was to President Kennedy; but most of his Democratic colleagues, and even occasional Republicans, found that it was positively agreeable, from time to time, to work with the White House. It was nice to be on the winning side. O'Brien kept the president in reserve: he wanted it always to be an honour and an event to receive a telephone call from Kennedy; but he saw to its that the members of Congress, and particularly the leaders, got to know the president better; for as they did so they all discovered, as had Sam Rayburn, that they liked him a lot. O'Brien became a master at pushing through the presidential programme: as he liked to boast, he had a good year in 1961 and a better in 1962. In 1961, of fifty-four presidential bills sent to Congress, thirty-three were passed ('more than had been passed in the final *six* years of the Eisenhower administration'),[7] a success rate of 61 per cent. In 1962, out of another fifty-four, forty were passed: 74 per cent.[8] To someone used to the British system, in which a government can normally expect to pass every bill it submits, these figures may seem less than impressive; but in the US system, with the separation of powers and far less party discipline, the figures effectively demonstrate the skill of O'Brien and the congressional Democratic leaders (Senator Mike Mansfield, Speaker John McCormack and others) and, incidentally, Kennedy's legislative activism.

Yet they are not to be taken entirely at face value. The bills which the president signed into law often differed substantially from those which he had sent up to the Hill (as Washingtonians call the Capitol); in spite of O'Brien's claims, not all the bills which passed were of great importance; and some of great importance were lost or (like civil rights proposals before 1963) not even submitted. Kennedy was never in a position to command Congress; few presidents ever are. His task was to nibble away at the opposition, to gain ground steadily, if he could, in the hope that a triumphant re-election in 1964 would sweep away the last resistance and make the enactment of the complete Kennedy programme certain. Meanwhile the author of *Profiles in Courage* never forgot his maxims that 'a fair or poor bill is better than no bill at all, and that only through the give-and-take of compromise will any bill receive the successive approval of the Senate, the House, the President and the nation.'[9]

Larry O'Brien's figures do at least demonstrate that the view, widespread at the time of Kennedy's death, that the administration had failed with Congress was wrong. It was a myth, related to another, which presented Kennedy himself as relatively uninterested in domestic politics and uncommitted to his programme: a myth which saw something sinister in Kennedy's faith in compromise. This was profoundly to misread the man. Like Joe Kennedy and all his children, Jack liked battle and victory, and if it was a battle to get laws through Congress, then it was one he could not avoid and wanted to win. When, in 1961, he heard that his proposal for a universal minimum wage of $1.25 had been lost in the House by one vote, he was so furious that he jabbed his letter-opener into his desk.[10] But there was more to it than that. In essence, Kennedy was a deeply reserved man: he held back something of himself in all relationships (except possibly with Bobby and, at the very end, with his wife); his charm, his humour, his ironical approach to life, all protected this hidden self; but his impulses were human and generous. He was intensely curious about life, in part because he knew from how much his moneyed upbringing had shielded him: he had not experienced the Depression and the New Deal from below, as had Larry O'Brien and Lyndon Johnson. Inevitably, most of the legislation he recommended to Congress had to go forward without deep emotional commitment on his part: he was no doubt intellectually convinced of its merits or its political necessity, but probably not even Hubert Humphrey could have believed with equal passion in every single bill. There were simply too many of them. But Kennedy could be educated into passion by direct experience. As we saw in Chapter 2, he had been horrified by the poverty he encountered in West Virginia; he committed himself to doing something about it, and his first executive order was to speed up the distribution of food to the poor. At the time of his death he was preparing a programme which later, much expanded, in Lyndon Johnson's time, became the War on Poverty.

The most reliably educative force in the president's life was his family. His eldest sister, Rosemary, had for years been an invalid: mentally retarded as a child, she had been lobotomised, in obedience to the best (or at any rate the most expensive) medical opinion in 1941; the operation destroyed her. She was sent to a 'home' for incapables, where she has since remained, while her parents and siblings tried to come to terms with their guilt and grief. When Joe Jr was killed, a foundation was set up in his memory, of which Eunice Kennedy Shriver became the effective head: it disbursed some $1.5 million annually to programmes to help mentally retarded people. Mrs Shriver, thought by some to be the ablest of all the Kennedys, made no bones about seeing Jack's election to the presidency as a godsend for her causes. They included the treatment of mental illness, and prenatal care ('more money is spent on pregnant cows than on pregnant women,' she would say),[11] but the related problem of mental retardation was always her chief concern. Prodded by her, Kennedy first set up a committee to investigate the treatment and prevention of mental retardation, and to make recommendations; and then, when as a result bills began to move through Congress (launched by a special presidential message on 27 February 1962),[12] advertised his support for them on every possible occasion. He agreed to everything that Mrs Shriver asked of him and, Congress finding her equally irresistible, the bills became law.

They revolutionised arrangements for mentally retarded people in the United States, but like all laws their consequences were variously good, bad, indifferent and unforeseen. For example, the last congressional bill that Kennedy ever signed into law was one 'for the construction of mental retardation facilities and community mental health centres'. He was warm in his commendation of the bill: it was, he said, the most significant effort in the field that Congress had ever undertaken. 'I think that in the years to come those who have been engaged in this enterprise . . . will recognise that there were not many things that they did during their time in office which had more of a lasting impact on the well-being and happiness of more people.' And indeed the bill sponsored research into the causes of mental retardation and the causes of premature birth, and promised to train more nurses and open new therapeutic centres. 'It should be possible, within a decade or two, to reduce the number of patients in mental institutions by 50 per cent or more.' It all sounded truly splendid.[13]

Unfortunately, as Senator Daniel Patrick Moynihan pointed out thirty years later (he had been one of the authors of the programme), things did not work out entirely as they should. The research was undertaken and the therapeutic system improved, but although the public mental hospitals were emptied, so that in New York state alone the number of inmates had been reduced by more than 90 per cent by 1995, community health centres were not built in anything like sufficient numbers; patients were simply tipped from public institutions into private ones, which were no improvement.[14]

It is a tragic story, which illustrates the limitations of human foresight and of the liberal reforms of the 1960s, and the wisdom of Christ's maxim that, having set your hand to the plough, you must not look back. But Kennedy is hardly to be blamed for the abandonment of America's commitment to the weak: he has not been around to resist it. The worst that can be said of him and his sister is that they meant well, which is more than can be said of those who dominate Congress today. His course in office was honourable and characteristic. He was fond of children: charming photographs show him receiving a handicapped boy at the White House during Mental Retardation Week. Child health was another of those issues which struck home to him through his personal experience: when he asked Mrs Shriver why a new institute of child health was necessary ('he was having trouble with the budget') she said: 'What about your own son? You probably wouldn't have lost one of your children if we knew more about prematurity.'[15] He took the point: in August 1963 Jacqueline Kennedy had given premature birth to a boy, hastily christened Patrick Bouvier Kennedy, who died within forty hours of hyaline membrane disease, to his parents' intense distress. In similar vein Kennedy came to labour for peace because he wanted the world to be safe for Caroline and John Jr.

Other tales of his attitude to legislation might ring a note of aristocratic largesse – *noblesse oblige*. But causes like mental retardation were taken up by a man who shared the ordinary fate of humanity. Ambassador Kennedy's stroke in 1961 was disaster enough in itself, and it left the family with heavy medical and care bills to meet for the rest of his life. The Kennedys could meet them without difficulty, but the president reflected that the burden would be intolerable to most families, who had not a millionaire's wealth. It stiffened his resolve to set up a system of federally backed medical insurance ('Medicare'), which had anyway been part of the Democratic programme since 1945. It did not pass Congress in his lifetime, nor indeed until after the 1964 election; but the president's identification with the proposal (immensely popular with elderly voters, though not with the American Medical Association) clarified and strengthened his position and that of his party in American life and prepared the way for Lyndon Johnson's great victory. Running through all Kennedy's public papers is his earnest belief in the possibility and desirability of educating the American voting public by never wearying in laying the same arguments before them, again and again, until they were convinced. Where mental retardation was concerned, for instance, he repeatedly made three or four simple points: that whereas in Sweden only 1 per cent of the population was mentally backward, in the United States 3 per cent were, a difference which demonstrated unarguably that improvement was possible; and that prevention made more economic sense than present conditions, for mental retardation cost the country far more dollars than a programme to reduce it ever would; and that scientific advances, of the kind which the Kennedy Foundation sponsored, could make an enormous difference. Again and again he told the story of how he was visited in the White House by two little girls, sisters, one of whom was condemned to a lifetime of backwardness while the other was not because, although she had exactly the same medical vulnerability as her sister, in the two years that separated their births science had discovered the key dietary changes which could make her safe. In this way Kennedy hoped to teach the people the possibility, and therefore the desirability, of action; or if not the people (it never became a great popular cause) then Congress. It was a typical Kennedy approach.[16]

Meanwhile there was the daily business of dealing with the two chambers. The House was the more intractable prospect, although the death of Speaker Rayburn in the autumn of 1961 did not prove so damaging as was feared. Rayburn was succeeded by his veteran deputy, John McCormack of Massachusetts. The Kennedys and the McCormacks were rival Boston tribes,[17] and in 1962 the new Speaker's son Eddy entered the Democratic primary as a candidate for the Senate seat that had been vacated by Jack Kennedy. The youngest Kennedy brother, Teddy, was also a candidate, and walloped McCormack before going on to a landslide victory in the general election. This might have made for bad blood between the president and the Speaker (Jack had had his doubts about letting Teddy put himself forward) but in fact seems to have done no harm. McCormack and his team (Carl Albert of Oklahoma and Hale Boggs of Louisiana) worked loyally and effectively with O'Brien from start to finish. All agreed that the secret of progress lay with the southern Democrats. As representation in the House is allocated according to population, rather than by state,[18] northern and urban Democrats carried much greater weight than they did in the Senate; they provided a fairly reliable core of support for the president; but in neither the 1961 nor the 1963 Congress could they make a majority overall. Republican party loyalty and discipline (always much greater than Democratic) ensured that even liberal Republicans would seldom help. So O'Brien set out to woo the least intractable southerners: not only could they give him the essential margin for victory, however narrow, but also, thanks to the seniority system, they controlled most of the important committees. The Rules Committee might have been tamed (though it could still bite occasionally), but there was still the Ways and Means Committee to manage. Its chairman, Wilbur Mills of Arkansas, was so powerful that O'Brien's routine test of any proposed political move (for instance, over Medicare) was always 'How will this play with Wilbur?' He knew where the power lay, and did not disguise (at any rate in retrospect) that he was prepared to leave the liberals in the lurch, hard though they might be working for the presidential proposals, if that meant getting Mills and others like him on board. He was so successful that he finally broke, he believed, the southern–Republican coalition: by the autumn of 1963 at least half the southern Democrats were voting regularly with their party.[19] The House was never a liberal body in Kennedy's time, but it became a manageable one.

The Senate was a significantly different proposition. It was smaller than the House, senators were elected to six-year terms (as opposed to representatives' two years), and the Democrats, during Kennedy's presidency, had 65–67 seats to the Republicans' 35–33. All this made co-operation easier to secure. But in terms of population the South and the West (also a conservative region) were grossly over-represented: the senators from New York, then the largest state (population 16,782,000 according to the 1960 census) had the same two votes as the senators from North Dakota (population 618,000). This was the underpinning of the conservative coalition; it was further reinforced by the Senate principle of open debate, which meant that a resolute group of senators could filibuster an unacceptable bill to death, unless two-thirds of the senators present and voting agreed to 'cloture' – the ending of debate. But Kennedy knew the Senate well, and he had advisers who were more expert than he (though Lyndon Johnson does not appear to have offered his advice very frequently) and before long he had discovered the key to making progress. He set out, as unobtrusively as possible, to replace the permanent coalition between the Republicans and the southern Democrats with an occasional one between the Republicans and the northern Democrats.

The Republican party in the early 1960s was perhaps as heterogeneous as it had ever been since its great split in 1912. Rising on the Right was the conservatism then associated with Senator Barry Goldwater of Arizona; still buoyant on the Left (until Governor Nelson Rockefeller blew his chances of a presidential nomination)[20] was the New York Republicanism that owed its success, such as it was, to a 'Yes, but –' attitude to the New Deal. In between was the miscellaneous Republicanism of the Middle West, representing everything from the business interests of Chicago to the unreconstructed isolationism of rural Iowa. In the Senate the majority of this motley army followed their leader, Senator Everett Dirksen of Illinois. Dirksen could regularly deliver twenty votes or so, and these, added to the votes of the liberal and moderate Democratic senators, would make a Senate majority. Kennedy did not expect such a coalition to manifest itself very often (normally he relied on O'Brien to bring in southerners as he did in the House) but he would need it on great occasions. So he himself undertook to cultivate Dirksen.

He and Bobby had also tried to 'stroke' J. Edgar Hoover, the formidable head of the Federal Bureau of Investigation (FBI), with no success. Dirksen was a much easier proposition. He represented a state with large industrial and urban interests, so he could not afford to get too far out of line with what Chicago wanted: and Chicago was controlled by an alliance of big business and the Democratic machine. His economic and social views were conservative, but he was not unreasonable, unintelligent or unpatriotic. A man of considerable personal charm, he got on very well with Jack Kennedy. Finally, as Minority Leader he knew that only through collaboration with the White House could he hope to effect much (it was not enough for him simply to stop things). No doubt he would have preferred to have a Republican in the presidency, but failing that, Kennedy would do very well. He became a regular visitor to the White House, and the horse-trading never ceased.

Kennedy never advertised or explained his relationship with Dirksen: that would have been to invite trouble. But its manifestations could not go altogether unnoticed. In the congressional elections of 1962, for instance, Kennedy campaigned vigorously for his party's candidates, saying wherever he went that the New Frontier needed more Democratic congressmen and senators. But he conspicuously failed to deliver more than a formal endorsement of Dirksen's opponent in the Illinois senatorial election (which Dirksen won). In the same year the president did a deal with Dirksen that nearly wrecked Senator Kefauver's drugs bill, and did strip it of its price-control mechanisms. These manoeuvres were incomprehensible to the pure-minded; but the fact was that Dirksen's collaboration was worth far more to the president than the success of the odd Democrat.

The calculation paid off stupendously. Whether it was the Nuclear Test Ban Treaty in 1963 (which needed the support of two-thirds of the senators present to pass) or the Civil Rights Act of 1964 (passed after Kennedy's death, but essentially his Act, got through by the strategy which he devised) Dirksen came across. The process involved give and take on both sides: the legislation that was put through Congress by Kennedy, and after him Johnson, was seldom just what the executive wanted, and sometimes had been drastically modified from its White House original. But the alternative was no legislation at all; anyway it is a curious liberalism which denies the right of Congress to make its contribution to reform and new law according to its own sense of its duty. Congress, after all, has the constitutional job of drawing up and passing on legislation; it is also the originating body of most of the reforms that eventually find their way into the statute book. The president is an energising rather than a creative force, and except when a quite exceptional congressional leader emerges, such as Lyndon Johnson between 1955 and 1960 (which hardly ever happens), his chief job is to find the compromises which successfully steer bills to enactment. When he pleases, he is the most important legislative leader; but he is not the only one, and he cannot, in the last analysis, do Congress's work for it.

The institutional and personal constraints of dealing with Congress (which always has its share of vain and intractable individuals) may be matched by a president's own complicating obligations. This was certainly the explanation of Kennedy's most undeniable congressional failure. His success as a legislator was largely to be explained – taking a large view – because he was cutting with the grain: what he wanted was what America wanted, and was coming to expect (this was true even of such

an apparently quixotic campaign as his mental health undertakings).[21] America wanted, decidedly, improved education,
whether in junior or high schools, in colleges or in universities.
Kennedy was anxious to supply it, and brought education bills
to Congress in every session; but he found that he was hopelessly hampered by his religious identity and the pledges he
had given as a candidate. He had told the ministers at Houston
that he believed in an America where the separation of church
and state was absolute, and Protestant America would certainly
hold him to that. As he remarked to Sorensen, the real test
was not his election, but his administration: if he proved by
his actions that a Catholic president was not the tool of the
Catholic hierarchy, the religious issue would be dead for ever;
if not, not.[22] He was right, and the story of educational reform
during his presidency was the demonstration.

Kennedy was deeply committed to the educational programme which he had announced during the 1960 campaign.
The national birth-rate had ballooned since 1945; partly for
that reason, and partly because there had been no fresh investment in the public school system during the Depression and
the Second World War,[23] there were not enough teachers and
not enough school buildings for the millions of children who
needed them; such teachers as there were were underpaid and
often underqualified, and the buildings were all too generally
decayed. Furthermore, thanks to the baby boom, 'a veritable
tidal wave of students is advancing inexorably on our institutions of higher education',[24] although far too many of them
would be unable to pay for undergraduate study, and most universities and colleges were unable to cope with such numbers.
Kennedy knew all the discouraging statistics by heart:

> only six out of every ten students in the fifth grade would finish
> high school; only nine out of sixteen high school graduates would
> go on to college; one million young Americans were already out
> of school and out of work; dropouts had a far higher rate of un-
> employment and far lower rate of income.[25]

Only the most reactionary believed that the federal government should do nothing about this crisis, but leave it to the
states: even Senator Taft had abandoned that position years
before his death.[26] President Kennedy had never believed in it.
It is not surprising that, according to Sorensen, one-third of all

the principal Kennedy programmes made some form of education a central element.[27] Nor is it surprising that one of the most conspicuous proposals of his first month in office was a bill to bring the resources of the federal government to the aid of the state governments, which had exhausted their tax-base in their attempts to pay for education.

Even before his inauguration Kennedy knew that he was running into trouble: Cardinal Spellman of New York, a notoriously illiberal prelate, had fiercely attacked the report of Kennedy's educational task force. (These 'task forces', which as somebody said might as well have been called committees, had been set up by the president-elect to help him prepare for the job of governing: there were a dozen or so of them.) The difficulty was that while half of the United States' 10 million Catholic children went to public schools, and would benefit directly from any money spent on those schools, half did not, going instead to schools run by the Catholic Church, which, according to the Supreme Court's interpretation of the Constitution, might not be subsidised by tax dollars, for that would violate the First Amendment.[28] As a practical man, Kennedy was unintimidated by this constitutional fetish: he knew it could be got round; but he also knew that he, the first Catholic president, jealously watched, was not the man to get round it: 'Eisenhower could have dealt with this whole problem, but I can't.'[29] So his bill for aid to schools excluded the parochial schools, and the wrath of his Church fell on his head. The strength of Catholic views was made known to Congress, and to the House of Representatives. The message was, no money for us, no money for anybody.

Kennedy never had much trouble with the Senate over this issue. States are so large and varied that on most issues no one group is in a position to tell a senator what to do: there is always countervailing pressure. A senator's instinct is therefore to search for a middle position. So on education Kennedy always had a majority in his old chamber. Matters were far more complicated in the House. There, not only were a higher proportion of the Democrats themselves Catholics, but also many of them came from districts where Catholics were in the overwhelming majority. Even that might not have mattered, but the Republicans were delighted to exploit a Democratic split: they voted solidly against the Kennedy bill. And lurking not far from the surface was the race issue. Conservative southern

Democrats opposed federal intervention in education because they believed (quite rightly) that it would lead to intervention against segregation in southern schools. Administration pressure was fatally weakened by the president's need to hold aloof. What all this amounted to was shown when the reconstituted Rules Committee voted on whether or not the bill should go to the floor of the House. The administration could not appease the Catholics without enraging the Protestants, and vice versa. So Representative James Delaney of New York city, a Catholic and a Democrat, cast his vote with Judge Smith and the Republicans to kill the bill, in spite of all Larry O'Brien's pleadings ('He didn't want a thing,' said O'Brien afterwards. 'I wish he did').[30] The bill was dead for 1961. Kennedy resubmitted it, in even stronger form, in 1962, but was defeated more roundly than before: in particular, the National Education Association, a schoolteachers' lobby, threw its considerable weight against the proposals to aid higher education, apparently on the grounds that public money should not subsidise private institutions, such as Harvard and Notre Dame.[31] The president was enraged by this. Both the Secretary for Education, Abraham Ribicoff, and the Commissioner of Education resigned, completing the rout of the administration's not very effective leadership.

Before resigning to run for the Senate, Ribicoff had lamented, 'there is not a full commitment to education in this Nation.'[32] Kennedy refused to accept this, and in 1963 sent up yet another education bill. He made two great concessions to the opposition: he dropped for the time being his plans to help the schools and to provide scholarships for needy college students. His 1963 bill was solely concerned with higher education facilities. It sailed through. All sides were rather ashamed of themselves, and the educational crisis was worse than ever. The Catholics withdrew their opposition, because their colleges and universities were eligible for funds under the bill; and Wayne Morse, guiding the law through the Senate, cunningly dodged the threat of a southern filibuster. The bill was signed into law before Christmas; as President Johnson remarked, the credit for it was chiefly President Kennedy's. But it took Kennedy's death and the election of 1964, when the Democrats gained thirty-seven seats in the House, to bring about the passage of the measure to aid America's schools which he had had so much at heart.

Congressional relations, though central to any assessment of a president's domestic leadership, are by no means the whole matter. No president can forget for a moment that beyond Washington looms the vast mysterious entity known as the American people; nearer at hand are the great baronies of society. No president can hope to please all the people all the time, or to gratify every interest simultaneously; indeed some presidents have made a successful career out of picking the right enemies and fighting them; but the good government of the United States demands that the modern president work towards some sort of stability in his relations with the churches, the corporations and the great agencies of the state (to give but three examples). Certainly, to understand Kennedy it is necessary to examine his record in all these matters, and also to inquire how he managed to win and keep the confidence of the voters.

Perhaps his most difficult partner in the slow waltzes of democracy was the business community. Here the tradition of the Democratic party was partly responsible. American business leaders had never been eager to accept the blame for the 1929 crash and the consequent Depression, and in the Roosevelt and Truman years the stock-in-trade of the Democrats had been their regular denunciations of the 'malefactors of great wealth' whose greed and incompetence had brought such misery upon the American people. By the 1950s this no longer made sense. For good or ill, what Roosevelt called 'the American profit system' had survived (partly because of his own policies), the corporations had regained their self-confidence and much of their influence, and the task of the US government was now to make sure that the system worked as well as possible for the benefit of all. Adlai Stevenson was the first national Democratic leader to attempt a rapprochement with big business, and Kennedy, not surprisingly, given his father's eminence as a businessman, was prepared to go a great deal further. One of his first acts as president was to offer huge 'investment credits' to businesses which modernised their plant or launched new enterprises. The costs could be set against taxation. This scheme was one of the president's plans to make the US economy fully competitive in the world market, and he expected business people to be appreciative. No Republican president would have dared, at that date, so blatantly to favour the business interest.

The response was grudging at best. Kennedy should not have expected anything else. American financiers, industrialists and traders, in spite of their pretensions, are curiously stupid about politics. Intensely conservative for the most part, they judge everything through a haze of ideology (which usually turns out to be whatever nonsense the *Wall Street Journal* is spouting this week) and are poor judges of the motives and actions of other people. Immovably convinced of their own rectitude and ability, they are unable to understand that from time to time they are greedy and corrupt, just like lesser mortals. Understanding their own affairs very well, they do not easily grasp that there is a world elsewhere: they mistake the part for the whole. They also mistake obsolete prejudices for genuine principles. In 1961 this meant that they were suspicious of Kennedy, and their reaction to the investment credits was to ask both why he had not done a great deal more for them, and why he had done anything at all. They were psychologically incapable of believing that any good could come to them from a Democrat, or any ill from a Republican, though President Eisenhower's parting warning against a 'military–industrial complex' was the most memorable thing he ever said, and although Kennedy, in reducing taxes on business, was blatantly continuing the trend of Eisenhower's policies.

Not every businessperson was so obtuse, and indeed business itself was deeply divided: the interests of big business and small, for example, were not identical, and some individuals and companies were comparatively quick to comprehend the administration's policies. But if Kennedy was to establish a satisfactory partnership with business (he wanted it to be a three-hander, including also organised labour) he would have to work at it ceaselessly, and with more than all his usual vigour.

The defining crisis came in the spring of 1962, in the affair of United States Steel. Kennedy's economic policy was shaped by various preoccupations. The most important was the balance of payments and the gold drain. Under the Bretton Woods system the dollar was pegged to gold, and was the chief stabiliser of world trade; this had been no disadvantage in 1945, when the United States was in a position of overwhelming economic predominance; but with the revival of other trading nations, and the outflow of gold to pay for America's Cold War exertions, the American position dangerously weakened. Kennedy had no intention of cutting back on expenditure on national security, in which he included his programmes of foreign aid (such as the Alliance for Progress); the alternative was to stabilise the domestic economy by keeping costs down, restoring the United States' international competitiveness; it was no disadvantage that this policy was also anti-inflationary. One consequence was that he and his advisers kept a close eye on the steel industry, for at that time rises in the price of steel quickly drove up the price of everything else.

The triennial wage agreements in the industry were due for renewal in 1962, and Kennedy used all his influence with the unions to keep their wage claims down to a minimum. In return for such restraint on labour's part he expected the big steel companies to absorb the small cost of the actual increases and forgo a rise in the price of their product. The general argument for this course was that it would help promote economic stability; the immediate argument was that by keeping prices low economic activity would be encouraged: more steel would be sold, to the companies' profit. This was clearly the administration's policy, and had been explicit for months. It was on this understanding that the Steelworkers Union had accepted wage restraint, and Kennedy believed that he had a gentleman's agreement with the companies to abide by his policy.

He was, therefore, furious when the president of US Steel, Roger Blough, looked in at the White House on 10 April 1962, four days after the wage settlement, to say that he would be putting up the price of the steel produced by his company by six dollars a ton. Blough did not need to say that since 'Big Steel' was the dominant force in the industry, most of the other steel companies would immediately do the same. Kennedy does not seem to have expressed the full measure of his wrath to Blough, telling him merely that he was making a mistake; but Arthur Goldberg, the Secretary of Labor, whose skilful diplomacy had deserved most of the credit for securing the wage agreement, said bluntly that it was a double-cross.[33] He and the president were confronted with the impending collapse of the stabilisation policy, a renewed threat to the US balance of payments, and, worst of all, the destruction of the president's authority: if US Steel were allowed to get away with this defiance, no union or corporation would ever take Kennedy seriously again.

So as soon as Blough had left the Oval Office Kennedy

mobilised the full power of the presidency to force a climb-down. It was probably then that he made a remark which soon became notorious: 'My father always said that steelmen were sons-of-bitches, but I never believed him until now.'[34]

Many a book (such as those of Richard Neustadt) and many an article have been written to demonstrate the limited power of the US president. The steel crisis shows that the limits derive more from the president's political needs than from institutional constraint. Kennedy was determined to defeat Blough; he thought that the costs of not doing so would far outweigh any disadvantages in giving battle; so he hurled the full might of presidential authority at his opponent. His chief weapon was the federal government's purchasing power: he ordered the Department of Defense and all other federal agencies to deal only with those steel companies which had not followed Blough's lead. Kennedy also encouraged the Senate's anti-trust subcommittee (headed by Estes Kefauver) to launch an investigation into possible violations of the law; the Attorney-General turned the FBI loose on its own investigation; by means of the press and television the American people were told how mean was the behaviour of Big Steel; within two days Blough had rescinded the objectionable price rise. All Kennedy had to do was to pay the price of victory.

On the surface, it was a stunning display of presidential power, but it may not have been all that it seemed. Kennedy may once more have been cutting with the grain. There were good economic reasons for thinking that Blough's price rise was indeed a mistake: he seems to have acted merely to please his share-holders, and the subsequent history of US Steel gives little reason to respect the business ability of that corporation's leaders. At any rate the administration had had no difficulty in finding steel companies that did not follow Blough's example: Inland, Kaiser and Armco all held back.[35] But business people can hardly be blamed for seeing in Kennedy's behaviour only a renewal of the old Democratic threat, as it had been posed by Roosevelt's taxes and Truman's seizure of the steel mills. Relations between the administration and the corporations were suddenly as bad as possible.

That was not at all what Kennedy wanted, and he devoted much time for the rest of his presidency to restoring good relations. Senator Kefauver was left in the lurch, and every possible opportunity was taken for emphasising that the administration was not 'anti-business'. A break in the stock market which occurred a month after the steel crisis did not make the job any easier – it was tempting to blame the president for it; but by the autumn Kennedy had succeeded in clawing back much of the credit that he had lost. Having demonstrated his power and determination to shape economic policy he felt free to advertise, yet again, his commitment to working in partnership with businessmen. On 7 June 1962 he made public his plans for a substantial tax cut.[36] He rightly calculated that nearly everyone would welcome this proposal. It should take away the nasty after-taste of the steel crisis and the market fall. And then he expounded his mature philosophy of economic management in one of his most notable speeches, his address on receiving an honorary degree at Yale on 11 June.

It began with a pleasing joke ('It might be said now that I have the best of both worlds, a Harvard education and a Yale degree'),[37] but is chiefly notable for its calmly urged and strongly felt plea that old myths and prejudices should no longer be allowed to deflect attention from the technical, rather than the ideological, nature of most of the economic problems confronting a modern government.

> The unfortunate fact of the matter is that our rhetoric has not kept pace with the speed of social and economic change. Our political debates, our public discourse – on current domestic and economic issues – too often bear little or no relation to the actual problems that the United States faces.[38]

The myth that he was particularly anxious to kill was the belief that, if possible, the federal budget ought always to be in balance; for the tax cut which he was proposing was certain to plunge the budget into deficit, and many of his advisers thought it would be a good thing if the deficit were permanent.

He had in many respects an easier task ahead of him than he supposed. The federal budget had been in deficit in most years since 1929, and although Congress, the Junior Chambers of Commerce and the *Wall Street Journal* still resounded with the old rhetoric (the *Journal* had a strong article on the subject on the very day that Kennedy went to Yale) nobody really believed it any more. As the economist historian Herbert Stein was to remark, the deficits of the Depression and the Second World War had done no harm: 'No one was struck by lightning. The country did not "go bankrupt", whatever that meant.'[39]

And everyone liked the idea of tax cuts. But because neither Kennedy nor anyone else knew quite how weak the balanced budget ideology had become, it took courage for him to commit himself to deficit financing, and as usual it required skill and patience to get the proposal through Congress. It was an authentic Kennedy success (though as in so many instances it was Lyndon Johnson who finally secured it, in February 1964); but looked at in a thirty-year perspective its meaning does not seem to be what was believed at the time. It has become something of a myth itself.

No one can doubt that a tax cut was in order. Taxes dating from the Second World War and the Korean War still pulled in large revenues, which were of little use except to pile up a budget surplus and pay off the national debt, which was hardly urgent, for as Kennedy pointed out in his Yale speech, it had increased only by 8 per cent since 1945, while private debt had gone up by 305 per cent and the debt of state and local governments by 378 per cent. True, the revenues might and perhaps should be used to pay for public works of various kinds, as J.K. Galbraith urged: his *Affluent Society*, with its theme of 'private affluence and public squalor', was the most influential work of political economy to have been published since 1945. Kennedy and many of his advisers tended to agree with him: he and they, all Democrats together, were inheritors of the Rooseveltian tradition. Unfortunately there were two bulky difficulties. The first, which Roosevelt himself had faced in the early days of the New Deal, was that there were not enough practicable schemes for public investment, and it would take years to develop any. Even more serious, Congress stood in the way, as the education affair showed, and as was to be shown again in the great liberal Congress of 1965–67, when even Lyndon Johnson could not persuade the two chambers to fund his programmes adequately. So in 1961–62 Galbraith's advice could not be taken, and he was packed off to India as ambassador. He continued to bombard Washington, and especially the president, with witty and intelligent comment, but on economic matters Kennedy listened rather to his Secretary of the Treasury, Douglas Dillon, a Republican who nevertheless became part of the president's inner circle, and the 'New Economist', Walter Heller, Chairman of the Council of Economic Advisers.

Heller and his team believed that it was their mission to

teach Kennedy Keynesian economics, and they regarded the strength of the US economy between 1961 and 1965 as proof of their wisdom and their success. Their professional competence cannot be doubted, but how much their fiscal manipulations had to do with Kennedy prosperity is uncertain. They believed that it had been brought about by what came to be called 'the fiscal revolution' (deficit spending; 'compensatory fiscal policy';[40] budget-unbalancing); but as Herbert Stein has pointed out, their theories have never actually been proved,[41] and by the 1970s the rival theories of monetarism would be sweeping the field, with equally dubious claims, while in the 1990s the atavistic cult of the balanced budget came roaring back. In the real world of jobs, trade and politics Kennedy prosperity may well have received a stimulus from the $10 billion tax cut, which put money in people's pockets either to spend (as Heller hoped) or to invest (as Dillon wanted). (Kennedy used both arguments.) The underlying stagnation of the later Eisenhower years became only a memory. But this recovery may have been caused as much, or more, by the immense vitality of the gigantic US economy as by any policy of the US government; and if business and overseas confidence was restored, it may have been simply because the world saw that economic policy was in Dillon's prudent and capable hands – which was why Kennedy had appointed him. Nor did it hurt that the commanding heights in Congress were still occupied by rigid fiscal conservatives.

Kennedy was undoubtedly lucky in inheriting an economy which was essentially in sound condition, and perhaps lucky that his policies seemed to work so well or, at least, did nothing to weaken that condition. He cannot be precisely described as lucky in being in power so short a time that the contradictions in his policy – between, for instance, his desire to staunch the outward flow of gold and his expensive resolve to 'pay any price, bear any burden ... to assure the survival and the success of liberty'[42] – could not make themselves felt, but it is a fact that he did not have to grapple with the problems that plagued Johnson and Nixon after him. But in the short term at least he well performed the housekeeping task of economic policy which, as he pointed out in the Yale speech, is laid on him by statute. The gold drain ceased, the balance of trade righted itself, unemployment went down, production went up, inflation was minimal. None of his successors has yet (1996) done so creditably. Whether he can be reckoned a success in the long term, as he hoped, is a different matter. The myth of balancing the budget was scotched, not killed. In 1994 Herbert Stein actually felt it necessary to publish an article urging, once again, that budget-balancing was not actually prescribed in the Bible[43] – and he had no effect. Republicans swept the 1994 congressional elections while supporting a movement to add a clause to the Constitution making balanced budgets mandatory on Congress and the president. This development would have been more surprising had not Ronald Reagan, during his years in the White House, encouraged a spree of tax cutting, federal borrowing and lavish expenditure which dwarfed anything that Kennedy dreamed of (or would have thought sane). As a result interest on the national debt became the second largest charge on the federal revenues, and left the country's immediate future in the hands of the holders of the debt, who were mostly foreigners such as the Japanese. The United States still did not 'go bankrupt', but the Reagan deficit undermined business confidence and faith in the dollar, and the debt-charges grievously limited the government's freedom of action, as President Bush found when he had to persuade foreign powers to pay for the US campaign in the second Gulf War. President Clinton had to make reduction of the deficit his first priority, which seriously injured his relations with his Democratic party. On the whole it cannot be said that the era allegedly inaugurated by the Yale speech has been marked by great financial wisdom: taxpayers and politicians have alike tended to grab whatever money was going and run, leaving posterity to sort out the mess. Only the Chairman of the Federal Reserve has stood between Americans and the consequences of their folly.

Kennedy would have been appalled by this development. He was at heart a conservative financier: he liked getting value for money, and in his private life was notoriously a tightwad, which led to some amusing clashes with his wife, who was not.[44] He found little difficulty in working with Wilbur Mills, the extremely powerful and traditionally conservative Chairman of the House Ways and Means Committee. Thus, Mills was persuaded to endorse the proposed tax cut, but insisted on linking it with tax reforms: measures to close various loopholes in the system and thereby bring in some $3 billion of fresh revenue. Mills thought in this way to offset some of the fiscal effects of the tax cut. Kennedy eventually made the Mills proposal his own, and the

House passed the whole package in September 1963; but, in a hint of things to come, the Senate proved less amenable. Harry Bird, Mills's counterpart – he was Chairman of the Finance Committee – refused to accept the tax reforms, and was in a strong position to get his way as the civil rights bill was also running into trouble and Kennedy did not want two simultaneous major parliamentary battles. Nevertheless, he had not given in to Byrd at the time of his death; it was left to Lyndon Johnson to surrender in January 1964. In return he got the tax cut. He signed it into law in February.

It is worth remarking that had Kennedy lived and made the same concession (as he would probably have been forced to) his critics would have said this showed how weak he was as a congressional leader, while LBJ's reputation as a congressional wizard meant that no one noticed his defeat. Three years later Johnson put up taxes again, to help pay for the Vietnam War. It may be legitimate to suggest that had Kennedy lived, and had he avoided the war, his tax policy would have continued successfully.

Prudent, yet unafraid of intelligent innovation: this humdrum style explains why Walter Lippmann said that the Kennedy administration was simply the Eisenhower administration again, only thirty years younger[45] (Lippmann meant it as an insult; today it looks more like a compliment), but it was hardly what most people saw, or wanted to see, when they looked at the Kennedy White House. Young, handsome and rich, Jack and Jackie put on a dazzling show: they made Washington, for perhaps the only time in its history, fashionable and fun; budget policy seemed far less characteristic of the Kennedy style than the president's appeal to young idealists with his Peace Corps and his project of sending a man to the moon.

These were the ventures which, most of all, seemed to flesh out the visions of the New Frontier and give the Kennedy administration a glow of noble excitement which has not yet quite worn off. Certainly Kennedy had a knack for this kind of leadership, but a close examination of the Peace Corps and the Apollo programme brings out several familiar, and equally authentic, traits.

> The 1950s made ancient mariners of us all – becalmed, waiting and a little parched in the throat. Then we picked up momentum on the winds of change that Kennedy brought in – the New Frontier,

the fresh faces in government, the vigorous, hopeful speeches, the Peace Corps.[46]

The birth of the Peace Corps is a striking example of what energetic political leadership can achieve. The idea of sending young Americans abroad, to work on aid projects in poor countries, had been current for years. As far back as the 1930s, Kennedy's brother-in-law, Sargent Shriver (Eunice's husband), had been involved in something called Experiment in International Living, and two of the most successful New Deal agencies had been directed at 'Youth' (that wonderfully period word); the Civilian Conservation Corps and the National Youth Administration, which last had given a start in life and politics to Lyndon Johnson. In the 1950s Congress had toyed with the idea and Hubert Humphrey had made it his own: he introduced a bill in June 1960, which first gave currency to the phrase 'peace corps' (peace is a period word too). This bill was part of Humphrey's drive to put his stamp on the Democratic party programme. A peace corps would educate America about the world and the world about America. It might even do some practical good: most aid programmes of the 1950s had been concerned with capital investment, not with people. Kennedy was sympathetic to the proposal, which fitted in well with his concern to increase American influence in the Third World. As his campaign went on and its appeal to young voters, particularly college students, became more evident, the desirability of tapping all the enthusiasm by some specific commitment became more obvious. The turning-point came at Ann Arbor, at the University of Michigan campus, on 14 October 1960, when ten thousand students waited until two in the morning to hear the candidate. Kennedy, who had just come from his third debate with Nixon, was tired, but his reception stimulated as much as it astonished him. Off the cuff he asked his young admirers if they were willing to sign up for a peace corps (though he did not use the phrase).

> On your willingness not merely to serve one or two years in the service, but on your willingness to contribute part of your life to this country, I think will depend the answer whether we as a free society can compete.[47]

It was a variation on his favourite theme, the need for self-sacrifice to win the Cold War; but his hearers received it as a call to adventure. They were full of patriotic and personal self-confidence: nothing in their experience had taught them to doubt themselves or their country. In three wars the United States had vindicated its claim to be the champion of liberty and progress, and also in the long confrontation with communism and in the fantastic abundance which it had realised. They were the first of the 'baby boom' generation to reach adulthood, and were looking for a cause to give them some greater fulfilment than the prosy respectability of the Eisenhower years offered. They were also, not so consciously, looking for a leader; and suddenly he appeared. As so often, Kennedy was lucky in his timing: a year or two later, and the Peace Corps might have been less of a magnet to the idealists who were drawn into the civil rights movement. But as it was, he and his hearers gave each other great satisfaction. Kennedy told Dave Powers that he had hit a winning number,[48] and in one of the last great speeches of his campaign, at San Francisco on 2 November, he explicitly committed himself to establishing 'a peace corps of talented young men and women' and also of mature teachers, doctors, engineers and nurses, who would live abroad for three years as missionaries of freedom by joining the worldwide struggle against poverty, disease and ignorance.[49] This did not nail down the California vote, but it may be seen as confirming Kennedy's link with the young; as soon as he took office he set about keeping his promise.

He handed the problem to Sargent Shriver, who had performed splendidly as director of the task force which had looked for talent to staff the new administration, and with some prodding from the impatient president Shriver had a scheme ready by the end of February. Speed was necessary not only to confirm the administration's claim to be vigorous and innovative, but also because without it the Peace Corps would not be ready to take the graduates who would be leaving college in the summer of 1961; for that reason Shriver recommended that the president should not wait for congressional action but set up the corps under an executive order, though the director should seek Senate confirmation. Kennedy accepted these suggestions, and on 1 March issued the executive order for a temporary corps while simultaneously asking Congress to authorise a permanent body. He also induced Shriver to accept appointment as the corps' first permanent director. This, as much as anything else, ensured the programme's success, though Shriver pretended that he was given the job because 'no one thought it could succeed and it would be easier to fire a relative than a friend.'[50] Shriver was probably the most idealistic of the Kennedy clan: they called him the family communist. He was wholly committed to the somewhat Franciscan ethos of the Peace Corps. None of the volunteers was to enjoy any diplomatic privileges while on service; they were all to live in the same way as the people they were helping; they were not to be exploited by the CIA, and were not to be allowed to carry guns. Even the administrators were to live low off the hog: a routine State Department memo which referred to their need for chauffeurs threw the director into a fearful rage.[51] At the same time Shriver had a great capacity for worldly business. Thus equipped, he lobbied Congress successfully for the corps, which became statutory on 22 September 1961 (and rapidly became almost as much a favourite of Congress as it was of the president – even Barry Goldwater came round);[52] with help from Lyndon Johnson he successfully fought off a bureaucratic move to subordinate the corps to the main foreign aid agency; and at Kennedy's suggestion he travelled the world to persuade foreign heads of government to accept his volunteers, which, again, he did with conspicuous success. It was less than a year from Ann Arbor to the Peace Corps Act; Kennedy and Shriver could congratulate themselves that its establishment beautifully exemplified the New Frontier's wish to hit the ground running. The disgruntled might, if so disposed, say that it was the only thing which did.

The Peace Corps, then, was a success. If, to its founder, it symbolised 'the idealistic sense of purpose which I think motivates us',[53] today it appears as a useful educational experiment which benefits both America and host-countries, but America, probably, rather more. Its spring is over, but it had a spring. 'I'd never done anything political, patriotic or unselfish,' said one volunteer, 'because nobody ever asked me to. Kennedy asked.'[54] What he and the corps meant to young America is perhaps best illustrated by what happened after his murder: the next day the Peace Corps office was overwhelmed by applications to serve, and in the week following 'the all-time record was reached: 2,500.'[55] All concerned felt that they were responding to their leader's call to do what they could for their country.

But the Peace Corps, after all, was no more than a marginal

enterprise, a grace-note, a flower in Kennedy's button-hole, a clean handkerchief in his breast-pocket. It was a reminder of a better world than the one in which presidents pass their days. Kennedy himself had no illusions about its importance. His own idealism was much more alloyed with scepticism and the realism of south Boston than was Shriver's. He liked and respected his brother-in-law, but sometimes felt impatient with him. He knew that he neither should nor would be judged in the end simply by his establishment of the Peace Corps, any more than by his plans to make landings on the moon.

As with the Peace Corps, the wildly romantic moon project had a long fore-history before Kennedy took it up. The launching of *Sputnik*, the first space satellite, in 1957, had excited and alarmed American opinion, although Eisenhower, characteristically, had been unimpressed both by the achievement and by any military threat which it might be said to represent. Not so Lyndon Johnson: James N. Giglio quotes a wonderfully wild speech made by that statesman in which he asserted that

> control of space means control of the world. From space, the masters of infinity would have the power to control the earth's weather, to cause drought and flood, to change the tides and raise the levels of the sea, to divert the Gulf Stream and change temperate climates to frigid.[56]

Spurred on by such dreadful visions, and perhaps by the more enticing glimpses of large appropriations to be spent in congressional districts, the legislature did its best to overcome Eisenhower's inaction in the matter, without success; so Kennedy was able to make lagging in the space race another charge against the administration in 1960.

Once in office he hesitated. His vice-president was eager for a lunar landing, but the cost would be stupendous (in the end it came to more than $30 billion), enough to give any thrifty president pause. But as so often events forced his hand. On 12 April 1961 the Soviet Union put Yuri Gagarin into space: the first man ever to orbit the earth. It was a great deed, exciting worldwide enthusiasm. It was immediately followed by the Bay of Pigs fiasco. Kennedy, who at this stage saw space exploration (like most things) entirely in terms of the superpower competition, and was particularly sensitive to the attitudes of the uncommitted nations – he did not want them to conclude that communism was the way of the future – decided that the best means to claw back some prestige was to commit the United States to putting a man on the moon by the end of the decade. Addressing Congress on 25 May, in a firmly reiterated context of 'the great battleground for the defense and expansion of freedom' in the southern half of the globe, he asserted that 'No single space project in this period will be more impressive to mankind, or more important for the long-range exploration of space,'[57] while conceding that none would be more expensive. The response of Congress, listening to him in joint session, was cool; but the large appropriations for which he asked were voted through in near unanimity. In 1969 the first man landed on the moon. As Kennedy had planned, he was an American.

The exploration of the universe by means of such space-swung wonders as the Hubble telescope is one of the most magnificent achievements of the twentieth century, and the United States has played the leading part in it. Kennedy's contribution was to see that the somewhat haphazard and underpowered space programme of the United States needed a sharp focus to energise it, and that the Apollo enterprise (why it was not named Artemis or Diana is a question never answered) was the very thing to do so. His contribution was essential, but so were those of many others (including the German war-criminals whose expertise built the rockets). He also deserves credit for the resolution and enthusiasm with which he followed up his commitment. He had told Congress that this was something which could not be carried out half-heartedly, and he lived up to his own prescription. But it is equally interesting to observe how his attitude to the space adventure changed: not in the sense that his commitment ever wavered, but in his perception of its political and diplomatic possibilities.

Even at the beginning of his administration, when his crusading fervour was at its height, he hoped to make space an international effort, and to draw in the Soviet Union as a partner. Understandably, Khrushchev did not at first respond. He became more co-operative after Colonel John Glenn of the United States emulated Gagarin's feat in February 1962, though nothing much came of this change in Kennedy's lifetime. But after Glenn's flight Kennedy always emphasised the possibility of international reconciliation through space, rather than the importance of outperforming the communists, although he never withdrew from his patriotic position that 'this is the new ocean, and I believe the United States must sail on it and be in a position second to none.'[58] It was a characteristic change of emphasis. Equally characteristic was his increasing stress on the splendour of the space enterprise itself. He did not drop the security argument, that the United States could not safely leave space to the Soviet Union, and he loved to emphasise the economic benefits of the multifarious space technologies, as in his speech at Rice University:

> What was once the furthest outpost on the old frontier of the West will be the furthest outpost on the new frontier of science and space. Houston, your City of Houston, with its Manned Spacecraft Center, will become the heart of a large scientific and engineering community.[59]

But his final point was emphatically romantic:

> Many years ago the great British explorer George Mallory, who was to die on Mount Everest, was asked why did he want to climb it. He said, 'Because it is there.'
>
> Well, space is there, and we're going to climb it, and the moon and the planets are there, and new hopes for knowledge and peace are there. And, therefore, as we set sail we ask God's blessing on the most hazardous and dangerous and greatest adventure on which man has ever embarked.[60]

It made a suitably uplifting end to his address, but there is no reason to doubt the sincerity of this emphasis. As Robert Kennedy was to say after his death, he thought of the exploration of space as being analogous to the exploration of America by Lewis and Clark, and 'he was always pleased when the United States did something extraordinary. Where it required not only brains and ability but courage.'[61] It was for this reason that he and his wife made so much of John Glenn; though it also helped that Glenn was potentially (and, after Kennedy's death, actually) an attractive Democratic candidate for office.

Yet, looking back, we can hardly say that it was Kennedy who turned a possibility into an inevitability. The times demanded the space programme. No president (not even Eisenhower) could long have allowed the Soviet Union to monopolise the glory of exploring heaven. The technological rewards of satellite technology were overwhelmingly tempting to world business. The intellectual rewards were equally alluring to the scientific profession; as Kennedy remarked at Rice, 'most of the scientists that the world has ever known are alive and working today', and the United States' scientific personnel doubled every twelve years.[62] These effective lobbies would also have been heard by any other president. Finally, it cannot be overlooked that one of the chief cultural expressions of the age was science fiction (SF). It was the medium through which humanity wrestled with the threat of nuclear extinction and the apparently unlimited promises – or were they threats also? – of human science; space exploration was equally an expression of these fears and aspirations. I know of no evidence that Kennedy was much of a reader of SF, but his speeches show that he too felt the tension, the anxiety and the hope, and he made himself the instrument of their reconciliation. The space programme was SF made fact. No other president would have reacted to the forces at work in quite the same way, for none would have perceived them identically; but the outcome would have been the same. Like much else of Kennedy's work, the space programme was overdetermined.

Such was Kennedy's record as the national housekeeper. It was a respectable one; it showed him as competent yet idealistic, prudent yet courageous. On the other hand it was not, on the whole, dramatic (the landings on the moon were not to occur on his watch). We have to look elsewhere for the crusades and crises which were to make the Kennedy presidency passionately memorable.

.   .   .

NOTES

1. Richard E. Neustadt, *Presidential Power*, first published, with immense success, in 1960 (Kennedy enjoyed it, and roped the author in as an adviser on the presidential transition); reissued, with revisions and additions, as *Presidential Power and the Modern Presidents* (New York: Free Press 1990).
2. KOH: Larry O'Brien.
3. The other occasions were the steel fight and the civil rights bill.
4. *PP* i p. 11: news conference, 25 January 1961.
5. Theodore C. Sorensen, *Kennedy* (New York: Harper & Row Perennial edn 1988) p. 341.

6. KOH: Larry O'Brien.
7. Lawrence F. O'Brien, *No Final Victories* (New York: Ballantine 1974) p. 130.
8. Ibid., p. 138.
9. *PC* p. 5.
10. O'Brien, *Victories*, p. 127.
11. KOH: Eunice Kennedy Shriver.
12. *PP* ii pp. 165–73. The final version of this message was largely written by Eunice Shriver.
13. *PP* iii p. 825: Remarks upon signing Bill for Construction of Mental Retardation Facilities and Community Mental Health Centers, 31 October 1963.
14. D.P. Moynihan, *Congressional Record*, 12 December 1995; also printed in the *New York Review of Books*, 11 January 1996, pp. 33–6. Dr Colin Samson has given me valuable advice on the history of Kennedy's mental health policy.
15. KOH: Eunice Kennedy Shriver.
16. James W. Trent Jr, *Inventing the Feeble Mind: a history of mental retardation in the United States* (Berkeley: University of California Press 1994) usefully discusses the Kennedy programme and its outcome.
17. See p. 26.
18. Though each state, under the Constitution, must have at least one Representative, however scanty its population.
19. O'Brien, *Victories*, p. 138.
20. When a fire broke out at the governor's mansion in Albany, NY, Rockefeller was observed climbing down a ladder from a bedroom with a lady who was not yet his wife (after both he and she were divorced she became so).
21. See Trent, *Feeble Mind*, pp. 225–55.
22. Sorensen, *Kennedy*, p. 358.
23. By 'public schools' Americans mean what the British call 'state schools'. What the British call 'public' or 'independent' schools the Americans call 'private'. 'Parochial schools' are those built and maintained by the Catholic Church.
24. *PP* iii p. 108: special message on education, 29 January 1963.
25. Sorensen, *Kennedy*, p. 358.
26. Irving Bernstein, *Promises Kept: John F. Kennedy's New Frontier* (New York: Oxford University Press 1991) p. 219.
27. Sorensen, *Kennedy*, p. 359.
28. See Bernstein, *Promises Kept*, p. 221.
29. Ibid., p. 224.
30. Sorensen, *Kennedy*, p. 361.
31. To a British eye it is curious that this argument, which would have been very powerful in Britain, had almost no resonance in the United States, and was taken up by nobody else.

32. Bernstein, *Promises Kept*, p. 234.
33. Sorensen, *Kennedy*, p. 448.
34. The version which first became current was that Kennedy had said that all 'businessmen' were sons-of-bitches, and it caused immense resentment. The president always denied this version, and it is indeed an unlikely utterance for either Joseph P. Kennedy or his son.
35. For all this see Jim F. Heath, *Kennedy and the Business Community* (Chicago: University of Chicago Press 1969) pp. 70–1.
36. *PP* ii pp. 456–8: news conference.
37. Ibid., p. 470.
38. Ibid., p. 473.
39. Herbert Stein, *The Fiscal Revolution in America* (Chicago: University of Chicago Press 1969) p. 459.
40. Ibid., p. 463 and elsewhere.
41. Herbert Stein, *International Herald-Tribune*, 14 September 1994.
42. *PP* i p. 1: Inaugural Address. David P. Calleo, *The Imperious Economy* (Cambridge, MA: Harvard University Press 1982) pp. 11–24, is severe on such contradictions.
43. Stein, *International Herald-Tribune*, 14 September 1994.
44. Benjamin C. Bradlee, *Conversations with Kennedy* (London: Quartet 1976) pp. 118–19, 186–7.
45. Herbert S. Parmet, *JFK* (New York: Dial Press 1983) p. 303.
46. Gerard T. Rice, *The Bold Experiment: JFK's Peace Corps* (Notre Dame, IN: University of Notre Dame Press 1985) pp. 30–1.
47. For all this, see ibid., pp. 1–12.
48. Ibid., p. 21.
49. *LTW* pp. 120–1.
50. Rice, *Bold Experiment*, p. 138.
51. Ibid., p. 93.
52. Ibid., p. 89.
53. Ibid., p. 269.
54. Ibid., p. 299.
55. Ibid., p. 169.
56. James N. Giglio, *The Presidency of John F. Kennedy* (Lawrence, KS: University Press of Kansas, 1991) p. 149.
57. *PP* i p. 404: special message to the Congress on urgent national needs, 25 May 1961.
58. *PP* ii p. 150: Remarks following the orbital flight of Col. John H. Glenn Jr, 20 February 1962.
59. Ibid., p. 670; 12 September 1962.
60. Ibid., p. 671.
61. RK, *Words*, pp. 340–1.
62. Ibid., p. 668.

Chapter 5

THE MISSILES OF OCTOBER

The Bay of Pigs affair and the Berlin crisis had between them taught John F. Kennedy much that he needed to know, and had initiated him fully into the arcane and dangerous world of high diplomacy. The Bay of Pigs, in particular, was a calamity from which he learned much. Later events suggest that he did not learn quite enough.

It confirmed his belief in the importance to the United States of Latin America. His policy towards that region had been settled before he took office; the Bay of Pigs made it seem urgent. He did not want to be written off as just another *Yanqui* imperialist. Apart from anything else, memories still lingered of Franklin Roosevelt's 'Good Neighbor' policy, and Kennedy did not want to fall short of his great predecessor in any respect. More potent was the Cold War mind-set. To Kennedy, who believed that communism and Soviet power were on the march throughout the world, Central and South America seemed to be especially at risk. The Cuban revolution seemed to make the danger concrete and immediate. Castro's rapid transformation from guerrilla hero to communist dictator was alarming enough; the likelihood that he and his henchman Che Guevara (an Argentine by birth) would incite other Latin American countries to follow their example was worse; and it was assumed that when they did they would receive effective support from the Soviet Union. The whole world south of the Rio Grande might suddenly go Red, and then what would happen to the United States? Something had to be done. This was one of the few points on which Eisenhower, Nixon and Kennedy all agreed. It would have been better for Latin America if they had not.

Not that in this area Kennedy's policy was simply a continuation of Ike's. As a liberal Democrat Kennedy saw clearly enough that Eisenhower's warm support for the corrupt military dictatorships of Latin America was both dishonourable and counter-productive. These regimes offered no hope to their peoples, they were feebler than they appeared, and as barriers against the spread of communism, which was Kennedy's chief concern, they were quite ineffective. The fall of Fulgencio Batista of Cuba and his replacement by Castro illustrated all these points. Clearly the United States must launch a fresh policy; an attractive thought in itself to the young president, with his desire to show that a new, more creative generation had taken command. The outcome was the so-called Alliance for Progress, promised in the inaugural address, and set up with great fanfare on 13 March 1961. It was formally agreed to and organised at an inter-American meeting in August at Punta del Este, Uruguay.

Kennedy had high hopes of the Alianza (as insiders liked to call it); he devoted much time to it during its early stages. And compared to US policy since his day, which has too often been irresponsible, hypocritical and callous, when not actually criminal (as in El Salvador during the 1980s), it looks enlightened and generous. Nevertheless it failed: in part because Kennedy's insistence on schemes for training soldiers and police officers in counter-insurgency ran contrary to the ostensible ethos of the Alianza (though not to the president's conception of it),[1] and in part because it was too ambitious. Had Kennedy been content to announce a revision of policies, committing the United States only to support for the more decent and democratic forces in Latin America and to a break with the military oligarchs, he would have achieved as much as possible and indeed, to the extent that this actually was US policy, did achieve it. Seen as a propaganda stroke the Alianza was a triumph, greatly encouraging reformers and modernisers throughout Latin America, and enhancing Kennedy's reputation much as did the Peace Corps, which was launched at the same time. But Kennedy and his men wanted more than that. A fashionable book of the period was *The Stages of Economic Growth*, by W.W. Rostow, which professed to be a democratic riposte to the *Communist Manifesto*. The Rostow analysis seemed to promise that with the application of the right techniques and sufficient money, backward countries could be accelerated into the stage of 'take-off' and become self-sustaining capitalist democratic societies. The author was given a job in the Kennedy administration, and the New Frontiersmen began excitedly to apply his notions. They reminded themselves of 1776, and announced that the United States was the one truly revolutionary country in the world; it would bring about a revolution of abundance and put the communists' noses out of joint for ever. But the idea of revolution is not one which can be misappropriated, stretched, pummelled and redefined at will, and essentially conservative statesmen (even if they are liberals) exhibit a certain frivolity if they use the term. The Kennedy men were no exception to this rule. The Rostow thesis did not work.

The New Frontiersmen were tempted to blame Congress, which year by year grew more reluctant to vote the large foreign aid programmes requested by the White House, and was apparently indifferent to the special claims made for the Alianza. But the shortfall in appropriations was as nothing to the shortfall in resources. The United States, gigantic though it loomed in its own eyes and everyone else's, simply did not command the means to make over Latin America as completely and as speedily as was hoped. Furthermore, even if it had been far richer, it was ill equipped in other ways to steer its neighbours to harbour. There could only be general and superficial agreement as to ends and means, and whenever the North Americans tried to go beyond that they necessarily ran into resistance, not all of it ill motivated or ill informed. Yankee idealism and energy were inextricably blended with Yankee self-assurance and cultural prejudice: an unattractive mixture. It gradually became clear that any success which the Alianza might achieve would be slow in coming.

Kennedy was too intelligent to have expected immediate results, but he seems to have been understandably disappointed by the discovery of how very small and belated the achievements of the Alianza were actually going to be; and in one matter he desired results at once. His feud with Castro could not wait.

The Bay of Pigs had left behind some irritating political problems that would not go away. Fidel Castro had humiliated Kennedy and the United States; although American public opinion had rallied loyally to the president after his misadventure, here, nevertheless, was an issue which the Republicans were certain to exploit as long as it was unresolved. They might do so with deadly effect in both the mid-term elections of 1962 and the next presidential election of 1964. For the country's leaders had been trying, ever since 1947, to scare the hell out of the people about communism and its international ambitions. They had been all too successful, and when Castro announced himself a communist, conditioned reflexes did the rest. It was partly concern with public opinion (which he himself had done much to inflame) that had led Kennedy to endorse, rather than to cancel, the Bay of Pigs scheme; and the scheme's failure did not lessen the pressure. Furthermore, Kennedy felt that by sanctioning their adventure he had in a sense assumed the leadership of the Cuban exiles; the débâcle did not eliminate his obligation to them, quite the contrary. Neither he nor any other American of the establishment saw Castro for what he was: a national leader who for the time being had won the firm loyalty of the vast majority of his people and could not be dislodged without a major military effort by the United States. His client relationship with the Soviet Union was at best a secondary trait of limited importance. Kennedy and his advisers saw it as primary, and Castro as a mere tool of Soviet imperialism. Finally, in 1961 both the Kennedy brothers felt a personal rage at Castro. They were not used to defeat, and at such hands. During the summer they took steps which they hoped would before long end in his overthrow. They were not deterred by the proved difficulty of tackling Castro. They merely resolved that next time they moved against him they would succeed.

As we have seen, the president was determined to profit from his Cuban mistakes, and thought to guard against any repetition by making his brother his watchdog and deputy. This was not altogether wise. Jack Kennedy, though of a cool and friendly disposition, could take men into aversion (as he did Adlai Stevenson) and seems to have felt vindictive towards Castro. But it was the vindictiveness of a man who seldom allowed his emotions to run away with him. The Attorney-General, on the other hand, was a notoriously good hater, and when he decided to 'get' someone went after him with relentless energy and not too many scruples, as malefactors such as Jimmy Hoffa, the corrupt and criminal head of the Teamsters union, could testify. Jack had a great deal to attend to; Castro was a strong preoccupation during the summer and autumn of 1961, but by the summer of 1962 Kennedy seems to have become much more indifferent to what happened in Cuba. His rage had cooled. His policy had not changed. He still hoped for Castro's fall, and worked strenuously to check the spread of his influence in Latin America, but the matter had ceased to be one of his first priorities. He had put Bobby in charge, and before long was content to leave the business entirely to him.

Bobby had a clear notion of his role: he had to energise the execution of the president's Cuban policy, and protect his brother against bad advice. His technique became legendary in the Kennedy administration. In its extreme form he would burst into a meeting, denounce all present for their sloth and inefficiency, and then storm from the room. Having no time for striped pants diplomats and spineless liberals he did not want to listen when they expounded the complexities of the Cuban question: to his mind they were only making excuses for inaction. On one dreadful occasion soon after the Bay of Pigs he savagely attacked Chester Bowles, then the Undersecretary of State, who was tactlessly expounding two State Department papers on the real difficulties of overthrowing Castro. This was not what the Kennedys wanted to hear, and anyway they both found Bowles a brilliant bore, though he had been of great value in the 1960 election. Besides, he had been much too ready to let his friends in the press know that he had opposed the Bay of Pigs adventure. Jack, who had not yet recovered his poise, bitterly resented this disloyalty, and since it was not his way to lash out himself he unleashed Bobby. Bowles lost his job soon afterwards.[2]

These *blitzkrieg* methods at least kept everyone alert, and in the Justice Department Bobby showed himself an inspiring leader; but as applied to the Cuban question his style was significantly inappropriate. What Bobby (and, behind him, the president) wanted was a direct, dynamic, 'vigorous' approach to the problem of toppling Fidel Castro. He did not want to be told that this was too simple-minded. He did not want to apply himself to the details. As Arthur Schlesinger was to remark, 'Castro was high on his list of emotions, much lower on his list of informed concerns.'[3] He was as busy as the president with other matters; too busy to scrutinise plans for attacking Cuba with the necessary thoroughness. He was content to act as a cheerleader, leaving the details to the operatives, just as the president left them to him. Yet this was the very pattern which had led to disaster at the Bay of Pigs.

Things went wrong again almost at once. Since a renewed invasion was ruled out, and no one had any confidence in mere diplomacy, Bobby turned for help to the CIA, which naturally leapt at the chance of redeeming itself. Even Richard Bissell was employed again. A 'task force' was set up, and by the end of summer 1961 it had been given a mission of sabotage and the fostering of general paramilitary activities within Cuba. Thus was 'Operation Mongoose' born. Early in November it was all explained to the president and Robert McNamara at a White House meeting. Bobby wrote a memo afterwards:

> My idea is to stir things up on the island with espionage, sabotage, general disorder, run & operated by Cubans themselves. . . . Do not know if we will be successful in overthrowing Castro but we have nothing to lose in my estimate.[4]

The CIA set to work, and among its other activities revived a scheme, originally hatched as part of the Bay of Pigs plans, to assassinate Fidel Castro. Controversy has raged as to what, if anything, the Kennedys knew about this idea. It was never officially part of Operation Mongoose, and John McCone, the new head of the CIA, was unswervingly opposed to assassination as a policy; a devout Catholic, he said that he would be excommunicated if he agreed to anything of the kind.[5] No close Kennedy associate has ever admitted to any knowledge of the assassination plots, and all assert that it would have been quite out of character for Jack Kennedy to approve them. When, in May 1961, he discovered that the CIA had been giving weapons to dissidents in the Dominican Republic to enable them to assassinate the dictator Rafael Trujillo, he tried unsuccessfully to extricate the United States from the plot (which achieved its aim the very next day), laying it down that the 'US as a matter of principle cannot condone assassination. This last principle is overriding.'[6] On the other hand there is some circumstantial evidence that he knew that assassination was part of the Bay of Pigs plan, and he remarked to a visitor in November 1961 that he was under 'terrific pressure . . . to okay a Castro murder'. He also said (perhaps on realising that his visitor, Tad Szulc, a journalist, was unsympathetic) that 'for moral reasons' the United States should never do anything of the kind, which is consistent with his Trujillo statement, but is also unhappily reminiscent of Richard Nixon's 'it would be wrong' during the Watergate affair. As Richard Reeves has remarked, all the pressure to 'get rid' of Castro (whatever that might mean) had been coming from the Kennedys themselves.[7] In January 1962, according to Richard Helms of the CIA, Bobby was insisting that 'the top priority' in the US government was the overthrow of Castro,[8] so it would not be particularly astonishing if the CIA believed that it had authorisation to do whatever seemed necessary.

Jack Kennedy, who had a deplorable weakness for covert activity of all kinds, at least toyed with the idea of murdering Castro, but he again disavowed assassination as an instrument of policy, this time publicly, if unemphatically, in a speech of 16 November 1961, a few days after Szulc's visit:

> as the most powerful defender of freedom on earth, we find our-selves unable to escape the responsibilities of freedom, and yet unable to exercise it without restraints imposed by the very freedoms we seek to protect. We cannot, as a free nation, compete with our adversaries in tactics of terror, assassination, false promises.[9]

Probably he had been tempted, but in the end stuck to com-mon decency and common sense: as he remarked to Tad Szulc, 'We can't get into that kind of thing or we will all be targets.'[10] (Perhaps he had not yet learned that the President of the United States is always a target.) As to Bobby, he was probably giving Helms one of his little pep talks, and did not realise how it would be taken. This is suggested by an incident in the spring of 1962. The CIA believed that the leaders of organised crime, who had lost vast amounts of money in the Cuban revo-lution, might be able to help in rubbing out Fidel: they had always been very good at rubbing out each other. One of those approached was Sam Giancana, eminent in the Chicago syndic-ate. He was also the current protector of Judy Campbell, one of the president's discarded mistresses. This overlap had come to the attention of the head of the Federal Bureau of Investi-gation, J. Edgar Hoover, and it seems to have been his rep-resentations to the president that induced Kennedy to break with the woman in March 1962. Then in May the CIA was at last forced to tell the Attorney-General about its dealings with the mob, since the Justice Department was conducting a vigor-ous campaign against organised crime which was inconveni-encing Mr Giancana and his friends (one of them protested, 'here am I, helping the government, helping the country, and that little son of a bitch is breaking my balls'). The CIA officer who had to tell Bobby had an uncomfortable half-hour; as he said later, 'If you have seen Mr. Kennedy's eyes get steely and his voice get low and precise, you get a definite feeling of unhappiness.' 'I trust that if you ever try to do business with organised crime again – with gangsters – you will let the Attorney-General know,' said Bobby. He put a stop to the Giancana caper immediately, and was so upset by the business that he even complained to J. Edgar Hoover about it, a choice of confidant so unlikely that of itself it shows how disturbed he was. But with his brother's backing he did not let up his pressure for somewhat less atrocious action against Castro. The trouble was (as was later to be the case in Vietnam) that however unsuccessful Mongoose was and was likely to remain, nobody had an alternative, the president having ruled out a US invasion. McGeorge Bundy saw what this meant: 'we should either make a judgment that we would have to go in militarily or alternatively we would have to live with Castro and his Cuba and adjust our policies accordingly.' The Kennedys hated both alternatives, and so Mongoose was still going on in October 1962; Bobby even tried to intensify it during the missile crisis – fortunately (for it might have made the resolution of the affair even more difficult than it was) without any greater success than usual.[11]

Read over today, the plans to topple or murder Castro (none of which came near success) have a strongly farcical air. One idea was to make Fidel's beard fall out and thereby destroy his charisma; another was to slip him a poisoned cigar.[12] (I remember how in happy days of childhood my brother and I spent hours earnestly preparing a bottle of poisoned beer – made of dirt, water and ivy-berries – for Hitler to drink.) But it was not really a laughing matter, and nor was the much more effective programme of sabotage. Thousands of tons of sugar, Cuba's chief export, were destroyed weekly, a shipload of the commodity was contaminated, attempts were made to wreck the Cuban copper-mines, huge sums were spent on anti-Castro propaganda and espionage, help was given to guerrilla groups in the mountains.[13] More damagingly than anything else, the embargo on trade between the United States and Cuba continued. It should have struck the Kennedys that all this was bound to have the one result that nobody wanted: it drove Fidel Castro closer to the Soviet Union. Since Castro was already in the communist camp, the brothers perhaps assumed that matters could not be worse. If so, they were wrong.

The Mongoose policy was also a self-conceived trap for the president in a second respect. Outside a small circle in Washington, nobody knew exactly what was going on, but Kennedy's posturing was visible enough to encourage American hostility to Castro to a dangerous point. 'We were hysterical about Cuba,' said Robert McNamara years later, and as is the way of things in the United States the hysteria spread from Washington through the country.[14] The American people are all too inclined to make bugbears of unfriendly foreign leaders and by the summer of 1962 far too many of them were almost obsessive about Castro, to the profit of the Republicans, who insisted that the president was fainthearted in the matter. In this way, and by Kennedy's fault, communist Cuba began to change from being a mere thorn in the flesh to being indeed a dagger in the heart – to use again Senator Fulbright's images.

Once more, as before the Bay of Pigs, Kennedy was not thinking through his plan of action. His 'Special Group (Augmented)', which was the instrument of his Cuban policy, committed the elementary strategic error of not considering what might be the reaction of its opponent to its offensive. Fidel Castro was not easily intimidated. As American sabotage began to make itself felt he protested publicly, loudly and repeatedly; and when, in the summer of 1962, the US Navy began vast manoeuvres just outside Cuban territorial waters, he did not take fright, as no doubt he was meant to, but announced that the United States was clearly planning an invasion (he knew that there were some in Washington arguing vigorously for just that). Understandably suspicious, he tightened his regime's control and accelerated Cuba's transformation into a Leninist state. If Kennedy's concern was really to rescue Cuba from communism he could not have chosen a less apt policy.

There is an old folk-tale of the sun and the wind, who went out for a walk together. Seeing a man on the road ahead they amused themselves with a bet as to who could soonest get his coat off. The wind blew and blew, but the man simply huddled deeper into his garment. Then the sun shone with summer warmth. The man took his coat off and slung it over his arm.

Castro knew that he could not stand up against the colossus of the New World without serious aid, and there was only one quarter where he could hope to find it. Cuba was already a favourite with the Soviets: the first state ever to go communist of its own accord (more or less). They would certainly not let it be recaptured for 'capitalism' if they could help it.

They had other motives. In particular, Khrushchev did. Here the historian must step carefully. The exploration of the Soviet archives has only just begun and will no doubt yield surprises. But the main lines of the 1962 crisis seem to have been established. In the winter and spring of the year Khrushchev was still smarting from the Berlin stand-off. The unimpressive young man whom he had met in Vienna had succeeded in thwarting the often-proclaimed Soviet designs on Berlin; it was time he was taught a lesson. Besides, Khrushchev's personal position was beginning to look shaky. His Berlin initiative had backfired on him. His great campaign to increase Russia's agricultural production by opening the so-called 'virgin lands' to cultivation was faltering: the harvest of 1961 had been the smallest for five years. The breach with China was becoming ever wider and more serious, and even Albania, then an unreconstructed Stalinist state, was defying Soviet leadership.[15] Kennedy's men had humiliated the Soviet Union by showing that the missile gap was a myth and that in fact the United States enjoyed overwhelming preponderance in nuclear weaponry. Khrushchev was looking for a quick, cheap and easy way to regain the initiative; in the current state of the Cuban problem he thought he saw his opportunity.

The island's economy could be rescued from the worst effects of the American embargo by Soviet subsidy; the question of preserving Cuba's independence against the possibility of an invasion was more difficult. Any move to send arms or soldiers to Havana would be denounced by the United States as a breach of the Monroe Doctrine. The Soviet Union could live with that, as its action would not contravene international law, but its government had to consider how far it was safe to go in provoking the Americans. And just as Kennedy had feared, Khrushchev miscalculated.

He really believed that one day, in the not too distant future, Soviet communism would triumph over the West: he thought it was intrinsically the stronger system, and believed that it had reached what Walt Rostow would have called the point of take-off. The United States should be compelled to recognise the Soviet Union as its equal, which meant that it should renounce the unilateral privilege it claimed to do as it liked. John Foster

Dulles had once told Andrei Gromyko, the Soviet Union's semi-permanent foreign minister: 'Matters involving the establishment of American military bases are decided by the United States, and only the United States, at its own discretion, and by agreement with the country on whose territory these bases are established.'[16] Such language must never be used again; or, at least, what was sauce for the goose must be acknowledged to be also sauce for the gander. For instance, why should the USSR tolerate nuclear missiles in Turkey, on its very borders? It maintained no missiles on the borders of the United States. Khrushchev had been complaining about this point for years. In 1958 he asked Adlai Stevenson, 'What would the Americans think if the Russians set up bases in Mexico or some other place? How would you feel?'[17] Brooding on these matters, and on Castro's request for help, Khrushchev thought he began to see his way. Nuclear missiles in Cuba might solve several problems: they might safeguard Castro, compel the United States to acquiesce in Soviet ambitions, and restore Soviet prestige. They might make it possible to reopen the Berlin question. The logic came to seem unanswerable, and not only to Khrushchev: the new initiatives had the unanimous backing of the Politburo. In May 1962 the first moves were made.

The Russians were making the same mistake as the Americans: they were not considering seriously enough what the reaction of the other side might be. And like the Kennedys, they may have been misguided by pique. There is a decidedly spiteful tone in Khrushchev's memoirs when he puts the cap on his arguments for emplacing the missiles by observing:

now they would know just what it feels like to have enemy missiles pointing at you, we'd be doing nothing more than giving them a little taste of their own medicine. And it was high time. . . . America has never had to fight a war on her own soil, at least not in the past fifty years. She's sent troops abroad to fight in two World Wars – and made a fortune as a result. America has shed a few drops of her own blood while making billions by bleeding the rest of the world dry.[18]

If this was Khrushchev's attitude, it is no surprise that he misjudged Kennedy as completely as Stalin misjudged Hitler in the months before June 1941.

He also failed to see the fantastic opportunity before him.

Had he been content only to send conventional weapons to Cuba he could have rescued Castro from all threat of a US invasion and nullified the Monroe Doctrine at the same time. He would have plunged Kennedy into an appalling political fix. The president would have had to explain to his indignant electorate why he had allowed Cuba to become a major Soviet base, and why he intended to do nothing about it. No Latin American nation, no neutral, no ally, even, would have liked a Yankee invasion of Cuba just to overthrow Castro. Few Americans would have welcomed a war with the Soviet Union, with all its terrible risks, for such a cause. The same factors which had deterred the West from supporting the Hungarian revolution would have come into play; Kennedy would have suffered a major defeat, all the worse for being largely self-inflicted, and Khrushchev could have crowed his heart out. But none of these things happened, because Khrushchev also wanted to get Western missiles out of Turkey.

That the Russians knew their enterprise to be somewhat provocative is demonstrated by the care they took to conceal it from the world until all was complete. This was another mistake: had they proceeded openly it would have been much harder, perhaps impossible, for the United States to rally international opposition. Khrushchev supposed that if he could conceal the missiles until after the congressional elections on 6 November Kennedy would feel himself under no particular pressure and would accept the *fait accompli* (so Khrushchev may have felt that he was telling the truth when he sent a message that he would do nothing to affect the outcome of the elections). But complete concealment was unattainable, as he was warned by Anastas Mikoyan, the Politburo veteran who had handled much of the diplomacy with Castro. By August rumours were beginning to fly in Washington, complicated by the fact that the Soviet Union was pouring conventional armaments into Cuba and building a deep-water harbour there. Voices (mostly Republican) were raised alleging that strategic nuclear missiles were being delivered to Cuba, but the administration on the whole dismissed these assertions as mere electioneering. Only John McCone said that the evidence pointed to ground-to-ground nuclear missiles, and he did not help his case by going off with his new bride on a European honeymoon.

Nevertheless, by September the dangerous possibilities seemed actual enough to necessitate presidential action. So

Kennedy issued a warning statement on 4 September, and another, more explicit, on the 13th; in the latter he told the Soviet leadership unequivocally that to set up 'an offensive military base of significant capacity' (i.e. nuclear weapons) in Cuba would provoke the United States to do 'whatever must be done' to protect its security.[19] The Soviet government responded both publicly (on 11 September), and through back-channels from Khrushchev to Kennedy,[20] that it would never install anything but defensive weapons in the island, a line it stuck to even after the truth had been made public. If you must lie, do so boldly and plausibly; and after all, what is offensive, what defensive, is a subjective question, or so the Kremlin reasoned. The fact that the American people would pay no attention to such niceties was overlooked.

The CIA intensified its reconnaissance of Cuba; for many days cloud cover impeded the flights of the famous spy-plane, the U2; but by Sunday 14 October, the sky was clear enough for the cameras to do their job. The resultant photographs, when developed and interpreted, proved beyond doubt that the Soviet Union was hurriedly installing intermediate range ballistic missiles (IRBMs) which, if fired, could destroy any major city in the United States except Seattle. McGeorge Bundy was informed on the evening of Monday 15 October. He decided to let the president get a good night's sleep, passing on the news the following day as Kennedy breakfasted. Thus began the president's gravest test, perhaps the gravest of the twentieth century, indeed of all human history to that date: never before had statesmen possessed the power to obliterate most of humanity, all of civilisation, and perhaps the planet itself as a home of life.

By 11.45 a.m. on Tuesday 16 October, Kennedy had assembled his advisers around him, and the group began to function which, during the next two weeks, would determine US policy (it became known as Ex-Comm – short for Executive Committee of the National Security Council). It consisted of some twenty men, of whom eight were only occasional participants, coming and going as they could and as required. Kennedy himself was the most conspicuous irregular member: after the first meeting Sorensen suggested that members would speak and argue more frankly in his absence, and he agreed. Proceedings were informal, in the Kennedy manner, with good results: according to Sorensen, 'one of the remarkable aspects of those meetings was a sense of complete equality.'[21] Dean Acheson, one of the occasional participants, greatly disliked what he later called a 'floating crap game for decisions'.[22] He believed that either the president or the Secretary of State should have given the meetings firm chairmanship. But Kennedy had absented himself precisely to avoid giving firm chairmanship; he did not want, because of his authority, to deter anyone from speaking his mind. All ideas and information had to be elicited, all angles scrutinised, and the junior were perhaps as likely as the senior to spot essential points. It was indeed one of the youngest men present, Bobby Kennedy, who took the lead, for Dean Rusk was as self-effacing as ever.[23] Bobby had great weight in the committee because he was the president's brother, but his essential function, as ever, was to nag, to ask the obvious questions which no one else thought of, and not to lose sight of basic principles. Over the next few days Ex-Comm was to do an excellent job, whatever its methods, and by its success was to add greatly to the Kennedy administration's self-confidence.

The committee's first task was to define the nature of the crisis and the choices open to the president. The possibility of doing nothing, of standing by and letting the missile installation go ahead, was soon dismissed. The missiles might or might not increase the danger to the United States, but while there was uncertainty it was Kennedy's duty to do what he prudently could to remove them, for the national safety. Failure to act might have brought about his impeachment, as he feared; he was under constraint. There were some lesser but still formidable considerations. Passivity would wreck his presidency, which was more than a personal matter: with him would sink all the hopes that his election had raised. Khrushchev might not expect or want to break Kennedy, but if he did so, even inadvertently, it would be a spectacular demonstration of Soviet power that would have incalculable consequences. At the very least, Democratic defeat in the elections of 1962 and 1964 would become almost certain, and the United States would be handed over to the mercy of the right-wing Republicans. Abroad, the blow to American prestige might shake the Western alliance to pieces. Kennedy could not tamely acquiesce in the Soviet move, for if he did so he would leave the world an even more dangerous place than he had found it on taking office. On the other hand, had Kennedy or any of the others understood the full measure of the risks they were to run in the next two weeks they might reluctantly – very reluctantly – have settled for acquiescence. The danger of miscalculation or mischance, which weighed so heavily on the president, was even greater than he supposed.

As it was, the risks seemed appalling. One of the nightmares for Ex-Comm was the incalculability of the Soviet leadership. Kennedy was furious at all the lies he had been told (and was still being told: on Thursday 18 October, he received Andrei Gromyko, and had to sit impassively in his rocking-chair while listening to yet more assurances that the USSR was up to nothing very much in Cuba) but still more worried: why had Khrushchev suddenly launched this uncharacteristic and enormous gamble, putting the whole future of the world in danger for such a paltry stake? Dean Rusk thought that it might be a fake punch, meant to distract the United States while the real blow fell on Berlin, 'But I must say I don't really see the rationality of the Soviets pushing it this far unless they grossly misunderstand the importance of Cuba to this country.'[24] Baffled in this way, the Americans would have to take decisions in the dark. The joint chiefs, as usual, had no doubt: bomb Cuba at once and then invade was their advice. Except for Maxwell Taylor they seemed to be incapable of grasping that there might be unacceptable consequences to such a strategy: for instance, all-out war with the Soviet Union. But if it was unsafe both to do nothing, and to do too much, where was the happy medium?

Ex-Comm's deliberations established that the arguments for and against all plausible choices were exquisitely balanced: every course had demonstrably serious drawbacks.[25] So the personal factor became decisive. The American constitutional system left the final responsibility with one man: the president. Everything turned on John F. Kennedy's judgement (his favourite word): on his character, intelligence and training. He knew it, too. Gazing out of the window of his office he said to Dean Acheson, 'I guess I better earn my salary this week.'[26] His wry humour seldom deserted him, even in crisis. But he could not hide from his brother, at least, how much he felt the strain. Watching him at the worst moment, on Wednesday 24 October, when they were waiting to see if the Russians would respect the American blockade, Bobby was reminded of how he had looked in the dreadful days immediately following the death of their elder brother, or in the moments when his own life had hung on a thread: 'His hand went up and covered his mouth. He opened and closed his fist. His face seemed drawn, his eyes pained, almost gray. We stared at each other across the table.'[27] Jack Kennedy had imagination enough to understand the full measure of his responsibility. It is to his credit that he did not crack under it. Indeed, throughout the crisis he was, to all seeming, the calmest person in the White House.

He had just been reading *The Guns of August*, Barbara Tuchman's masterly account of the mistakes of the various governments which had brought about the First World War. He was determined not to fail in the same way, if he could help it. If anybody survived to write *The Missiles of October*, he said, 'they are going to understand that we made every effort to find peace and every effort to give our adversary room to move. I am not going to push the Russians an inch beyond what is necessary.'[28] Probably any president, at such a moment, would have felt the same; but Kennedy stuck to the point throughout the crisis with notable firmness and consistency, and followed through its implications with equally notable dexterity. His commitment to peace was not simply the common reaction of his generation, which had borne the brunt of the Second World War and had lived ever since under the nuclear shadow. Still less had the author of *Why England Slept* been converted to the neurotic anti-militarism of Britain and America in the 1930s. His desire to secure peace corresponded to what was deepest in his nature: to the responsibility which he had felt for the crew of *PT 109* and now felt for the whole of humanity; to his sense that as a Kennedy, and the leader of the Kennedys, he must not, at this challenge, dishonour the family name by imprudence or glib judgements; to his happiness in his children, whose future he wanted to secure (in this he was very much his father's son); and to his knowledge that if things went wrong his own life, and those of everyone he knew, would be ended horribly. In 1962 the fate of the world did not lie in the hands of a shallow man; the missiles of October would have compelled any man to think deeply.

He was not the competitive warmonger that some of his posthumous critics have depicted. As a candidate on the stump he had uttered many unwisely bellicose speeches, and would do so again, speaking for Buncombe County in the bad old tradition. At bottom he was temperamentally incapable of acting except on the presumption that all men of power were susceptible to good sense and accurate reasoning (it was a repeated shock to him when he discovered, as he regularly did, that this presumption was too optimistic). He believed that the Soviet Union was an aggressive state which had to be vigorously resisted, and the missiles affair confirmed him in this perception; but he also believed that if he tried hard enough the Soviet leaders would one day see sense. The Republicans were right to mistrust him: he was by choice a negotiator, as he had said in his inaugural, not a crusader against the Red Menace.

All this qualified him excellently to handle the crisis; but more was needed. He would require the judgement and skill of a poker player; a cool head as well as a decent heart, to come through. What this meant was perhaps best demonstrated on the fifth day of the crisis, Saturday 20 October, when Adlai Stevenson strongly argued that the United States should offer to withdraw its missiles from Turkey and Italy if the Soviet Union withdrew its missiles from Cuba. He also suggested the abandonment of the US base in Cuba at Guantanomo Bay. Stevenson was to pay dearly for making these proposals,[29] but, apart from Guantanamo, something very like them was to be the real, if most secret, basis for settling the dispute. But on 20 October Kennedy saw that the United States could not afford to apparently abandon two allies under Soviet threat. It was not yet time to put the cards on the table.

It was, however, time to act. Every day brought nearer the moment when the missiles would be operational. After long and heated discussion Ex-Comm had rejected the proposal to invade Cuba, at any rate as a first step. Bobby Kennedy had argued passionately that a surprise attack would discredit the United States in the eyes of the world. Others, perhaps remembering the Bay of Pigs, were dissuaded by the certainty that an invasion would entail heavy US casualties, and by the uncertainty of the outcome: once American soldiers started fighting Soviet ones, where would it end? Their concern would have been even greater if they had known that there were 43,000 Soviet troops on the island, not the 10,000 estimated by the CIA, and that in a supreme act of reckless folly the Soviet government had actually sent tactical nuclear warheads, as well as strategic ones, to Cuba, and would most probably have used them in the event of an American attack.[30] It had already become clear to the intelligent that the distinction between tactical and strategic nuclear weapons was false: the use of the former must inevitably bring about a swift escalation to the use of the latter.

The point was hardly an esoteric one in this instance. Had Soviet forces used tactical nukes to annihilate an invading US Army Kennedy would probably have ordered a nuclear counter-attack, likely to provoke a strategic exchange, and the world would have come to an end. That Khrushchev should have added to the dangers of his adventure in such a way was completely contrary to established Soviet practice and is still almost incredible; contemplating the fact today helps us to re-capture the sense of outraged incredulity with which Kennedy reacted to the first news of the missiles. He had never imagined that Khrushchev could be so reckless, so defiant of good sense, which explains his own slowness (and that of his advisers) to believe in the approaching threat.[31]

Ex-Comm came to the view that the only realistic alternative to an immediate invasion was a blockade – which Kennedy preferred to call a quarantine, thereby evading certain problems in international law. A strictly enforced embargo on Soviet military shipments to Cuba would prove that the US government meant business, and perhaps persuade the Russians to remove the missiles, which they could do with a minimal loss of face. If they stood firm an invasion could be launched. Kennedy accepted this recommendation on 20 October, and instantly all the political, diplomatic, military and naval pre-parations were set on foot. So much activity could not be hidden from reporters, but the few newspapers which discovered what it meant were persuaded, on patriotic grounds, to keep silent. All that the American people knew was that the pres-ident had suddenly abandoned the campaign trail (the con-gressional elections were in full swing) because he had a cold; and then that he would address the nation on television on the evening of Monday 22 October. It was the seventh day of the crisis.

It was the most important speech of his life, and as a per-formance was masterly. The language used was devoid of any literary flourish: matters were too serious for that. As ever, the speech had been drafted by Sorensen and then revised in the light of others' suggestions; but the chief reviser was Kennedy himself, who made dozens of alterations, some of them long (for a short speech) and substantial.[32] The final product was blunt, spare, and to the point. It told of the grave danger that had suddenly arisen, of the Soviet lies, of what the administration meant to do, and of how much it still hoped for Soviet second thoughts. The only false note struck was an appeal to 'the captive people of Cuba', which betrayed the standard misconceptions. For the rest, the appeal was to the people of the United States:

> The path we have chosen for the present is full of hazards, as all paths are – but it is the one most consistent with our character and courage as a nation and our commitments around the world. The cost of freedom is always high – but Americans have always paid it. And one path we shall never choose, and that is the path of surrender or submission.[33]

The speech rallied the Americans, perhaps not surprisingly, considering how firmly Kennedy pressed the right buttons – 'freedom', 'surrender', 'submission', 'peace'. His comparative frankness – 'this Government feels obliged to report this new crisis to you in fullest detail'[34] – was also impressive; and he renewed his familiar call to sacrifice and self-discipline. The citizens' faith in their country and its institutions, including the presidency, was still substantially intact; twenty-one years of war and Cold War had taught them what to expect and how to behave in such emergencies. In short, they came very well out of the crisis. There was some alarm, and in some quarters panic, but the majority accepted their president's case and resolved to stare down the Russians. Possibly they could not entirely realise how dangerous the situation was, but patriotism was undoubtedly their controlling emotion; Kennedy had been warning them of danger, and vastly increasing defence expenditure, ever since he became president. This was the crisis they had been prepared for. There was also a special factor at work. All over the United States that autumn journalists and politicians had been whipping up agitation over Cuba; the popular temper, if letters to the press are any guide, was inflamed about this as about no other international issue. The missile crisis came as a safety valve for much emotion: at last Kennedy was acting. In a sense this was the pay-off for his alarmism about Castro.

Foreign reaction was more mixed. Harold Macmillan's immediate response was 'Now the Americans will realize what we here in England have lived through for this past many years.'[35] British public opinion was divided (the unilateralist agitation was at its height) and, mingled with natural alarm, there was a certain scepticism about American allegations. But the British government stood firm; so, even more conspicuously, did the government of France, although anti-Americanism was so powerfully corrosive a force there; so did that of West Germany. Adroit US diplomacy rallied the Organisation of American States to give a retrospective legitimacy to the quarantine; Adlai Stevenson denounced the Soviet Union effectively at the United Nations. Perhaps none of this mattered very much. Everything turned on the response of the Soviet government; and for nearly a week that seemed to be undecided. Nerves grew taut in Washington.

They seem to have been far tauter in Moscow. Khrushchev, that virtuoso of the bogus ultimatum, was distraught to find himself on the receiving end of a real one. The gambler had gone a bluff too far, and was now being called. He dared not raise the stakes (it is important to remember that throughout the crisis the United States never threatened to use nuclear weapons) but he could hardly endure the humiliation of climbing down. He seems to have been genuinely bewildered, as well as angry and astonished, by Kennedy's actions. No doubt he had committed, along with all his other blunders, the mistake of believing his own propaganda. But writhe as he might, there was no escaping the choices the United States was forcing on him. Unless he was to increase the already high risk of war, and of that US invasion of Cuba which it was his central purpose to avert, the quarantine must be respected; all Soviet vessels shipping nuclear weapons must turn back to port. On Wednesday 24 October (the ninth day of the crisis) they did just that. 'We are eyeball to eyeball,' said Dean Rusk, 'and the other fellow just blinked.'[36]

So far so good. But the main point was to remove from Cuba those weapons already installed, and that would involve a far more palpable Soviet climb-down. And there was so little time. The US government was determined that the nukes be removed before they became operational. Work went on feverishly at the missile sites, as Kennedy pointed out in a statement on Friday 26 October: 'The activity at these sites apparently is directed at achieving a full operational capacity as soon as possible.'[37] It had to stop, or the United States would send in its forces: by Monday 29 October, at latest, was the advice of the joint chiefs.[38] And there were other dangers in delay, dangers beyond the control of the high command on either side. Kennedy had ordered the grounding of all U2s, except those surveying Cuba, but on Saturday one of the planes based in Alaska not only took to the air but also strayed into Soviet airspace, over Siberia. 'There is always some sonofabitch who doesn't get the word,' said Kennedy;[39] it was just as well that the Soviets had not mistaken the flight for the precursor of an attack. On the same day a U2 flying over Cuba was shot down by a surface-to-air missile: the local Soviet commander had acted on his own authority (with the warm approval of Fidel Castro) in case the Americans were launching a surprise attack (Moscow was furious).[40] It was clear that if Kennedy and Khrushchev were to keep control of the crisis it would have to be ended immediately.

Luckily it was by now also clear on what terms it could be ended. The missiles would have to go; in return the United States would agree not to invade Cuba. It had not intended to do so, so the concession was a small one; but its sabre-rattling had understandably alarmed the Soviets; Kennedy's public renunciation of any such project distinctly improved international relations. It was also made clear, in immensely secret conversations between Bobby Kennedy and the Soviet ambassador, that the Jupiter missiles in Turkey, on the Soviet border, to which Khrushchev so much objected, would be removed, since the analogy with missiles in Cuba was all too clear. The Kennedy administration was more than ready to make this concession, fearing that otherwise Khrushchev would make a new move against West Berlin; besides, the missiles were technically obsolete, and might already have been removed had it not taken so long to induce Turkey to accept them in the first place. Turkish susceptibilities must if possible still be respected (though the president was ready to disregard them if he absolutely had to, whatever damage that might do to European confidence in America).[41] Fortunately the Russians accepted both the offer and the need for secrecy. Kennedy published his official terms on Saturday 27 October; Khrushchev accepted them in a broadcast the next day. Kennedy publicly welcomed the statement, and the crisis was suddenly over. The missiles were removed during the next few weeks.

'He plays a damn good hand of poker, I'll say that for him,' commented Lyndon Johnson.[42] When Ex-Comm met on 28

October to register the Russian climb-down the members all rose to their feet as the president entered the room: he had earned his place in history.[43] Not everyone thought so. On 29 October the rejoicing president thought it might be a good idea to stroke the chiefs of staff whose belligerent counsels he had so firmly rejected. He invited them to the Cabinet Room – and there the naval chief said, 'We have been had!' and the air force chief of staff, the notorious General Curtis Le May, pounded the table and cried, 'It's the greatest defeat in our history, Mr. President. . . . We should invade today!' No wonder that the next day Kennedy told Arthur Schlesinger that the chiefs were mad, and two weeks later remarked to Ben Bradlee, his journalist friend, that 'The first advice I'm going to give my successor is to watch the generals and avoid feeling that just because they were military men their opinions on military matters are worth a damn.'[44] But this was the only blemish on an otherwise dazzling scene of achievement and hope. He could afford at last to smile at the Republicans, who as soon as the danger was passed returned to their attack (some even suggesting that he had got up the whole crisis in order to carry the November elections). He had at last won the initiative from the Soviet Union, and could begin to steer international relations the way he thought they should go.

The difficulties of negotiation with the Russians largely remained; patience, ingenuity and resolution were still essential when dealing with that stubborn and unpredictable government; but success was now possible as it had not been before. Both sides had learned some essential points about the world they lived in, and about each other. They had learned that it did not do to play games with nuclear weapons, and the supreme importance of not backing your opponent into a corner; they had learned that neither side desired war; they had learned the supreme importance of not misjudging each other's wishes and intentions. All this vindicated what Kennedy had been saying since he took office. He summed it up yet again in a speech given at the American University, Washington, DC, on 25 July 1963, in which it is easy to see what moral he drew from the missile crisis both for the Americans and the Russians:

Above all, while defending our own vital interests, nuclear powers must avert those confrontations which bring an adversary to a choice of either a humiliating retreat or a nuclear war. To adopt that kind of course in the nuclear age would be evidence only of the bankruptcy of our policy – or of a collective death-wish for the world. To secure these ends, America's weapons are nonprovocative, carefully controlled, designed to deter, and capable of selective use. Our military forces are committed to peace and disciplined in self-restraint. Our diplomats are instructed to avoid unnecessary irritants and purely rhetorical hostility.[45]

Yet again he insisted on the importance of avoiding miscalculation, welcoming the proposal to install a 'hot line' between Moscow and Washington 'to avoid on each side the dangerous delays, misunderstandings and misreadings of the other's actions which might occur at a time of crisis'.[46] (And which, he might have added, had been among the most alarming aspects of the missiles affair.) Above all, he urged,

> let us not be blind to our differences – but let us also direct attention to our common interests and to the means by which differences can be resolved. And if we cannot end now our differences, at least we can help make the world safe for diversity. For, in the final analysis, our most basic common link is that we all inhabit this small planet. We all breathe the same air. We all cherish our children's future. And we are all mortal.[47]

These may be called the Kennedy theses, and their cool and obvious good sense at last found a receptive audience in Moscow. If his memoirs are to be trusted, Khrushchev persuaded himself, either at the time or in the melancholy years of his retirement, that 'the Caribbean crisis was a triumph of Soviet foreign policy':[48] Castro's survival had been assured, and the Jupiter missiles had been removed from Turkey. But even Khrushchev must have realised that the same ends might have been attained by much less dangerous means; the stark fact was that the Soviet Union, confronted by a resolute United States, had meekly climbed down, after the merest flurry of bluster. The all-too-lively epoch of Soviet adventurism was at an end: a new policy must be adopted. So the Kennedy theses were accepted, and became the basis of US–Soviet relations (though they were not always strictly observed by either side) until the end of the Cold War. They ushered in the second phase of that conflict, and explain why there was never to be another Berlin crisis, or indeed another major rupture of Russo-American intercourse until the invasion of Afghanistan in 1979;

and why, for good or ill, the United States did not seriously oppose the Russian intervention in Czechoslovakia in 1968, nor the Soviet Union make more of an issue of the war against Vietnam. Whether, in all this, the great powers were making the world safe for diversity is more than doubtful, but at least world war was averted. And there were other benefits. From the day of his inauguration Kennedy had been hoping to obtain a comprehensive Nuclear Test Ban Treaty, which the USSR had steadily rejected on the grounds that the United States wanted too many inspections of Soviet installations. This objection remained, but now the way was open for a treaty renouncing atmospheric nuclear tests, which would be greatly to the advantage of the world's health, and advertise the new relationship between Russia and America. On 25 July 1963 such a treaty was agreed in Moscow. It was a moment of great hope, and could not have been achieved but for the authority which Kennedy's handling of the missile crisis had brought him.

Kennedy wanted the Test Ban Treaty to be the precursor of even better things, and indeed in due course a Non-Proliferation Treaty was to be signed and, later on, the first Strategic Arms Limitation Treaty. They were both in the tradition. But the root difficulty could not be got over. The Soviet marshals, for example, learned one very simple lesson from the missile crisis: never again ought the USSR to be so decisively outgunned by its rival. So they accelerated the arms race; on both sides the stockpile of nuclear weapons was enormously increased (it had already been large enough to worry Kennedy); in this respect, if in no other, the Soviet Union attained parity with its rival. The two superpowers glared at each other for more than twenty years through a grid of rockets. It made no economic sense; it appallingly increased the risk run by the human race; it was a permanent barrier to better understanding between East and West. In this respect the missile crisis did not end happily. Not until the implosion of the Soviet Union in the late 1980s was it possible to negotiate a real end to the nuclear competition; and the very break-up of the communist regime which made such a denouement possible also created a risk that chaos would prevent its realisation. All of which suggests that Kennedy would not have got very much further in his attempt at détente had he lived, even though Khrushchev seems to have been as eager as he was himself to make progress towards peace and co-operation. This prompts the further thought, that perhaps a purely diplomatic approach to the missiles problem, such as Adlai Stevenson advocated, might have been better in the long term. In the short term, to be sure, Kennedy had little choice, as we have seen, to act otherwise than he did; but then, as we have also seen, it was in part his own provocations which brought about the crisis at all.

Nor did the missile crisis help with the problems besetting the Western alliance. General de Gaulle, the President of France, had supported Kennedy stoutly, but he saw at once that if the President of the United States and the Chairman of the Soviet government could between them bring the world to the brink of destruction without more than courtesy calls on their partners,[49] then a country as determined as was Gaullist France to be the mistress of its own destiny needed to rethink its alliances; and so the way was open to the French withdrawal from NATO, the French independent *force de frappe*, and the French veto on Britain's entry to the European Community – all of them blows at US policy. By contrast, a similar crisis with Britain in the early winter of 1962, immediately after the missile crisis, when the United States thoughtlessly knocked away the central prop of Britain's so-called independent nuclear deterrent by cancelling production of the Skybolt missile, was not directly caused by the Cuban affair; on the other hand, given the Macmillan government's loyal support of the Kennedy administration, not just during the days of October, but during the Bay of Pigs and at all other times too, the Americans could hardly say No when Macmillan asked to be given the Polaris submarine-based launcher instead of the once-promised Skybolt. As Dean Rusk explained, 'we have to have *somebody* to talk to in the world.'[50] But the immediate consequence was to alienate De Gaulle still further; at longer distance it kept alive British politicians' misconception of the proper place of their country in the world. Perhaps that need not matter very much to a President of the United States.

What should have mattered to him was that the missile crisis did nothing, in the end, to rationalise US relations with Cuba. Castro had been furious at the way the Russians had handled the affair, pressing him to accept the missiles as an act of communist solidarity, then making all the decisions without consulting him, and finally caving in to the *Yanquis*, whom Castro was more than ready to defy. (Cuba, he said, was prepared to be annihilated rather than surrender, and if he really intended to use the tactical nuclear weapons at his disposal, annihilation would no doubt have been the outcome of an armed collision.) Being a Soviet satellite clearly had its disadvantages; it might be preferable to seek an accommodation with the United States. An opening occurred when, after intense diplomatic efforts by the Americans, Castro agreed to return the last Bay of Pigs prisoners to the United States in return for $50,000 worth of medicines. The prisoners were restored to their families by Christmas, and Kennedy might well have felt that he had now liquidated his obligation to the Cuban exiles. He chose instead to renew it, appearing with his wife at a grand rally for them in Miami on 29 December 1962 where he accepted the banner of the exile brigade and announced that

> this flag will be restored to this brigade in a free Havana. . . . Under the *Alianza para el Progreso*, we support for Cuba and for all the countries of the hemisphere the right of free elections and the free exercise of basic human freedoms. . . . I am confident that all over the island of Cuba, in the Government itself, in the Army, and in the militia, there are many who hold this freedom faith, who have viewed with dismay the destruction of freedom on their island.[51]

The old romanticism still flourished; its expression on this occasion was highly injudicious, and was made worse by other developments.

As part of the Kennedy–Khrushchev agreement the United States had promised to lift its blockade once the UN had verified that the missiles had all left the island, but Castro refused to allow the UN inspection, so the blockade continued; this failure on the communist side to keep their side of the bargain liberated Kennedy also from his promise not to invade. Having apparently learned nothing in this respect from the missile crisis he welcomed this opportunity to renew his sabre-rattling. Although the National Security Council had put an end to Operation Mongoose as soon as the missile crisis was over, attempts to sabotage the Cuban economy continued, with the energetic encouragement of the Attorney-General. Worse still, the CIA continued to dabble in mad schemes to murder Fidel Castro – and was still at it in November 1963;[52] possibly without the Kennedys' knowledge.

In this context Kennedy's professed willingness (made in discreet contacts with trustworthy go-betweens) to negotiate with

Castro amounted to very little, and since the terms on which he insisted amounted to Castro's abdication (a breaking-off of all political ventures into Latin America, the expulsion of all Soviet military personnel from Cuba, and the discontinuance of his experiment in socialism) it is hard to believe that negotiations, even had they been undertaken, would have led to anything: for them to have been successful, one side, or both, would have had to swallow too many words.[53] Possibly Kennedy would have modified his policy in a second term; possibly his tough stance was motivated solely by the need to carry Florida in the 1964 election (he knew the state well); possibly he would have been ashamed of himself had he lived to discover that thirty years after he failed to grasp the nettle the US blockade was still in position, and if anything even tighter than it had been when he instituted it; while in spite of, or even because of, continuing US aggression, Castro was as firmly in power as ever. The Kennedy-induced sufferings of the Cuban people have achieved precisely nothing. The disgusted Cuban exiles long ago took back their flag.

If Kennedy was conscious that his Cuban policy was perhaps his worst failure, he never showed any sign of it. Rather he was chiefly conscious of the solid gains that the missile crisis and, in the summer of 1963, the Test Ban Treaty had brought him with American public opinion. The people of the United States were not on the whole so bellicose as the leaders of the Right, such as Barry Goldwater, liked to pretend. There was never a serious nuclear disarmament movement in the country, but everyone knew what a nuclear exchange would entail, and welcomed the respite now secured them, it seemed, by the president (who had spent the previous two years doing his best to frighten them). By September 1963 Kennedy was thinking seriously about his re-election campaign, and began to make 'non-political' trips to test the waters and consolidate, if he could, his support. The first of these trips took him to the West, where he had not done particularly well in 1960; he thought some speeches about conservation might do some good. But he soon found that the treaty was a far better card. The old isolationist pacifism which had once been so pronounced a feature of the region's politics might be dead, but there was nevertheless a widespread, acute and conscious yearning for peace and security. To his astonishment a speech extolling the treaty was a wild success in Salt Lake City – the very place where, in 1960, he had felt it most necessary to beat the Cold War drum. He went back to Washington convinced that he had found his winning issue, especially if the Republicans were so insane as to nominate Goldwater, one of the tiny band of senators who voted against the ratification of the Test Ban Treaty when it came before them on 24 September. He was still capable of striking a sternly patriotic note when necessary: the speeches he gave in Texas in November, and those which he intended to give, were full of anti-Russian fire. But Texas was another doubtful state, like Florida. On the whole, it is fair to say that in the course of 1963 the whole tenor of his presidency changed, in foreign policy as in some other things; and the quest for peace replaced the crusade for freedom as the defining concern of the Kennedy administration. It was a new phase; how consistently it would have been adopted, how long it would have lasted, and with what success, will never be known.

. . .

NOTES

1. Kennedy's determination to use the Alianza for counter-insurgency is abundantly illustrated in Edward B. Claflin (ed.) *J.F.K. Wants to Know* (New York: William Morrow 1991), for example pp. 224–6, which gives the text to NSAM 206, 'Military Assistance for Internal Security in Latin America'.
2. Richard Reeves, *President Kennedy: profile of power* (London: Papermac 1994) pp. 104–5.
3. Schlesinger, *RK*, p. 480.
4. Ibid., p. 476.
5. Michael R. Beschloss, *Kennedy v. Khrushchev: the crisis years 1960– 63* (London: Faber 1991) p. 418, text and footnote.
6. See, for example, Schlesinger, *RK*, pp. 488–94, and Theodore C. Sorensen, *Kennedy* (New York: Harper & Row Perennial edn 1988) p. 631. For the Trujillo incident see Schlesinger, *RK*, p. 491.
7. Reeves, *President Kennedy*, pp. 264–5.
8. Beschloss, *Kennedy v. Khrushchev*, pp. 5–6.
9. *PP* i p. 725.
10. Beschloss, *Kennedy v. Khrushchev*, p. 140.
11. For all this see Schlesinger, *RK*, pp. 488–98, and Christopher Andrew, *For the President's Eyes Only* (London: HarperCollins 1995) pp. 274–90.
12. Schlesinger, *RK*, pp. 481–2.
13. See Beschloss, *Kennedy v. Khrushchev*, pp. 376, 412, 639.
14. Andrew, *For the President's Eyes Only*, p. 274.

15. See Beschloss, *Kennedy v. Khrushchev*, p. 356.
16. Ibid., p. 392.
17. Ibid., p. 382.
18. Nikita Khrushchev, *Khrushchev Remembers* (London: Book Club Associates 1971) p. 494.
19. *PP* ii p. 674: president's news conference, 13 September 1962.
20. Beschloss, *Kennedy v. Khrushchev*, pp. 420–7.
21. Sorensen, *Kennedy*, p. 679.
22. Douglas Brinkley, *Dean Acheson: the Cold War years, 1953–71* (New Haven, CT: Yale University Press 1992) p. 159.
23. The roles of Bobby Kennedy and Dean Rusk during the crisis are somewhat debatable: neither man had much respect or liking for the other, and each recorded his views. See Beschloss, *Kennedy v. Khrushchev*, pp. 451–2. Their mutual criticisms should be used cautiously.
24. Ibid., pp. 434–5.
25. Robert F. Kennedy, *Thirteen Days: the Cuban Missile Crisis October 1962* (London: Macmillan 1968) pp. 37–8.
26. KOH: Dean Acheson.
27. Kennedy, *Thirteen Days*, p. 71.
28. Ibid., pp. 66, 125.
29. When the storm was safely over various members of the administration used this incident to suggest, quite falsely, that Adlai Stevenson had somehow flinched from the challenge. Kennedy tacitly encouraged this slander, which surfaced in a magazine article, partly because he disliked Stevenson, partly because he wanted to cut him down to size (his performance at the United Nations had greatly impressed the American public) and partly, Beschloss suggests (*Kennedy v. Khrushchev*, p. 569), to throw a smokescreen over the secret fact that he had actually adopted Stevenson's position. It was a characteristic manoeuvre of the kind that does not increase respect or liking for the president.
30. Robert S. McNamara, *In Retrospect* (New York: Times Books 1995) pp. 340–1.
31. Beschloss, *Kennedy v. Khrushchev*, pp. 420, 448, is severe on Kennedy for issuing his warning in September, when it was too late to do any good (the missiles were already being delivered) and served only to restrict his freedom of action. This is to be misled by hindsight. In September the American political situation seemed to demand a strong public stand against something which Kennedy, Bundy and the rest were sure was not going to happen. They were wrong, but whose fault was that?
32. See Sorensen, *Kennedy*, especially pp. 698–700.
33. *PP* ii p. 809: proclamation interdicting the delivery of offensive weapons to Cuba.
34. Ibid., p. 806: radio and television Report to the American People.

35. Beschloss, *Kennedy v. Khrushchev*, p. 477.
36. Dean Rusk, *As I Saw It* (New York: Norton 1990) p. 237. Rusk explains that this famous phrase arose from a game he used to play in his childhood in Georgia: 'we would stand about two feet apart and stare into each other's eyes. Whoever blinked first lost the game. It is not an easy game to win.'
37. *PP* ii p. 812: White House statement on the Soviet missile sites in Cuba.
38. Beschloss, *Kennedy v. Khrushchev*, p. 530.
39. Ibid.
40. See ibid., pp. 531–2.
41. Ibid., p. 538.
42. Ibid., p. 543.
43. Sorensen, *Kennedy*, p. 717.
44. Beschloss, *Kennedy v. Khrushchev*, pp. 544–5; Schlesinger, *RK*, p. 524; Benjamin C. Bradlee, *Conversations with Kennedy* (London: Quartet 1976) p. 122. Bradlee writes of Kennedy's 'forceful, positive lack of admiration for the Joint Chiefs of Staff, except for Maxwell Taylor'. He also liked the Marine Commandant, General Shoup.
45. *PP* iii p. 462: commencement address at American University.
46. Ibid., p. 463.
47. Ibid., p. 462.
48. Khrushchev, *Khrushchev Remembers*, p. 504.
49. Dean Acheson was Kennedy's emissary to De Gaulle during the missile crisis:

> he said, 'In order to get our roles clear, do I understand that you have come from the President to inform me of some decision taken by your President – or have you come to consult me about a decision which he should take?' And I said, 'We must be very clear about this. I have come to inform you of a decision which he has taken'. (KOH: Dean Acheson)

50. Quoted in Richard E. Neustadt, *Report to the President on the Skybolt Affair*, p. 71. This immensely instructive document has only recently been declassified, and has not been published. I am deeply grateful to Dr Neustadt for giving me a copy.
51. *PP* ii p. 911: remarks in Miami.
52. Beschloss, *Kennedy v. Khrushchev*, p. 674.
53. See ibid., pp. 638–9.

Chapter 6

REVOLUTION

To look back at the United States in 1961, when Kennedy took office, is to see that the country was about to undergo a deep and sudden change, as profound as any since the abolition of slavery. The infamous system of racial injustice was collapsing, and the only choices before Americans and American politicians were either to hurry the fall, or vainly to resist it, or apathetically to stand aside. No choice was cost-free. It is therefore to the permanent credit of the intelligence and principles of the Kennedy and Johnson administrations that they decided to help along the change as rapidly as, taking all things into consideration, they prudently might. Neither Kennedy nor Johnson was prepared to sacrifice the prospect of success to the mere exhilaration of self-righteousness. Neither forgot that the President of the United States had other duties besides that of doing what he could to secure racial justice, which made their more radical allies impatient; but in the end their judgement was vindicated, and the once-formidable structure of segregation and white supremacy was totally overthrown. It was one of the brightest moments in American history, and Kennedy's part in bringing it about is the brightest part of his record.

It was not an achievement that seemed to lie clearly before him when he took office. His publicly stated views on the race question were those of his party, but his sense of its true importance might reasonably be questioned. As a frequent visitor to Washington, a segregated city, before 1947, and a permanent resident there afterwards; as a regular visitor to Florida; as a candidate travelling throughout the United States, he had seen for himself that the system of white supremacy was wrong, cruel, ridiculous and unsustainable. But he does not seem to have known Negroes (as that people then preferred to be called) except as servants or as political activists. He supported their cause, but also thought it necessary to work with white southern leaders, respecting their views and their interests (this attitude explains why he was so acceptable to southern Democrats in 1960). He did not identify himself with the black cause (the Negro constituency in Massachusetts was small). He was capable of flashes of instinctive generosity and leadership, as when he telephoned Coretta King during the 1960 campaign, but he did not see the United States from the Negro point of view, which, indeed, he hardly knew. It was his brother Bobby who later on remarked of this period that 'I didn't lose much sleep about Negroes, I didn't think about them much, I didn't know about all the injustice,'[1] but Jack might have said much the same. The Kennedys' world was comfortable, northern and white. Jack had little sense of urgency about the race question. He believed that the most pressing problems facing him in 1961 were those to do with foreign policy. He thought that segregation mattered to presidents chiefly because it was becoming impossible for the United States to sustain its role as the banner of democracy while a regime of atrocious injustice prevailed in one-third of its territory. He supposed that it would be his record on foreign policy that determined the outcome of the 1964 election, and he also thought that his re-election would be unlikely if he alienated the white South. Nor did he expect to be controlled by events. The president should be master.

Yet the United States stood on the brink of a revolution. That word is used too lightly by historians, as well as by others, but if it ever means anything it does so here. The story of African Americans is long and complex and far from finished, but can best be understood as unfolding (so far) in four phases. The first was that in which the forced importation of labour from Africa gradually turned into the notorious Atlantic slave trade, which in turn generated a slave society that was at its height in terms of power, oppression and apparent solidity at the end of the eighteenth century. Then came a period of hectic expansion, during which, nevertheless, the forces making for the destruction of slavery also developed powerfully: the Civil War came as the climax and decisive conclusion of this phase. In the third period the pattern was repeated: a new system of racial oppression was set up (not only, though worst, in the South) which after nearly a century (that is, by the time that Jack Kennedy was elected president) was ready to collapse. After the Second Reconstruction black Americans, who in the nineteenth century helped to put an end to slavery, can say that in the twentieth they have claimed effective citizenship and political equality. A fourth phase has opened, but it is all too obvious that the work of attaining substantive social and economic equality will be achieved only in the twenty-first century; given the sluggish growth of the US economy since 1973,[2] the effort required may well turn out to be as huge and long-drawn-out as in any of the earlier periods. Yet there is no reason to despair, for in both the nineteenth and twentieth centuries the necessary energy was eventually forthcoming, and with astonishing speed social transformations were brought about, that can only be called revolutions.

The possibility of overthrowing the old order in the South was slowly becoming apparent, at any rate to a few, during Eisenhower's second term. The obstacles were enormous. The structure of white supremacy was formidable; with very few exceptions (Estes Kefauver,[3] Albert Gore Sr, Lyndon Johnson and Claude Pepper are the only ones who spring to mind) the region's politicians were deeply committed to it; there was a dangerous minority of violent racists, all too ready to kill, wound, maim and burn to maintain the system; the white majority, though comparatively passive, were nevertheless ready, as fellow-travellers, to support the aims and ignore the methods of this minority; the legal system, whether local, state or, too often, federal, was part and parcel of the segregationist structure; economic power lay squarely in the hands of the whites; the culture of the South acquiesced in the status quo; and that status quo involved perpetual fear, humiliation and deprivation for all African Americans, even where they formed a local majority of the population, or when they had achieved a measure of economic independence.[4] Blacks lived under a constant threat; they were also shut out from opportunity in education, work and housing: from most of the chief benefits of being American, in fact. Things were not so bad in the rest of the United States, but there too a profound racial prejudice, all the worse for being largely unadmitted, hindered African American advancement: it was in the North that the civil rights movement would eventually meet defeat. But before then it met victory in the South.

It was a victory made possible above all because the Negroes had managed at last to get control of their own destiny. This was something that even many liberal whites – especially southern liberals – did not understand. They supported civil rights and an end to white supremacy (Democratic party platforms had been saying as much since 1948) but they thought that they controlled the timing, that it was up to them to decide when action should be taken, and that it was they who would decide what that action should be. They expected blacks to accept white priorities. By 1960 all these assumptions were obsolete. The really effective pressure for change was coming from black people themselves; and black leaders, such as those in the National Association for the Advancement of Colored People (NAACP), had to respond to this pressure. It was one of the marks of Martin Luther King's greatness that he knew when to follow: he began to go to jail because his young militants said it was expected of him. In short, the immediate future of the United States lay largely in the hands of the poor and the oppressed. This was the stubborn fact which President Kennedy would have to recognise, absorb and adjust to. So would the Attorney-General. It was not an easy process, but in the end it was complete, and led to their greatest achievement: one that was permanent, noble and unambiguous.

Jack Kennedy supported black rights as a matter of course, and on his way to the presidency he had taken pains to convince Roy Wilkins of the NAACP, and other Negro leaders, that he was sound on the issue.[5] But in 1960–61 he would have been best described as a moderate, and is so described by historians. This was only in part because he knew that he could win neither the nomination nor the election unless he made himself acceptable to the white South. He did not yet accept that only radical action (what he would have called extremism) would ever demolish segregation. Misled by tradition, which his Harvard education had done nothing to correct, he believed that it was southern pride, not southern racism, which lay at the root of the difficulty. He thought that the First Reconstruction had failed because it had been enforced by federal troops, who had inflicted bad laws, corrupt legislators and unqualified black rulers on a resentful South which otherwise would have behaved reasonably after its defeat in the Civil War. He had sharply and persistently criticised President Eisenhower for sending troops to Little Rock in the crisis of

1957: Eisenhower should never have let things reach such a pass. Kennedy, as president, would handle the South much more tactfully. Finally, like every other president, he regarded civil rights as only one of the problems which reached his desk; it would have to wait its turn for his attention and action. For one thing, as he remarked, if his economic programme failed to get through Congress, black workers would suffer as well as white ones. 'If we drive Sparkman, Hill and other moderate Southerners to the wall with a lot of civil rights demands that can't pass anyway,' he said to Sorensen, 'then what happens to the Negro on minimum wages, housing and the rest?'[6] He did not foresee that even on non-civil rights matters he was not going to get much southern Democratic co-operation, however considerate he was.

These were routine political views and calculations; but the politics of civil rights was no longer routine (if it ever had been). The movement had developed and was still developing a logic and strategy of its own. By 1961 it was relegating to a subordinate position the legal strategy of the NAACP that had succeeded in getting the courts to find segregation unconstitutional. The Montgomery bus boycott of 1955–6 had set the pattern which was to be followed until the late sixties, and had conferred exceptional significance on the boycott's leader, Martin Luther King.[7] King was a Baptist minister and a Gandhian, and as such had espoused a philosophy of non-violence: only so, he reasoned, could the weak black minority defeat the strong and violent southern white majority. The black movement must cling to the Bible and the Constitution and get the conscience of white America on its side. It mattered only to the committed where this philosophy came from, and what were the psychological arguments for it: to the rest, the point was that it seemed to work. The Montgomery buses had been desegregated, and ever since, in the name of King and non-violence, more and more Negroes – especially the young ones – had been claiming, by exercising, their people's right to travel, eat in restaurants, sleep in hotels, study and amuse themselves like any other Americans. This activism led directly and intentionally to spectacular clashes with the forces of white supremacy at their most brutal; it kept the issues alive in the minds of all the American people; it acted as a superb recruiting agent among the blacks, and, not least, forced the federal government to intervene on the side of the oppressed.

The activists proved wonderfully fertile in tactical ideas. They held the initiative and exercised it brilliantly.

What this would mean for the Kennedy administration first became clear during the early summer of 1961, when the Freedom Rides began. These were the logical sequel to the sit-ins of the previous year. Dedicated little groups of black and white young people, girls as well as boys, boarded Greyhound buses, claiming their constitutional right to travel together through the South from Baltimore to New Orleans. The further they went the uglier was their reception, especially after they had entered Alabama. In Anniston one of the buses they rode was burned out by a furious white mob. In Birmingham, where the notorious police chief, 'Bull' Connor, carefully kept his officers off the streets (he later pretended that he had given them all permission to stay at home because it was Mother's Day), another mob brutally attacked the Riders themselves, and anybody else who got in the way. In Montgomery John Seigenthaler, one of the Attorney-General's chief assistants, was hit on the head with a piece of pipe as he tried to protect a young woman against attack, and was kicked, unconscious, under a car. ('You did what was right,' said his boss later.)[8] The next night a mob besieged the Riders and their friends (Martin Luther King among them) in the church where they had taken refuge: only the arrival of the National Guard prevented a massacre. Then the Freedom Riders headed on into Mississippi.

The President and the Attorney-General had no choice: they had to protect the Riders, but they did not like the necessity. When Jack first heard about them he was preparing for his journey to Paris and Vienna, and thought that the news from the South would weaken his standing with De Gaulle and Khrushchev: 'Tell them to call it off,' he said to his civil rights adviser, Harris Wofford (who replied patiently, 'I don't think anyone's going to stop them right now').[9] Bobby was apparently more concerned with the damage that the affair might do to his brother's reputation in the white South.[10] But they could not stand back and let the Freedom Riders be murdered. Bobby was more or less ceaselessly on the telephone to Governor Patterson of Alabama, finally inducing him to send in the National Guard. Even the president was drawn in, not very successfully: at one point the governor – who had been a strong Kennedy supporter in 1960 – refused to take his call. The brothers began to learn an important lesson, that the bonds between fellow Democrats and politicians frayed and snapped all too easily when the issue was race; but even the dawning suspicion that there was no middle ground in the South did not put the Kennedys wholeheartedly on the side of the Freedom Riders: they thought they needed the Southerners in Congress too much. So in the end Bobby negotiated a deal with Senator Eastland of Mississippi: the Riders would be escorted safely through Alabama, and there would be no more mob violence, but once they crossed into Mississippi they would be arrested by the state authorities and sent to jail for violating state laws; and there, with any luck, they would slip out of the headlines. So they did; and although the Attorney-General was willing to look for a way to get them out of jail, most of them insisted on staying there to serve their sentences, for a witness (when at last they were released they were welcomed in the North as heroes). Yet in spite of this accommodation, the affair had alerted Bobby to the need for action. Taking up a suggestion made earlier by Martin Luther King, he put unprecedented pressure on the Interstate Commerce Commission, which had jurisdiction, and by the autumn the ICC had officially banned segregation in all bus terminals.[11] Soon after that railroads and airlines were also desegregated.[12] The Rides had been victories after all.

The story of the Freedom Rides epitomised the whole tale of the Kennedy administration's encounter with civil rights. In gross and in detail the Kennedys were to be pushed to go further, faster, than they had ever expected. Not that Jack had ever meant to be inactive in the struggle. He was determined not to risk a disastrous clash with the South in Congress by introducing a civil rights bill which, in 1961 or 1962, would certainly fail, but he did not mean to leave his black supporters out in the cold: after all, they had provided his victorious voting margin. The federal legislature might be, for the moment, a broken reed, but the executive had enormous powers of its own. Desegregating the federal government was a process with a long way to go:[13] Kennedy was horrified when investigation disclosed how very, very few blacks were in positions of responsibility, or indeed in any positions at all in the US government. On Inauguration Day his eagle's eye had noticed that there were no black faces in the detachment of the Coast Guard which paraded before him; he ordered immediate action to remedy the situation thus disclosed, and required a report from each Cabinet officer on how things stood in his department. The findings were appalling: Chester Bowles for the State Department reported that of the 3,647 Foreign Service officers, only 15 were Negroes; Bobby Kennedy found that only 10 of the 995 Justice Department attorneys located in Washington were black; at the FBI, which had 13,649 employees, only 48 were black (and those were mostly employed as chauffeurs). A later survey discovered that although 12.6 per cent of the entire federal government's employees were Negroes, there were only two in the highest ranks of the civil service, and the overwhelming majority were employed only in manual jobs.[14] This was something which Kennedy could and did tackle immediately; by 1963 he had appointed far more blacks to posts in the federal government than all the presidents before him, his two most significant appointees being Robert C. Weaver to head the Housing and Home Finance Agency, and Thurgood Marshall, the NAACP's most formidable lawyer, to the Second Circuit Court of Appeals in New York. Kennedy hoped to raise the Housing Agency into a department of Urban Affairs, with a seat in the Cabinet; but because it was well known that Weaver would be the secretary (and thus the first black member of the Cabinet in US history) the segregationists in Congress blocked the whole proposal. Being nice to them did not seem to get results.

Very occasionally there was a quid for a quo. The Senate Judiciary Committee might well have blocked Thurgood Marshall's appointment (and anyway took its time over it) had Kennedy not agreed to appoint Harold Cox to the federal bench in Mississippi: Cox had been Senator Eastland's room-mate in college, and Eastland was the committee chairman. Yet as Arthur Schlesinger remarks, 'Cox was a heavy price to pay.'[15] He was a brutal-mouthed segregationist, who did everything he could to obstruct the advance of civil rights in Mississippi. Nor was he alone. Three other judicial appointments in the South in 1961 turned out equally badly, and exposed the Kennedys to telling Republican criticism. They could only resolve to be more careful in future, and were.[16] It was one more proof that trying to work with the southern conservatives in Congress did not pay.

The Attorney-General had his own strategy for outflanking both the racists and the civil rights activists. The Justice Department would be unleashed. Bobby put together an outstanding team in the Civil Rights Division, which began to bring suit everywhere to give effect to the Civil Rights acts of 1957 and 1960 and further the cause of desegregation wherever it could. The structure of white supremacy rested, in the last analysis, on the fact that southern whites voted and southern blacks, because of intimidation, corruption, apathy and despair, by and large did not. So Bobby urged the civil rights movement to make black voter registration its prime objective. Funds in large amounts would be made available for registration drives and to train registration workers. The Justice Department would see to it that such a campaign was unmolested by the racists. In this way, over a period of a few years, a significant black vote might be created in the South; and once that had happened, Bobby knew, the southern white politicians would have no choice but to respond positively – or lose office.

It was a rational strategy, and had the far from incidental advantage, from the Kennedys' point of view, that it might be kept fairly dark: the participation of the administration in a registration campaign might be concealed, so there need be no trouble in Congress, and there need be no marches, demonstrations and riots either. Anything for a quiet life. Unfortunately the scheme was doubly flawed. As was quickly to emerge, the Deep South would as actively and viciously oppose voter registration as it would any other assertion of black rights. The murder in Mississippi in the summer of 1964 of three young registration workers (one black, two white) occurred after Jack Kennedy was dead, but some such grim climax was always predictable, and in the end it turned out that a special Voting Rights Act was necessary (it became law in 1965). So the Kennedy strategy, even if it had been wholeheartedly adopted by the civil rights movement, would not for long have kept the issue off the floor of Congress. However much President Kennedy wanted to avoid it, one day he would have to offer strong legislative leadership on the matter. Anyway there was no question of the movement simply settling for the Kennedy strategy. 'Civil rights' was the name of the game. The importance of voter registration was well understood, and the black organisations were happy to take the money which the Kennedys pressed upon them; in particular, the young militants of SNCC (the Student Non-Violent Co-ordinating Committee) eagerly started work in the most benighted corners of the South and complained bitterly when the Justice Department, from shortage of manpower, failed to protect them as promised;[17] but the logic of the movement, as it had developed, imposed quite different priorities, as the Freedom Rides had proved.

Yet at the end of 1961 Jack Kennedy's priorities were unchanged. He would continue to do what he thought he could for civil rights, but the question was clearly even more intractable than he had supposed; an attempt would now be made to keep it at a distance. Harris Wofford was gradually edged out of decision-making, and eventually gave up in disgust to join the Peace Corps.[18] The administration's only legislative initiative was the uncontroversial bill for a constitutional amendment forbidding the poll tax in federal elections, which passed Congress in August 1962 and completed ratification by the states in January 1964; but as Schlesinger points out, it only affected elections in five states, and state elections not at all.[19] There was no second intervention in the great struggle until the summer of 1962, when Albany, Georgia, became the focus of a big desegregation campaign.

Albany was not a success for the integrationists, though the tactics practised there were to be employed triumphantly in Birmingham the following spring. Bobby Kennedy eventually exploited it to try to show the white South that he administered the law impartially between races, which enraged the black leaders. But the episode did drive the president, who could not afford to be perpetually silent on civil rights, to remark at a news conference,

> I find it wholly inexplicable why the City Council of Albany will not sit down with the citizens of Albany, who may be Negroes, and attempt to secure them, in a peaceful way, their rights. The United States Government is involved in sitting down at Geneva with the Soviet Union [this was an allusion to disarmament negotiations]. I can't understand why the government of Albany . . . cannot do the same for American citizens.[20]

This was perhaps the strongest comment which he had made, so far, as President. Six weeks later he showed that he had taken another step when he remarked, at another news conference, apropos the burning down of Negro churches in Mississippi during a voter registration campaign:

> I don't know any more outrageous action which I have seen occur in this country for a good many months or years than the burning

of a church – two churches – because of the effort made by Negroes to be registered to vote. . . . I commend those who are making the effort to register every citizen. They deserve the protection
of the United States Government, the protection of the State, the
protection of local communities, and we shall do everything we
possibly can to make sure that that protection is assured and if it
requires extra legislation and extra force, we shall do that.[21]

It might seem that he could hardly say less (actually he said
even more), given what was occurring and how strongly the
Justice Department had pushed the registration campaign, but
the important point was that now, for the first time, the President was spontaneously mentioning the possibility of early legislation and the possibility of the use of force. A road was
opening, and Kennedy was learning.

The next lesson (which profited many besides Kennedy) came
at the end of September 1962, when James Meredith, a black
citizen, inspired by the Kennedy rhetoric, made good his application to study at the University of Mississippi. What followed
was perhaps the decisive battle in the civil rights struggle; the
turning-point, after which all conditions had been altered.

Meredith's personal position was the simplest element in the
confrontation. He was claiming rights which could not legally
be gainsaid; his stubborn, almost morose character made it
possible for him to maintain them in circumstances of hostility
and physical danger which might well have broken a weaker
man. But for his dour heroism the cause might have suffered
a grave setback, as it had done when Autherine Lucy (through
no fault of her own) was driven from the University of Alabama in 1956.

The attitude of the federal government was twofold. The
executive was constitutionally obliged to defend Meredith's
assertion of his rights, and there was every long-term, historical reason for doing so: the sooner that the South was made
to bite the bullet and accept desegregation, the better for all
concerned. What had to come, had best come swiftly. But the
Kennedy administration also had to consider the politics of the
matter. A Pyrrhic victory in Mississippi, which enrolled Meredith
at the university at gunpoint, but wrecked the administration's
programme in Congress, and lost the Democrats the 1962 and
1964 elections, would in some ways be worse than a defeat. As
in the affair of the Freedom Riders, the Kennedys hoped to

come to a reasonable agreement with the local politicians and avoid the use of troops. This quest for the reasonable was at the heart of Jack Kennedy's political style; 'let us reason together' might much better have been his motto than Lyndon Johnson's, for LBJ's idea of reasoning was largely indistinguishable from intimidation. But the passions now let loose in Mississippi and much else of the Deep South could not be checked by any such cool appeal. The Ku Klux Klan was loose again, and it smelt blood.

A generation later, it is perhaps easier to understand President Kennedy's angry bafflement than it was at the time. He seemed to be up against a bunch of lunatics.[22] The title of a book of the era, *The Deep South Says Never*, accurately stated an attitude, but the attitude made no sense. The power structure of the segregationist South had been sustained, as it had been installed, by violence and chicanery; both props were now collapsing under the application of superior power, by the federal courts, the federal executive, and even by Congress. African Americans, though still too much a people apart, were now able, as never before, effectively to claim their rights as American citizens, and could not be stopped. If the tide had to retreat one yard, it would advance three. The structure of the entire modern world was altering to accommodate the strength of non-European peoples (as the United States would soon discover in Indo-China); the civil rights movement was a local manifestation of a far wider upheaval. Finally, the South itself was changing, becoming more urban, industrial, modern: its business leadership could not afford, and the bulk of its white population no longer really supported, the rural system of injustice that was such a check on progress and prosperity. The segregated South, in short, was a house of cards, beginning to totter. Kennedy could see this clearly, and was as much perplexed as vexed by the refusal of southern leaders to do so.

He was up against exponents of that famous demagogy which had added so much to the liveliness, absurdity, corruption and brutality of southern politics since the end of the First Reconstruction. Such men as Vardaman, Bilbo and the Long brothers had been expert at playing on the loves and hates, hopes and fears, ignorance, prejudice and ambitions of their constituents, rather than appealing to their intelligence, good feelings and common sense. Demagogy, to be sure, was not confined to the South; it was to be found in the North, if in less extreme form, even in Boston. But southern demagogy was dangerous because it operated in a closed society.[23] In part because southern moderates had been so unwilling to take a lead, to speak up for reform, the scene had been dominated, since the Supreme Court's *Brown* decision, by those who believed, or pretended to believe, and at any rate proclaimed, that the cause of segregation was lost, and that staunch resistance would compel the new generation of damn Yankees to give up, as their forerunners had done eighty years before. Elections had been won repeatedly by the race-baiters; George Wallace of Alabama explained his tactics in the 1962 gubernatorial election, 'I started off talking about schools and highways and prisons and taxes – and I couldn't make them listen. Then I began talking about niggers – and they stomped the floor.'[24] Politicians and voters caught each other up in a hot fantasy, stewed up out of legends of the southern past, racial hatred, fear of the currents which were sweeping the old ways to oblivion, resentment of Yankees, and all the excitements of mob feeling and action. James Meredith had stepped into this vortex, and it would have taken a cleverer man than Governor Ross Barnett of Mississippi to control and dissipate the consequences.

But Barnett did not even try. He was caught up in the dream of resistance. The Kennedys wanted to do a deal with him. If he would allow Meredith to enter the university and graduate, other black students would come, and the crisis would be over for good. On what terms would Barnett agree to Meredith's admission? Not at all, said the Governor: 'I won't agree to let that boy get to Ole Miss. I will never agree to that. I would rather spend the rest of my life in a penitentiary than do that.'

ROBERT KENNEDY: Mississippi must obey, as it is part of the United States.
BARNETT: We have been a part of the United States but I don't know whether we are or not.
ROBERT KENNEDY: Are you getting out of the Union?[25]

Barnett seems to have been high on Confederate legend and the prospect of great popularity in his state. It proved impossible to make a bargain with him – perhaps, in the long run, fortunately: great issues are not best settled by covert deals, though the Kennedys had yet to grasp the point – the details proved impossible to arrange, and meanwhile the Governor's vicious publicity had whipped up a storm of anger and hatred which he could neither contain nor control. He appeared at a University of Mississippi football game (the home team was known as The Ole Miss Rebels) and announced, to roars and shrieks of applause, 'I love Mississippi! I love her people! I love her customs!' (*Pandemonium*).[26] The largely student crowd felt, after that, that it knew its duty. Meredith was smuggled onto the campus on the evening of 30 September 1962, and three hundred federal marshals ringed the administration building, partly, it seems, to act as decoys (Meredith had been installed in one of the student dormitories) and partly to advertise federal authority. Believing that all was well, the President made a television speech at 10 p.m. urging the people of Mississippi and, especially, the university students to accept that the law should be obeyed:

> The honor of your University and State are in the balance.... Let us preserve both the law and the peace and then healing those wounds that are within we can turn to the greater crises that are without and stand united as one people in our pledge to man's freedom.[27]

Since he was still pursuing the hope that white Mississippians could be induced to behave co-operatively he said nothing about the righteousness of Meredith's cause, only that the law must be enforced and obeyed ('Americans are free to disagree with the law but not to disobey it')[28] and he stroked their pride and vanity with admiring references to various white state heroes, such as L.Q. Lamar.[29] When, a couple of hours later, he signed the orders calling out the National Guard, just as Eisenhower had done at Little Rock, he remarked that he was doing so on a desk that had belonged to Ulysses S. Grant, but he gave an order that this was not to be mentioned to the press – he had no wish to stoke up neo-Confederate paranoia any further.[30] All these palliating efforts were useless. Few of the Mississippi students heard or heeded his appeal. Even before he began to speak, though he did not know it, the marshals were having to defend themselves with tear gas (they were under strict instructions not to use pistols): they were coming under a terrifying barrage of stones and bricks and other missiles. The state highway policemen had disappeared: Governor

Barnett later said that they had been ordered to stay and maintain peace, but he told so many lies during the crisis that it is hard to believe him; anyway, there had not been very many state policemen, and they were unarmed. Some of the rioters had guns (thirty years later it seems astonishing that they were comparatively few) with which they wounded 28 of the marshals and killed a journalist and a bystander. The regular troops finally ordered in by Bobby Kennedy were maddeningly slow to appear (another black mark for the Pentagon in the eyes of both the Attorney-General and his brother); it was touch and go until dawn. The President was up all night: 'I haven't had such an interesting time since the Bay of Pigs,' he remarked.[31] The Attorney-General bitterly blamed himself for not having had troops nearby, in greater readiness. But when the troops arrived with the dawn, the essential point was achieved: James Meredith was a registered student at Ole Miss, and another bastion of segregation had fallen.

And the Ole Miss affair had an even larger significance. It made everyone think again. Senator Eastland, while publicly attacking the marshals for bringing their troubles on their own heads by their 'amateurism' and ranting in the usual fashion about 'judicial tyranny', told Bobby privately that Barnett had behaved ludicrously.[32] Barnett found that his political career was over, and when his former Lieutenant Governor, Paul Johnson, took office as governor, he quickly showed that he had abandoned the defiant rhetoric which, as much as Barnett, he had hurled about during the crisis. Still more significantly, the authorities in Alabama drew the appropriate conclusions. The University of Alabama was now the last remaining unintegrated state university in the country; its turn would soon come; there must be no repetition of the Mississippi fiasco – it was bad for the university and bad for business. 'Most of us know the Southern cause is doomed and it's ridiculous to keep spouting defiance,' said one Congressman.[33]

The Kennedys had their own reckoning to carry out. The affair had hardly been an advertisement for their skills of crisis management: they had been extremely lucky that none of the marshals had been killed and that Meredith had not been lynched. Ole Miss had been, politically, exactly what Kennedy had most wanted to avoid, a repetition of Little Rock, with troops sent into a southern town (they stayed until Meredith graduated in the summer of 1963) and much of the Deep South

boiling with resentment at what it saw as yet another unjusti-
fied Yankee invasion. The outcome of so much sound and fury
could be construed as minimal: the integration of higher education in the South went forward, but at a snail's pace and in
only token numbers. Martin Luther King and other black leaders felt that the President had muffed matters by not making the crisis an occasion for a ringing call for justice: all he
had talked about was the importance of obeying the law. Civil
rights, King felt, 'no longer commanded the conscience of the
nation'.[34] The President sought to bury the Meredith episode
and its potentially disastrous political consequences for himself, his programme and his party by referring to it as seldom
as possible.

He maintained this stance for some months. He allowed the
centenary of the Emancipation Proclamation (1 January 1963)
to pass without presidential acknowledgement, and made sure
that a big reception for black leaders at the White House on
Lincoln's Birthday went virtually unreported in the white press.[35]
(Martin Luther King, A. Philip Randolph and Clarence Mitchell
boycotted it.) He occupied himself with the other business
of the presidency, especially the Cuban missile crisis and the
congressional elections. It is impossible to admire this ignoble
behaviour, but ignobility is one of the traits exacted of democratic politicians from time to time by their less than noble
constituents. Even as he signed the Voting Rights Act of 1965
Lyndon Johnson prophesied accurately that it would lose the
Democrats the South for thirty years; his predecessor is not
perhaps to blame for trying to avert that fate. Right or wrong,
he was not going to abandon the effort in all that remained to
him of life.

Yet a fundamental shift was occurring in both his attitudes
and his calculations. He was beginning to see the South as it
actually was. Thus, in the aftermath of the Meredith storm 'he
specifically wondered aloud whether all that he had been taught
and all that he had believed about the evils of Reconstruction
were really true.'[36] Already, in February 1962, he had met David
Donald of Harvard, one of the most authoritative historians
of the Civil War era, and begun to learn that his own knowledge of the period was about twenty-five years out of date. In
the wake of Ole Miss he began to read the works of C. Vann
Woodward, including no doubt *The Strange Career of Jim Crow*,
the historical Bible of the civil rights movement.[37] By the sum-

mer of 1963, as the list of murderous southern outrages lengthened, he was ready to confess to Arthur Schlesinger, 'I don't understand the South' – to recognise your own ignorance is the beginning of wisdom – 'I'm coming to believe that Thaddeus Stevens was right. I had always been taught to regard him as a man of vicious bias. But, when I see this sort of thing, I begin to wonder how else you can treat them.'[38] By then he had come to see that it was hopeless, even immoral, to try to compromise with the segregationist leaders any longer, and that his mission was instead to take up the banner of the old Radicals and secure a Second Reconstruction. Even politically it made sense: if he could not win over the South then he had to rally the North.

External forces continued to drive him along the path he must go. He was popular with the black rank and file, but the leaders, though still susceptible to his charm, were more and more sceptical as to his effectiveness. He was sensitive to charges that he was not doing enough, especially as the Republicans were beginning to take them up. On 28 February 1963, two weeks after the Lincoln's Birthday reception, he sent a special message on civil rights to Congress in which he boasted of the achievements of the last two years in that area, and called on the legislature to supplement the efforts of the executive by passing a new voting rights act to end literacy tests and speed up the progress of voting rights suits; and he asked for funds to assist the continuing desegregation of public schools. It was the first civil rights bill he had ever proposed, and the fact that he made any proposals at all showed how far he had moved since his inauguration. But to the civil rights leaders it was not nearly enough. Randolph began to make plans for a gigantic march on Washington to put pressure on Congress, and if necessary on the White House too; King put the finishing touches to his plans for a major campaign in Birmingham, Alabama, which he called 'the most thoroughly segregated big city in the U.S.'.[39]

The Birmingham campaign was the most heroic moment of the civil rights revolution. The aim was to defy the laws of white supremacy and to force the desegregation of the city by sit-ins, economic boycotts and mass marches; stores were to be emptied and jails filled; pressure was to be steadily increased until the power elite of the city gave in. After a slow and sticky start, against huge odds, the plan worked. Martin Luther King went to jail, where he composed his masterpiece, *Letter from Birmingham Jail*, vindicating his strategy and tactics. One exceedingly dangerous specimen of those tactics, a children's crusade, proved astonishingly effective: the jails were filled, crowds joined in, and Bull Connor gave way to rage, sending in armed cops, some wielding fire-hoses, some with batons flailing, and vicious police dogs against women and children. All America watched what was happening: television proved to be a powerful new ally for the movement. The President said the sight made him 'sick', and endorsed the rising to the extent of saying 'I am not asking for patience. I can well understand why the Negroes of Birmingham are tired of being asked to be patient.'[40] Martin Luther King's message had got fully home to him at last. But what would follow? An agreement between the two sides in Birmingham was eventually negotiated through the good offices of Burke Marshall, assistant attorney-general in charge of the civil rights division, but elsewhere the South exploded: 14,000 demonstrators were going to be arrested before the summer was out.[41] As Bobby Kennedy saw, it was impossible for the federal government to protect them all: it had neither the legal nor the physical means to do so.[42] The axe must be laid to the root of the tree. On 1 June, at a meeting of his closest advisers, President Kennedy announced that he was going to send a major civil rights bill to Congress. What had seemed unthinkable and unattainable two years earlier was now to be attempted. It was the only thing to do.

The President did not like it. At the 1 June meeting he was uncharacteristically irritable,[43] for he knew that he was taking a decision which might yet wreck his presidency. Even after his proposals had gone to the Hill he would say to the Attorney-General (who, alone in the inner circle, strongly supported the move), 'Do you think we did the right thing . . . ? Look at the trouble it's got us in.'[44] But his manner was half-jocular: in the Kennedy style, he was using flippancy to cope with the emotional strain of a crisis. As he was to show, he was fully committed. At Lyndon Johnson's suggestion the administration lobbied every member of Congress before the bill was formally presented; and the President waited for the politically opportune moment to announce his new stand. It was provided by George Wallace.

Two black students, James Hood and Vivian Malone, had applied for admission to the Tuscaloosa campus of the University of Alabama, and that institution, after dragging its feet as much as possible, had accepted them: it knew that it was futile to follow Ole Miss in defying the law. It hoped fervently that there would be no repetition of the Autherine Lucy riot or, worse still, of the Ole Miss affair; but it was not in control of events. Wallace had repeatedly sworn to resist and defy the federal government if it tried to register Hood and Malone as it had Meredith: 'When the Court order comes, I am going to place myself, your governor, in the position so that the federal court order must be directed against your governor. I shall refuse to abide by any such illegal federal court order even to the point of standing in the schoolhouse door, if necessary.'[45] In spite of enormous pressure from the federal government and from many level-headed Alabama businessmen, Wallace stood firmly by this pledge, and as the day of the students' registration approached, Kennedy once more mobilised the National Guard; and this time he made sure that there was no repetition of the Ole Miss inefficiency. He had an ally in his determination that there would be no trouble at Tuscaloosa: Governor Wallace himself. Wallace knew quite well that Alabama could not resist the federal government successfully, and that if there was a riot his political ambitions (which were immense) would be unattainable: he would go into oblivion, like Ross Barnett. He decided to play a charade: he would stand in the schoolhouse door (or at least, in the door of the university's administrative building) and protest vehemently, but that done, would step aside, the pathetic victim of Yankee tyranny. The hearts of all the rednecks in Alabama would go out to him, his reputation as a fervent bigot would be confirmed, and since the students would have been registered the question of integration would at last be moot. So Wallace exerted himself to make sure that the Ku Klux Klan stayed away and that the university students behaved themselves. Kennedy federalised the Alabama National Guard, and the show went ahead. Nicholas Katzenbach, Bobby Kennedy's lieutenant, appeared on campus with the students; Wallace appeared in the door, read out a defiant proclamation, and then stepped out of the way; James Hood and Vivian Malone registered. Kennedy was relieved and pleased, and impulsively decided to give a TV address that evening, proclaiming his decision to bring forward a big civil rights bill. He was a victor at last, commanding events, not merely reacting to them, and he meant to exploit the victory.

The speech was one of the most important and effective that Kennedy ever gave, but it was one of the least polished. His decision to give it took Ted Sorensen by surprise, and he had no time to do more than dash down a first draft. With only a few minutes to go, Kennedy and his advisers tinkered with the text, and then he was on camera live. It did not matter. He was now so experienced and self-confident an orator that he was able to improvise a compelling address out of scraps. It does not read so impressively as his other great speeches, but Kennedy's conviction that now was the time to act to repair a century's wrong still comes over, and at the time, delivered with ever-increasing force as he warmed to his task, it was urgent and compelling. Sorensen has pointed out that the speech contained little that Kennedy had not said before (except for the all-important commitment to a comprehensive civil rights bill), but he had never before said it with such urgency, at such length, before such a large audience: the American people.[46]

> We are confronted primarily with a moral issue. It is as old as the scriptures and is as clear as the American Constitution. . . . This is one country. It has become one country because all of us and all the people who came here had an equal chance to develop their talents. We cannot say to 10 per cent of the population that you can't have that right; that your children can't have the chance to develop whatever talents they have; that the only way that they are going to get their rights is to go into the streets and demonstrate. I think we owe them and we owe ourselves a better country than that.[47]

The speech was a huge success. Letters to the White House ran 4 to 1 in its favour. One of them came from Martin Luther King: 'It was one of the most eloquent, profound and unequivocal pleas for justice and the freedom of all men ever made by any President. You spoke passionately to the moral issues involved in the integration struggle.'[48] Indeed he had. John F. Kennedy had enlisted in that struggle for the duration.

It was far from over. On the very night of Kennedy's speech Medgar Evers was assassinated in Mississippi. During the long summer civil rights demonstrations erupted all over the United States; tempers began to rise on all sides. In September, with the opening of the new school year, schools in almost every state in the South were integrated peacefully; the exception was Alabama, where Governor Wallace was up to his little tricks again. He sent state troopers into four cities (including Birmingham) to stop the schools opening. The courts enjoined him; he withdrew the troopers, replacing them with national guardsmen; Kennedy federalised the guard, and ordered it to withdraw from the schools. Once more Wallace had grandstanded, achieving nothing except a renewal of his popularity among the diehards of Alabama and the rest of the South; but he had inflamed tempers which needed cooling, and on 15 September a bomb exploded under a black church in Birmingham, killing four little girls. A riot resulted, in which two more Negroes were shot – one while running away, another, a thirteen-year-old, by a couple of trigger-happy Eagle Scouts coming away from a segregationist rally. They could not, afterwards, explain their action: they had just obeyed the impulse to try out their new pistols on a boy riding a bicycle.[49]

America, clearly, was tottering on a terrible brink; but the centre of the action was now Washington. The target of the Kennedy administration and the civil rights organisations was Congress. The courts and the executive had done, or were doing, all that they could; it was the turn of the legislature. And the bill which Kennedy had sent up on 20 June had been carefully crafted to be irresistible: a bold measure which, nevertheless, the cautious and the conservative (whether Republican or Democrat) could support without sacrificing their principles or incurring the wrath of their constituents. It incorporated the February proposals (on which, as the President drily remarked in his Special Message, neither House had yet had an an opportunity to vote);[50] but it added proposals outlawing racial discrimination in public accommodations (hotels, restaurants, lunch counters, theatres, movie theatres, and so on); greatly strengthening the powers of the Attorney-General to intervene to further desegregation suits; forbidding racial discrimination in federally-assisted programmes, and setting up a Commission on Equal Employment Opportunity to monitor government contracts. As it turned out, the Civil Rights Act that was passed a year later was significantly stronger in the measaures it took against job discrimination;[51] it was weaker in that it took no steps against racial imbalance in schools or colleges, as Kennedy had wanted; but on the whole the Act was so like the bill as to vindicate the judgement of the man who first proposed it.

But if the President proposed, it was for the legislature to dispose. The great test of Kennedy's congressional management had come, and at moments it looked as if he was going to flunk it. From June to the end of October the focus was on the House Judiciary Committee, to which the administration had sent its bill for consideration. It proved to be the battle of the Rules Committee all over again: Kennedy again discovered the hard way (after Emanuel Celler, the Committee chairman, had entangled matters almost beyond rescue) that the famed congressional veterans, for all their power and experience, were frequently incapable of delivering on their sanguine promises. At one point even Larry O'Brien found that he had been much too optimistic. Yet in the end the central point was gained. Kennedy knew that too strong a bill had no hope of clearing the House, let alone the Senate too. Celler's mistake was in letting his sub-committee amend the administration's bill until it was far too radical to succeed; the situation could only be rescued in the full committee, and there only with the help of the Republican leadership – William M. McCulloch, and Charlie Halleck, the Minority Leader. They put a price on their assistance: not only would they insist on being full partners in writing the bill, but they must get public credit for doing so. It was not too high a price to pay, and Kennedy gladly came across, while putting all the pressure he could mount upon his own unruly Democrats. The result was that on 29 October the bill as amended was reported out of the committee, and the first congressional hurdle had been crossed. Kennedy was immensely pleased: the new bill was stronger than the one he had submitted, but not so much so as to imperil success. He immediately issued a public statement:

> The bill is a comprehensive and fair bill. . . . From the very beginning, enactment of an effective civil rights bill has required that sectional and political differences be set aside in the interest of meeting an urgent national crisis. The action by the Committee today reflects this kind of leadership by the Speaker of the House, John McCormack, House Minority Leader, Charles Halleck, the Committee Chairman, Emanuel Celler, and the ranking Minority Member, William McCulloch.[52]

The next battle would be that of getting the bill out of the Rules Committee, but with the Republican leadership supporting what was now a plainly bipartisan bill Kennedy could reasonably hope to get over that hurdle too, and he had Everett

Dirksen's promise that the Republicans in the Senate would support a cloture vote, thus removing the South's precious last-ditch weapon, the filibuster.

It is scarcely possible to say more on this topic. Nobody knows what would have happened had Kennedy not been shot. Clearly, much could have gone wrong, and it is noteworthy that even with Lyndon Johnson exercising his formidable skills the Civil Rights bill did not become law until the summer of 1964. The prize which President Johnson secured (partly by evoking his predecessor's memory) might have eluded President Kennedy. On the other hand, it might not. He and his team made some serious initial blunders when trying to get the bill through the Judiciary Committee, but they learned as they went along, and were successful in the end. There seems no particular reason to suppose that these highly intelligent, committed men, wielding the power and influence of the presidency, could not have done as well at later stages. Congressional liberals did not think so, but their political judgement was poor; their intractability was one of the chief obstacles in Kennedy's way.

At least no one can deny that Kennedy started the process which was to issue so triumphantly in the Civil Rights Act of 1964 and the Voting Rights Act of 1965. So it is perhaps best to remember him as he seemed during the great March on Washington of 28 August 1963. This event had been originally planned by A. Philip Randolph, as we have seen, as a means of putting pressure on the president. By August this was no longer necessary; Congress was the target of this huge lobbying demonstration, which would also have the merit of uniting all the various constituents of the civil rights movement in a single action (there was a real danger, that summer, that the movement would fly apart and dissipate its strength in unco-ordinated and possibly violent street turbulence, thereby alienating the essential white allies who had been brought on board by Bull Connor's cruelty). Kennedy was initially anxious about the March, fearful that it would do harm; but once it was made clear to him that it was going ahead whatever he thought he characteristically moved in and took it over. When more than 200,000 marchers appeared in Washington they were welcomed with everything except drum majorettes and a fly-past. The federal government made sure that every possible medical, sanitary, refreshment and other facility was available, and that the city received them peacefully; and after the speeches at the Lincoln Memorial, which culminated in Martin Luther King's celebrated 'I have a dream' oration, the leaders were received by a smiling President at the White House. Spirits were high; but Kennedy characteristically used the occasion for business. The March was a great lobbying occasion: what should they be lobbying for? Wilkins, Randolph and Walter Reuther wanted the President to lead a crusade and press for an even stronger bill. Kennedy (who, like his brother Bobby, wanted a bill, not an issue)[53] took them through the entire roll of the House and Senate, giving them Larry O'Brien's estimate of how each member of Congress would vote. It was going to be terribly tight, and there was no hope unless the movement backed a bipartisan bill – in other words, deferred to Republican attitudes. Neither side much swayed the other, but they parted on friendly terms, with a better understanding of each other's point of view. It was a microcosm of the processes which had gradually carried the President into the radical camp.

If Kennedy and the civil rights leaders found it difficult to work together, as practical politicians and idealists always do, there could be no doubt about his enormous popularity among blacks at large. They believed that he had done more for them than any other president since Lincoln, and they expected him to do more. His murder came therefore as a dreadful shock. A survey showed that half of them worried about how the event would affect their jobs, lives and careers; 81 per cent of the black children surveyed felt that they had lost 'someone very close and dear'. Coretta King (in 1969) would recall that nothing previously had affected her so much as Kennedy's death, not even the first attempt to murder Martin Luther King. Black activists felt once more betrayed by white society, and feared (unjustly, as it soon turned out) that Lyndon Johnson would not press forward with civil rights legislation. Fred Shuttlesworth, speaking in New York four days after the murder, paid tribute to Kennedy: 'The dedication to freedom and desire found in Negro leadership and the passionate yearnings of the oppressed masses in this country were matched by his own courage of convictions, grasp of the needs of the hour, and his devotion to making the U.S. Constitution become meaningful to all its citizens.'[54]

The sincerity and justice of such tributes make Taylor Branch's remark that there was something 'exogenous' about

Kennedy's involvement in the civil rights crusade seem rather mean-spirited. It is true that there was a wide gap between Kennedy's personality, outlook and priorities and those of the civil rights leadership, but that was nobody's fault, and both sides worked hard to overcome the gap, for they knew that they needed each other. The shocking fact that neither Roy Wilkins nor Martin Luther King was asked to the funeral mass was hardly Kennedy's doing, and King, though deeply hurt, stood on the pavement in Washington with tens of thousands of other Americans to see the coffin and the riderless horse go by. He knew what, in spite of all the friction, he and his people owed to the dead man.[55]

Kennedy entered the White House at a moment when the issue of racial oppression could no longer be dodged. He had to act, and did so effectively and (in the main) willingly. His successor inherited a great opportunity which it only needed his own conviction, energy and cunning to realise. There is no reason to believe that any other man who could have been elected President in 1960 would have done better than these two, and perhaps none could have done so well.

. . .

NOTES

1. Carl M. Brauer, *John F. Kennedy and the Second Reconstruction* (New York: Columbia University Press 1977) p. 90.
2. See Jeff Madwick, 'The End of Affluence', *New York Review of Books*, 21 September 1995, pp. 13–17.
3. Tennessee, his own state, remained loyal to Kefauver, but elsewhere in the South he was denounced as a traitor. His crime was to say that as desegregation had become the law of the land (because of the *Brown* decision) it had to be accepted. Like LBJ he had also refused to sign the Southern Manifesto. This led a Mississippi delegate at the 1956 Democratic convention to explain his support for Kennedy: 'we'd be for anybody against that nigger-loving Kefauver' (Brauer, *John F. Kennedy*, p. 19).
4. It was never a large measure. On one occasion Martin Luther King sought to raise $100 from every black Baptist church in the South; one minister replied that he and his flock could do better than that, and sent $500; neither sum was very big. See Taylor Branch, *Parting the Waters: Martin Luther King and the civil rights movement, 1954–63* (London: Macmillan 1988) p. 571.
5. Brauer, *John F. Kennedy*, pp. 25–8.

6. Theodore Sorensen, *Kennedy* (New York: Harper & Row Perennial edn 1988) pp. 475–6.
7. Taylor Branch *Parting the Waters*, p. 307, makes the point that this was not immediately apparent to white politicians. As late as 1960, during his campaign for the Democratic nomination, Kennedy was surprised to be told by Harry Belafonte that the one black leader it was essential for him to get on terms with was King.
8. Schlesinger, *RK*, p. 297.
9. Ibid., p. 295.
10. It turned out that the president's popularity in Dixie was not seriously reduced until the summer of 1963.
11. See Branch, *Parting the Waters*, p. 478. Unofficially, segregation lingered a little longer. During the fall of 1962 I discovered that in central Tennessee there was still at least one bus stop where there was one waiting-room for blacks and one (much better-appointed) for whites, and that only an imperceptive foreigner would go into the wrong one. But twenty years later I travelled by car from Tennessee into North Carolina with two black friends and had no difficulty of any kind at the restaurants where we refreshed ourselves en route.
12. Schlesinger, *RK*, p. 300.
13. See the excellent monograph on this topic, Desmond King, *Separate and Unequal: black Americans and the U.S. federal government* (Oxford: Clarendon Press 1995).
14. Brauer, *John F. Kennedy*, pp. 82–3.
15. Schlesinger, *RK*, p. 308.
16. Ibid., p. 310.
17. It was this feeling which touched off the extraordinary attack on Bobby Kennedy at his private meeting with some eminent Negroes in May 1963; though the young man who started all the trouble by saying that he was nauseated at being in the same room as the Attorney-General was a worker for CORE (Congress of Racial Equality) rather than the voter registration project.
18. But Kennedy told him that he was despairing too easily. See Harris Wofford, *Of Kennedys and Kings: making sense of the sixties* (New York: Farrar Strauss Giroux 1980) p. 125.
19. Schlesinger, *TD*, p. 858.
20. *PP* ii pp. 592–3: news conference, 1 August 1962.
21. Ibid., pp. 676–7: news conference, 13 September 1962.
22. Brauer, *John F. Kennedy*, p. 156, is not the only recent writer to question the sanity of Governor Ross Barnett.
23. For what this means, see James Silver, *Mississippi: the closed society* (London: Gollancz 1964). This classic work contains, among much else (Silver was a professor at Ole Miss during its great

crisis), a remark by William Faulkner which Kennedy would have liked: 'To live anywhere in the world of A.D. 1955 and be against equality because of race or color, is like living in Alaska and being against snow' (p. xi).

24. Brauer, *John F. Kennedy*, p. 141.
25. All this from ibid., p. 185.
26. Branch, *Parting the Waters*, p. 659.
27. *PP* ii p. 278: radio and television report to the nation on the situation at the University of Mississippi, 30 September 1962.
28. Ibid., p. 727.
29. Who had been celebrated in *Profiles in Courage.*
30. Brauer, *John F. Kennedy*, pp. 190–1.
31. Branch, *Parting the Waters*, p. 667.
32. Brauer, *John F. Kennedy*, pp. 187 and 198.
33. Ibid., p. 200.
34. Branch, *Parting the Waters*, p. 672.
35. Even the black press played it down, but still it was the biggest such reception there had ever been; Louis Martin, the organiser, boasted that Kennedy would be entertaining 'more Negro guests than had assembled in the cumulative history of the White House' (Branch, *Parting the Waters*, p. 694).
36. Brauer, *John F. Kennedy*, p. 204, quoting KOH: Sorensen. Curiously, this revealing comment is omitted from Sorensen's book.
37. Ibid., pp. 153 and 240.
38. Schlesinger, *TD*, p. 856. The particular outrage which prompted this reflection was the murder of Medgar Evers, the chief NAACP organiser in Mississippi. Kennedy received the Evers family at the White House, and the Attorney-General went to Medgar Evers's burial in Arlington Cemetery (where, before long, he and his brother would also lie).
39. Sorensen, *Kennedy*, p. 489.
40. Schlesinger, *TD*, p. 875.
41. Ibid., p. 879.
42. RK, *Words*, pp. 172–3.
43. Charles Whalen and Barbara Whalen, *The Longest Debate: a legislative history of the 1964 Civil Rights Act* (New York and Ontario, Mentor Book edition 1986) p. 17.
44. RK, *Words*, pp. 176, 179. 'He always felt that maybe that was going to be his political swan song ... he kept getting reports that it was going to affect all the other legislation' (p. 176).
45. E. Culpepper Clark, *The Schoolhouse Door* (New York: Oxford University Press 1993) p. 154.
46. Sorensen, *Kennedy*, p. 495.
47. *PP* iii pp. 469–70.
48. Branch, *Parting the Waters*, p. 824.

49. See Whalen and Whalen, *Longest Debate* pp. 33–4, and Branch, *Parting the Waters*, pp. 890–1.

50. *PP* iii p. 484: *Special Message to Congress on Civil Rights and Job Opportunities*, 19 June 1963.

51. And by a wrecking amendment offered by old Judge Smith, which backfired on him, it became the first federal statute to outlaw discrimination in the job market on account of sex.

52. *PP* iii p. 820: *Statement by the President Following Action on the Civil Rights Bill by the House Committee on the Judiciary*, 29 October 1963. For the whole story, see Whalen and Whalen, *Longest Debate, passim.*

53. See Whalen and Whalen, *Longest Debate*, p. 45.

54. For all this see Brauer, *John F. Kennedy*, pp. 312–14.

55. Branch, *Parting the Waters*, pp. 918–19.

Chapter 7

VIETNAM

If the civil rights revolution was to leave a deeper mark on American society, and perhaps on the history of the world, than any other event of Kennedy's time, it has nevertheless had to compete for posterity's attention with that other great crisis of the 1960s, the US war in Vietnam, which wounded the national consciousness as nothing else had done since the Great Depression or even, perhaps, the Civil War. Kennedy's part in this second crisis, though important, was less central than his part in the civil rights revolution, but it has been much more fiercely contested. Something like a consensus has grown up, if not among professional historians or the people at large, but at least in what may be called the opinionated classes, that Kennedy was as much to blame for the great national tragedy as anybody else, even Lyndon Johnson or Richard Nixon; but there is also a vocal minority opinion that he was the man who could and would have saved America from its fate, had he lived. No study of John F. Kennedy can be complete which does not inquire into the fairness and plausibility of these contradictory judgements.

We must begin with an outline of what the Vietnamese question actually was, since so much of the debate, both in Kennedy's lifetime and afterwards, and so many of the decisions taken, were determined by what statesmen, generals and journalists believed it to be.

Indo-China was that portion of South-East Asia, lying between Thailand, Malaya and China, which was colonised by France in the nineteenth century. It consisted of three countries, Laos, Cambodia and Vietnam, which lie along the lower courses of the great river Mekong. The French empire there collapsed under Japanese attack in 1941–42, and could not be successfully re-established after the Second World War was over, in spite of the old imperial power's most strenuous efforts. The Vietnamese won a decisive victory at Dienbienphu in 1954, after which France gave up. By the 1960s it was a settled French policy never again to get involved militarily in South-East Asia.

Thus summarised, the story is a fairly usual one. By 1945 the day of all the great overseas empires was done, whether the French, the Japanese, the British, the Dutch, the Portuguese or what little was left of the Spanish; all went through much the same dismantling process in the next thirty years or so. And immediately after victory over Japan the United States gave independence to the Philippines. The imperial powers seemed in the end to be none the worse for their abdication, though not all of them were wise enough to retire peaceably from the game. The French were particularly tenacious, fighting not one but two wars against decolonisation, in Algeria as well as in Indo-China. They lost both because French public opinion in the end rebelled against the enormous casualty-lists incurred in what seemed to be incomprehensible, unnecessary, unwinnable struggles. Onlookers should have found both episodes instructive (and some did). But in the grand sweep of history they were merely two among many.

The decolonisation of Indo-China had one feature which set it apart and which, to the sorrow of most concerned, was to have a determining effect on the future. The anti-imperialist, nationalist movement in Vietnam was captured by the Vietnamese communists. In the Asian context this was not surprising: at the same period communists were carrying the day in China. A powerful factor, ironically, was the prestige of Paris. Ho Chi Minh, the communist leader, knew France well. He had been a founder-member of the French Communist Party, which was the only French party that was even theoretically committed to decolonisation. He was also a great admirer of the American anti-imperial tradition, and launched his rebellion against Paris quoting the Declaration of Independence. He worked with American secret agents against the Japanese during the war, and afterwards tried repeatedly to arrive at an understanding with Washington. None of this moderated the alarm of the US government at his advance. France was clamouring for aid in its war against Vietnamese nationalism. As early as 1947 the State Department was telling the US ambassador in Paris that 'Ho Chi Minh has direct Communist connections and it should be obvious that we are not interested in seeing colonial empire administrations supplanted by philosophy and political organizations emanating from and controlled by [the] Kremlin.'[1] Besides, the French state seemed so weak that it might be necessary to support it in Indo-China in order to encourage it to stand fast against the Soviet Union in Europe. Then in 1949 Mao Tse Tung and the communists conquered the whole of mainland China. A monolithic worldwide communist conspiracy, of which Ho Chi Minh was a member, seemed to be sweeping all before it. The invasion of South Korea in 1950 by communist North Korea, acting under Stalin's orders, seemed a conclusive proof of the thesis, which explains Dean Acheson's otherwise baffling recommendation to President Truman that one of his responses to that invasion ought to be a substantial increase in aid to the French in Indo-China.[2] France was now seen as defending the southern front against a general advance of 'the Sino-Soviet bloc' in Asia, and so deserved to be supported. Traditional American anti-colonialism could not be allowed to stand in the way. Before long the United States was paying nearly 80 per cent of the cost of the French war-effort.[3]

The decision to help the French in Indo-China did not go quite unchallenged in the State Department. One of Acheson's officials, John Ohley, warned that 'these situations have a way of snowballing.' Acheson ignored this. American resources were poured into Indo-China: 'Although the French complained that our aid was never enough, it was more than Indochina was able to absorb.'[4] At least the State Department and the joint chiefs of staff were equally resolved against sending US armed forces to the theatre; but the United States was now committed to propping up a discredited imperialism. In spite of all the changes that occurred in the next fifteen years, it did not abandon this commitment: Ho Chi Minh must be resisted. If, then, there was a decisive moment in the United States' relations with Vietnam, it occurred, maybe, in 1950.

Ohley's warning began to be vindicated all too soon. The commitment showed a horrible staying-power, though the rationale was always changing. When in 1953 the Republicans replaced the Democrats the new Secretary of State, John Foster Dulles, argued that the purpose of American Indo-Chinese policy was to deter communist China: 'There is a risk that, as

in Korea, Red China might send its own army into Indo-China.'[5]
In 1954 President Eisenhower enunciated the famous domino
theory when at a press conference he was asked to explain 'the
strategic importance of Indochina to the free world'.

> You have a row of dominoes set up, you knock over the first one,
> and what will happen to the last one is the certainty that it will go
> over very quickly. . . . when we come to the possible sequence of
> events, the loss of Indochina, of Burma, of Thailand, of the Penin-
> sula, and Indonesia following, now you begin to talk about areas
> that not only multiply the disadvantages that you would suffer
> through loss of materials, sources of materials, but now you are
> talking really about millions and millions and millions of people . . .
> the possible consequences of the loss are just incalculable to the
> free world.[6]

Another argument which impressed even those who did not
accept the domino theory was that American prestige, a 'vital
national interest', was at stake. As late as 1966 Arthur M.
Schlesinger Jr, of all people, was writing:

> Our stake in South Vietnam may have been self-created, but it has
> none the less become real. Our precipitate withdrawal now would
> have ominous reverberations throughout Asia.[7]

In other words, we're here because we're here, and American
prestige, American credibility, demand that we stay.

In view of all that happened afterwards, it seems almost
incredible that the intellectual foundations of the American
commitment should have been so fragile. Robert McNamara
wrestles with the problem throughout his memoirs (it must be
said, to no great purpose).[8] The reason seems to have been the
unshaken dominance of what may be called the Cold War
paradigm.[9] The isolationist–pacifist paradigm of Kennedy's
youth had long been overthrown; few members of Congress
believed it any longer, and of leading American statesmen in
the 1950s and 1960s the one whose views bore traces of it most
clearly – only traces – was Eisenhower, who in other respects
embodied Cold War attitudes. The Cold War paradigm was
the full flower of that internationalist thesis which the Pearl
Harbor generation had struggled to win the American people to accept. Its major premise was that the peace and prosperity of the United States depended on an active assumption

of international responsibility, even to the point of going to war if necessary; its minor premise was that after 1945 the only serious challenge to that responsibility was the international communist conspiracy, energised by Russian power, centrally directed by Moscow, and active in all continents. The obvious consequence of this reasoning was that the United States must resist communism wherever it showed its face; a less obvious, indeed almost unconscious, but powerful inference was that all important world events could and should be explained in terms of the Cold War. As Henry Kissinger said in the 1970s, history revolved round an East–West axis, never around a North–South one.

This paradigm worked excellently while Stalin was alive, and for some years afterwards. It saved statesmen from the trouble of rethinking the nature of the international system at every crisis, and was a largely accurate guide to the interpretation and prediction of events. It began to break down when China and the Soviet Union quarrelled; and the extreme reluctance of many officials in Washington (especially in the CIA) to accept the reality of that quarrel – they argued that the business was merely a blind to bamboozle the West – illustrates very clearly how strong the grip of the Cold War paradigm had become.

That grip could not be broken until a new paradigm was ready, but one was at hand. To the greater part of the politically conscious human race the central theme of the post-1945 period was not the Cold War but what may loosely be called Third World revolutionism.[10] Outside the playgrounds of the West and the fortress of the Soviet empire, the whole population of the world was moving. Nationalists were challenging imperialists, the country was challenging the town, tribes were rebelling against states, Islam was beginning its war against Western values, peasants were warring against commercial elites (themselves deeply compromised by involvement with the old imperial system).[11] Events on the largest scale were impending; events which the Cold War paradigm could not accurately interpret and which, in the not too long run, neither communism nor capitalism could control. In this new world the power and the responsibility of the United States would be no less; what was in question was its wisdom. It proved to be in tragically short supply, and Vietnam was the place of the demonstration.

Yet Vietnam should have been an early and easy lesson in the obsolescence of the Cold War paradigm. As a nation it was deeply divided, fissured by the legacy of colonialism, by tribal differences, religious differences, political, social and economic differences. It was hardly surprising that as the French withdrew it lapsed into civil war: the situation was not unlike that which, in the 1990s, was to follow the collapse of the Yugoslav state. It should have been obvious that this calamity had very little to do with outside interference. For one thing, the Vietnamese were fiercely nationalistic, and throughout their history had vigorously resisted foreign domination. The idea that a communist Vietnam would be the puppet of China (or any other country) was fallacious: Ho Chi Minh and his followers were nationalists before they were communists, and deeply distrusted their northern neighbour, which had a long history of imperialist designs on Vietnam.[12] (China and Vietnam fought each other almost as soon as the Vietnam War was over.) A united, vigorous, communist Vietnam under Ho's leadership might have created difficulties for its neighbours; Vietnam had its own expansionist traditions; but in itself it posed no threat to American strategic interests. Nor has any such threat developed in the years since. Yet the domino theory insisted not only that there was such a threat, but also that it was a crucial danger to the United States.

It is tempting to attribute this obstinacy in error solely to domestic politics, and there can be no doubt that fear of the Republican Right, which had so bitterly denounced the 'loss of China' after Mao Tse Tung's victory in 1949, was an important factor in the calculations of all the presidents, from Truman to Nixon, who had to deal with the Vietnam question. But this was not the only, nor indeed a sufficient reason (even in their own eyes) for the decisions taken by these men. Eisenhower, for example, enjoyed an almost completely free hand politically, in the choices he made about South-East Asia, and to the degree that he faced serious opposition, it was from the Left. (In 1954 John F. Kennedy was one of his most articulate critics in the Senate.) The fact is that the decision-makers were guided by the Cold War paradigm, which was inapplicable to the situation in Indo-China, and bred further damaging illusions.

So in 1954–55, as the French retreated from Indo-China, the US government faced a largely self-imposed dilemma: how to maintain the southern bulwark against the spread of communism? It was constrained in its policy-making by three principles. The first was that no direct US military intervention be undertaken (memories of the just-ended Korean War, its casualties and its unpopularity, were still fresh). Of all the presidents only Lyndon Johnson departed from this principle; Richard Nixon's vaunted 'Vietnamisation' policy was a reversion to the norm. Second, the United States had no wish to replace French colonialism with its own;[13] not only would any such enterprise be inconsistent with its traditions, but also it would be anachronistic to the point of impossibility: as Ho Chi Minh remarked, 'the white man is finished in Asia.'[14] The third principle was that no agreement with Ho Chi Minh was possible, he being no true nationalist but a tool of the Kremlin. It followed from all three principles that the United States needed a 'real' nationalist to organise an effective anticommunist government and act as a reliable ally – the unkind would say puppet – of Washington. For similar reasons the French in their time had set up Emperor Bao Dai. The Eisenhower administration made the fatal choice of Ngo Dinh Diem.

Diem was not a man of straw – he was inflexible. A member of a leading mandarin family, he enjoyed a modest reputation in nationalist circles for his refusal to work with the French. Unfortunately it was equally significant that over the years he had refused to work with everybody else too. He emerged as the prime minister of Vietnam in the dying days of the French regime, when his authority barely extended over Saigon. A British observer called him 'the worst prime minister I've ever seen',[15] and US General J. Lawton Collins reported to the National Security Council that 'it is my considered judgement that the man lacks the personal qualities of leadership and the executive ability successfully to head a government that must compete with the unity of purpose and efficiency of the Viet Minh under Ho Chi Minh.' But Diem's success, during his first year in office, in extending and consolidating his authority 'by bribery, persuasion, and finally force', induced the Americans to back him enthusiastically. 'President Diem is the best hope that we have in South Vietnam,' said Hubert Humphrey in 1955. This continued to be the general view in Washington until 1961.[16]

The Americans never found a viable means of co-operation with Ngo Dinh Diem, and never really understood him. Attempting to explain him, their tone varies from the scornful to the despairing; it will take an Asian historian to make him fully intelligible to the West. Yet even through the distorting prism of American journalism and historiography it is possible to glimpse something of his point of view (the Pentagon Papers are very helpful). Head of one of Vietnam's greatest families (the Ngo had been emperors of Amman in the eleventh century) his political outlook seems to have been little affected by the Catholic Christianity to which the Ngo had been converted. He was a nationalist in the sense that he had opposed the French ascendancy and was determined to resist any attempt to impose a Chinese hegemony; but he seems to have had as little grasp of the modern idea of a nation as he did of the related idea of modern democracy (or he could hardly have accepted and furthered the partition of his country). In fact he was not modern in any way at all. He seems to have supposed that he had the equivalent of the traditional Chinese 'mandate from heaven' to rule. In spite of residence in the United States he had little idea of how a modern state must function: he had had little experience in administration, and had lived in retirement between 1933 and 1954. He relied solely on his family to help him rule, and especially on his brothers (there is a certain resemblance to the Kennedys here, but the Ngo were by far the more numerous and far less well adapted to their times). At all times he resented American pressure to reform: the Americans, he thought, were naïve, and he never did more than gesture compliance in response to their urgings. In reality, he himself was naïve. He did not understand that Third World revolutionism was directed against the *ancien régime* as well as against the imperialists; or rather, he fondly imagined that traditional ways could prevail against the new challenges, although they had failed to do so everywhere else since the Boxer Rising.

Admittedly, he had a most difficult task. The conference at Geneva in 1954 which ended the first Indo-Chinese war had decreed an armistice line along the seventeenth parallel: communists to the north, their opponents to the south. A huge exchange of populations followed, and Vietnam was partitioned, as Korea had been. Nationwide elections would supposedly be held in 1956 and unite the country again, but did not take place: neither side wanted them, at any rate if they were honest. Ho Chi Minh began the construction of a typical Stalinist state in the north, and Ngo Dinh Diem was supposed (at any rate by the Americans) to start building a nation out of the wrecked economy and shattered fragments of population in the south. Seen from the future, the undertaking looks to have been tragically futile from the first. South Vietnam was always more of a refugee camp than a state, but with that capacity for self-deception which marked their course from first to last, American officials soon persuaded themselves that it was working. After all, Diem had told them so.

Some sort of success was perhaps possible. Vietnam had suffered appallingly in both the Second World War and the war against the French; both Hanoi and Saigon had enough to do in reconstruction to keep them busy for years, and it was not until 1960 that the Viet Minh once more began to take a hand in southern affairs. But Diem was not interested in a real reconstruction, for that would have required major social reforms. He retained the old landowning and tax-collecting systems, bitterly though they were hated by the peasants who made up the great majority of the South Vietnamese population. Diem, they decided, was no more than a new Bao Dai, typical of the old master class which had collaborated with the French and adopted their religion. On his side Diem probably remembered that a hundred of his Catholic ancestors had been murdered by Buddhists in the nineteenth century. He turned more and more to his family and his co-religionists for support, thus confirming the peasants' suspicions (the Vietnamese population was overwhelmingly Buddhist). A new resistance movement grew up spontaneously, which the Americans came to call the Viet Cong (Vietnamese communists). Diem sent his army in to crush the rebellion, and to shift the peasants out of their villages into what were called 'strategic hamlets', supposedly safe from guerrilla attack or influence. This merely intensified peasant resentment and so helped the communists. In 1960 Ho Chi Minh began to send supplies and agents south to assist the insurgents. Diem soon had another cause for anxiety in the disaffection of the army itself. In November 1960 he was nearly overthrown by a conspiracy of generals and survived, it appears, only thanks to American support.

This was the bad situation which Kennedy inherited from Eisenhower, and it is evident that all the elements which led to the downfall of South Vietnam were already in place. The structure was inherently unstable, and nothing that the Americans could rationally do would prop it up for long, let alone give it permanence. Admittedly, the Americans might act irrationally, but no one knowing Jack Kennedy would bet on the likelihood. Once, during a meeting of the National Security Council to discuss South-East Asia, the chairman of the joint chiefs promised victory 'if we are given the right to use nuclear weapons'. Kennedy ended the meeting without comment, but remarked afterwards, 'Since he couldn't think of any further escalation, he would have to promise us victory.'

> They want a force of American troops [he said.] They say it's necessary in order to restore confidence and maintain morale. But it will be just like Berlin. The troops will march in; the bands will play; the crowds will cheer; and in four days everyone will have forgotten. Then we will be told we have to send in more troops. It's like taking a drink. The effect wears off, and you have to take another.[17]

He was absolutely opposed both to using nuclear weapons and to committing US troops, not just in South-East Asia but in every theatre. As both the Berlin and the Cuban crises showed, he always preferred negotiation – his enemies would say, to the point of weakness. On this point he had no intention of abandoning Eisenhower's policy.[18]

His qualifications for dealing with the Vietnam problem were excellent. In 1951 he had actually visited Saigon, and he was never taken in by the claims of French colonialism or the arguments given for supporting it. In the Senate, in 1954, he spoke out vigorously against John Foster Dulles's call for 'united action' in Indo-China (in other words, for America to go to the help of France with as many other allies as it could drag in):

> to pour money, materials, and men into the jungles of Indo-China without at least a remote prospect of victory would be dangerous, futile and self-destructive. Of course, all discussion of 'united action' assumes the inevitability of such victory; but such assumptions are not unlike similar predictions of confidence which have lulled the American people for many years and which, if continued, would present an improper basis for determining the extent of American participation.
>
> Moreover, without political independence for the associated states [of Indo-China], the other Asian nations have made it clear that they regard this as a war of colonialism; and the 'united action'

which is said to be so desperately needed for victory in that area is likely to end up as unilateral action by our own country.[19]

Prescient words! He was if possible even more acute two years later, in his once-notorious 2 July speech on the French war in Algeria. In a manner that strikingly recalls *Why England Slept* he relentlessly analysed French policy in Algeria and insisted that it was bound to fail, as it did; and in replying to his critics a few days later he spelt out explicitly what a refusal to accept the inevitability of Algerian independence would mean to France:

> Will it not mean that France will have suffered a weakened economy, a decimated army and a series of unstable governments only to learn once again – as she learned too late in Indochina, Tunisia, and Morocco – that man's desire to be free and independent is the most powerful force in the world today?[20]

All this shows that Kennedy was intellectually capable of confronting the Vietnam problem; unfortunately other passages also show that he had not fully understood the nature of Third World revolutions. He did not see that they challenged, not only the old imperial powers, but also the economic order, the class structures, which had grown up under them; the 'freedom' which they claimed was not commonly what Americans, who are too fond of trumpeting the term, understood by it. And unluckily he was among the many who were taken in by Ngo Dinh Diem. In 1954 he indicated publicly that he expected Ho Chi Minh to take over Vietnam, and did not seem especially agitated by the prospect; but by 1955 he had persuaded himself that Diem had worked a 'miracle' in South Vietnam, that he had begun 'to release and to harness the latent power of nationalism to create an independent, anti-Communist Vietnam';[21] that he was 'meeting firmly and with determination the major political and economic crises which had heretofore continually plagued Vietnam'.[22] He still believed in Diem when he became president; he thought that the difficulties which had palpably arisen between Saigon and Washington were the fault of the Eisenhower administration, which had not treated Diem sympathetically enough.

His education in the realities began almost at once. As we have already seen,[23] Eisenhower, as he left the presidency, did his utmost to persuade Kennedy that the most strenuous measures must be taken to defend Laos against communist imperialism:

189

'[he] said with considerable emotion that Laos was the key to the entire area of Southeast Asia. . . . He stated that we must not permit a Communist take-over. . . . President Eisenhower stated it was imperative that Laos be defended.'[24] Kennedy before long rejected this application of the domino theory and settled for what diplomacy could achieve – which was not very much; the people of Laos continued to suffer, in large part because of the continuing war in Vietnam; but the security of the United States and the strength of the 'Free World' seemed after all to be unaffected by this ignoble retreat from an indefensible position. In retrospect the application of this lesson is obvious; it was obscured at the time because, unlike Laos, Vietnam had a long coastline. It was all too accessible to American power.

There is little point in chronicling the ups and downs and comings and goings that marked the Vietnam policy of the Kennedy administration for its first thirty months. 'Money, materials and men' (American military advisers) were poured into South Vietnam; there was a steady stream of high-ranking visitors to Saigon, beginning with Vice-President Johnson in May 1961; repeated conferences were held in Washington, Saigon and Hawaii; the consensus emerging from all this activity was that on the whole things were going well and getting better, and so it was reported to the president. Kennedy, who had many other, seemingly more urgent preoccupations, was content to continue, in essence, with the Eisenhower policy, suitably improved by an infusion of more resources, New Frontier vigour and a greater initial willingness to co-operate with Ngo Dinh Diem. When he referred publicly to Vietnam (which was not often) it was always in terms of the Cold War paradigm and the domino theory: for example, on 11 April 1962, at a press conference, when a journalist raised the point that America soldiers were getting killed in South Vietnam, he replied:

> Well, I'm extremely concerned about American soldiers who are in a great many areas in hazard. We are attempting to help Viet-Nam maintain its independence and not fall under the domination of the Communists. The Government has stated that it needs our assistance in doing it. . . . it presents a very hazardous operation, in the same sense that World War II, World War I, Korea – a good many thousands and hundreds of thousands of Americans died. So that these four sergeants are in that long roll. But we cannot desist in Viet-Nam.[25]

In other words, he was sticking to the three principles, though they were rapidly becoming inconsistent with each other and with reality.

Officially, all was going well; officially, the president and all his men, the joint chiefs and all their subordinates, accepted and believed this line. Yet running through the documents which circulated in vast qantities between the White House, the State Department, the Pentagon and the US embassy in Saigon is an undercurrent of unease, doubt and anxiety; there is a subtext which shows that reality was trying to break through. The paradigm was not working as it should. But failure and defeat were still unthinkable; to mention the possibility was contemptible heresy, as J.K. Galbraith found. He visited Saigon in November 1961, and reported unfavourably to Kennedy on Diem:

> I am reasonably accustomed to oriental government and politics, but I was not quite prepared for Diem. . . . The political reality is the total stasis which arises from his greater need to protect himself from a coup than to protect the country from the Vietcong. I am quite clear that the absence of intelligence, the centralization of Army control, the incredible dual role of the provincial governors as Army generals and political administrators, the subservient incompetence of the latter, are all related to his fear of being given the heave.[26]

He thought it significant that whenever Diem left Saigon, if only for a day, all the members of his cabinet were required to see him off and welcome him back, 'although this involves less damage to efficiency than might be supposed'.[27] So concerned was Galbraith with the drift of events in South Vietnam that on a visit to Washington the following spring (after, as ambassador, he had escorted Jacqueline Kennedy round India on a highly successful visit, and so was in good odour with the president) he concocted a memorandum, with Averell Harriman, making dissentient noises about South Vietnam; warning, especially, that 'We have a growing military commitment. This could expand step by step into a major, long-drawn out indecisive military involvement,' and restating his doubts about Diem.[28] This memo was submitted to the Pentagon for comment, and got a firm rejection from General Lemnitzer:

> The effect of these proposals is to put the United States in a position of initiating negotiations with the communists to seek disengagement

from what is by now a well-known commitment to take a forthright stand against Communism in Southeast Asia. . . . The Joint Chiefs of Staff are aware of the deficiencies of the present government in Vietnam. However, the President's policy of supporting the Diem regime while applying pressure for reform appears to be the only practicable alternative at this time.[29]

Lemnitzer had noticed that Galbraith's policy proposals were not as cogent as his criticisms; but he did not face the criticisms at all. Matters went on as usual for another year and more. Diem made no reforms. What he wanted from Washington was unflinching support, cash and military supplies (troops, if necessary) as he requested them, and a free hand for himself. What is not clear is why he persisted so obstinately in a course that proved suicidal.

Diem would not allow his army to engage the Viet Cong seriously, fearing that high casualties would alienate popular support, and that too many victories might encourage a successful general to topple him. He refused to overhaul his command structure, for fear of losing control; for the same reason he would not hear of trying to broaden his political support. When visitors came – especially American visitors – with unwelcome news or advice he silenced them by the simple expedient of talking non-stop (on at least one occasion, for six hours at a stretch). Noting this, his entourage made sure never to tell him anything except what he wanted to hear, so it may well be that he did not realise how badly things were going: how much ground the communists were gaining, how ineffective and unpopular his government was, how radically disaffected his officers.[30] The one person he trusted implicitly was his brother Ngo Dinh Nhu, whose chief job was head of the secret police. Observers could not decide whether Nhu was mad or merely bad; they were pretty sure that he was an opium addict, given to wild flights of paranoid or megalomaniac fantasy. Whatever the truth, he was a disastrous influence on Diem. To cap matters, he had a beautiful but bloody-minded wife, a 'Dragon Lady' (as American journalists quickly named her) who went in for a disastrous frankness that might have been planned to alienate American opinion.

By May 1963 the South Vietnamese government consisted essentially of no more than Diem's coterie and Nhu's thugs. The generals, having decided that the war could not be won without Diem's overthrow, or perhaps simply disliking their exclusion from power and profit, were beginning to meditate a *coup d'état*, for which, they reckoned, they needed American support or, at least, neutrality. Neither might have been forthcoming, or not for a long time, but for the eruption of violent hostilities between the government and the Buddhist church. Soldiers under orders fired into a crowd celebrating Gautama Buddha's birthday on 8 May; nine people died and more were injured. Diem refused to accept responsibility or even to acknowledge what had happened: he said the explosion of a Viet Cong hand grenade had led to a panic. But the facts were known to all and could not be hidden. Led by their monks, the Buddhists began to demonstrate in every city in the South, and met ever more determined resistance by the government forces. On 11 June, as a gesture against religious persecution, the monk Thich Quang Duc burned himself to death at a crossroads in Saigon. Seen on the front pages of American newspapers and on American television, these incidents created a huge revulsion of feeling in the United States, which was intensified by Mme Nhu, who said that she clapped her hands on hearing the news of the first suicide, and offered a box of matches for the next 'barbecue'. In vain the US representatives in Saigon used every stick and carrot at their disposal to induce Diem to seek a reconciliation with the Buddhists. In a familiar pattern the retiring ambassador, Fritz Nolting, who incarnated the 'sink or swim with Diem' policy, was given assurances by Diem in person, but only a few days after Nolting left Saigon, Nhu ordered that all the pagodas should be stormed by his (American-trained) Special Forces. More deaths resulted, more injuries; monks were imprisoned, and when university students and then high school pupils began to demonstrate, there were mass arrests. In August a second monk burned himself to death.

The Kennedy administration now found itself facing a crisis like that of the Bay of Pigs, but on a larger scale. Once more its chosen policy was exposed to the world as a total failure. Once more the president had lost control of events. Once more the administration itself was split, only this time far more deeply and intractably. Nor, in the time left to him, did Kennedy ever regain control. To do him justice, he had much else to preoccupy him – the Test Ban Treaty and the civil rights revolution, to name two. His instincts, his experience, his historical knowledge, had begun to push him towards some sort of disengagement even before the Buddhist crisis occurred. Nor is he to be blamed for moving cautiously: not expecting his death, he thought he had time, and the situation was politically, as well as literally, explosive.[31] If his goal was now becoming a political, not a military, solution to the Vietnam question (as it probably was) we can safely assert that he was making progress. Robert McNamara was coming to share his doubts, and together they were determined to start withdrawing US troops: there were by now more than sixteen thousand in South Vietnam, and seventy had already been killed. Kennedy and McNamara were committed to bringing a thousand of them home, by way of beginning disengagement, and McNamara wanted the president to make a public pledge to do so by Christmas.[32] Perhaps, had John Kennedy lived, he would have successfully completed this movement, and in 1964 been able to repeat what, three years previously, he had said to Averell Harriman about Laos: 'A military solution isn't possible. I want a political solution.'[33] But he would have had to overcome a mountain of difficulties.

And the impression left of his administration's performance between May and November 1963, as to Vietnam, is one of frightful muddle. There is no trace of the incisive reasoning and coherent teamwork of the missiles affair. It is hardly surprising. The deepening Buddhist crisis demonstrated that the Diem government, on which two US administrations had depended to create a just and stable anti-communist state in South Vietnam, had succeeded only in uniting the whole population against itself. Its incessant blunders had greatly assisted the emergence of an ever-more vigorous and effective communist movement; no other convincing alternative to the regime was visible. If there had ever been a real opportunity to create a non-communist state in South Vietnam without American military commitment, it had gone long ago. The discovery of all this (and even the Pentagon was denying it no longer) was bad enough; but further difficulties were now apparent. Obeying Maxwell Taylor's orders, the US military mission to Saigon had been resolutely optimistic since 1961. This had meant shutting its eyes to the gloomy but accurate reports of its men in the field (of whom the best remembered is John Paul Vann)[34] and accepting instead the invariably rosy reports of the South Vietnamese commanders. These, knowing what the senior Americans wanted to hear, reported villages recaptured, Viet Cong killed, battles won, *ad lib.*, and General Harkins, the US military mission chief, in turn told McNamara that the war would be won in a year. By the summer of 1963 Kennedy realised that he could not trust any of the reports he was getting from the military. The war had already begun to corrupt the US Army. He was spared the further discovery that, for all the fashionable talk of counter-insurgency, none of his generals, not even Maxwell Taylor, really knew how to fight the Viet Cong. They thought in terms of set-piece battles, and had tried to train the South Vietnamese accordingly; for the rest, they expected firepower and saturation bombing to do the trick against the guerrillas. They dreamed wistfully of nuclear weapons; and they began to lobby discreetly for the dispatch of American ground troops to the theatre. The appalling failure of the US Army and US Air Force was already determined even before Kennedy's death, though no one suspected it.

At least it was apparent that the military were divided: that the men in the field in Vietnam bitterly disagreed with their superiors' appraisals. In Washington the State Department was split, between the followers of the cautious Cold Warrior Rusk, and those of 'the Crocodile', Averell Harriman, who had long ago despaired of the Ngo family, and was now ferociously biting those colleagues who disagreed with him. The CIA's intelligence reports contradicted those of the Defense Intelligence Agency, McNamara's baby. The vice-president was still rigidly loyal to Diem. Waiting in the wings was Congress. No wonder the White House dithered. It had gone along with the myth that the war was necessary and was being won; in public the president still did so; if the news of the real state of affairs, and the divisions in the administration, became known, there would be big trouble. And the truth was leaking out. David Halberstam, of the *New York Times*, was filling his paper with the gloomiest possible reports about conditions in the Mekong Delta (where the largest number of South Vietnamese lived) as well as about the near-civil war in Saigon.

At this stage the Vietnamese problem seemed to Washington – to the White House, the State Department and the Pentagon – to be the problem of Ngo Dinh Diem: the war could not be won if he continued in his present course, perhaps if he continued in power at all. Very few saw that the real problem was the American commitment to South Vietnam itself. Among the few was Senator Mike Mansfield, the Democratic leader in the Senate, who at Kennedy's request had visited South Vietnam in 1962 and reported:

> It is their country, their future that is at stake, not ours. To ignore that reality will not only be immensely costly in terms of American lives and resources, but it may also draw us into some variation of the unenviable position in Vietnam that was formerly occupied by the French.

Kennedy had not liked this analysis, but as he said to Kenneth O'Donnell, 'I got angry with Mike for disagreeing with our policy so completely, and I got angry with myself because I found myself agreeing with him.'[35] But that did not seem to be the issue in the summer of 1963. Kennedy sent out a new ambassador to Saigon, Henry Cabot Lodge Jr, whom he had beaten for the Massachusetts Senate seat in 1952 and who had been Richard Nixon's vice-presidential candidate in 1960. Lodge had lost all faith in Diem and was prepared to support a coup against him; he visited the presidential palace only once, and reversed Nolting's policy by excluding General Harkins from all knowledge of his dealings with Washington (to Harkins's rage): he regarded Harkins as Diem's stooge. Kennedy sent more special envoys to Saigon to look at the situation for him. One such mission consisted of Joseph A. Mendenhall of the State Department and Marine General Victor Krulak: they reported back in such contradictory senses (Mendenhall predicting disaster, Krulak victory) that the president asked, 'You two did visit the same country, didn't you?'[36] Maxwell Taylor and Robert McNamara were sent again, rather to Lodge's displeasure. There is distinct pathos in Kennedy's mollifying message to him: 'I quite understand the problem you see in visit of McNamara and Taylor. At the same time my need for this visit is very great indeed, and I believe we can work out an arrangement which takes care of your basic concerns.'[37] At least he realised that hard choices could not be avoided much longer; but he had still not made them.

His difficulties (and those of his advisers) were starkly illuminated by the affair of the Hilsman cable. Some of the South Vietnamese generals had approached the Americans about the possibility of a coup, and on 24 August 1963 the State Department sent Lodge a cable of guidance, largely drafted by Roger Hilsman and Averell Harriman. What was perhaps its key sen-

tence ran: 'If, in spite of all your efforts, Diem remains obdur-
ate and refuses, then we must face the possibility that Diem
himself cannot be preserved.'[38] The generals were thus being
given a green light. Unfortunately it was a weekend ('Never do
business on the weekend,' said McGeorge Bundy afterwards),[39]
and the senior members of the administration were scattered
far and wide (Kennedy was at Hyannisport). Not only that, but
by a muddle between Hilsman and a reporter the gist of this
immensely confidential message got into the newspapers.[40] All
those who had cleared the cable by telephone – Kennedy, Rusk,
McNamara, Taylor – were furious at this damaging leak, and
hot words were exchanged when the National Security Council
(NSC) met on the Monday (26 August). Kennedy had reason
to be displeased, but he would not allow his advisers to use the
leak as a means of having second thoughts about the policy.
He went round the table, polling them one by one: 'Do you,
Mr Rusk, wish to change? No. Do you, Mr McNamara, wish to
change the cable? No. Do you, General Taylor . . . ?'[41] The policy
remained as stated; but Kennedy remarked gloomily after the
NSC meeting, 'my government is coming apart.'[42]

The administration continued its debate during September,
since the South Vietnamese generals were unimpressed by the
evident American indecisiveness, and for the time being held
back; but the discussion was futile. Tragically, Bobby Kennedy
had largely withdrawn from deliberations on foreign policy, as
the work of the Justice Department grew more and more de-
manding; perhaps he was forgetting what had been, for him,
the chief lesson of the Bay of Pigs affair, namely that the president's back had to be guarded, and only he could do it. Had
Jack lived, Bobby would certainly have been drawn back as the
Vietnam question grew more and more pressing. His peculiar
talents were still in full working order. He asked all the right
questions at a meeting of the National Security Council in
September:

> As he understood it, we were there to help the people resisting a
> Communist take-over. The first question was whether a Commun-
> ist take-over could be successfully resisted with any government.
> If it could not, now was the time to get out of Vietnam entirely,
> rather than waiting . . . the basic question of whether a Commun-
> ist take-over could be resisted with any government had not been
> answered, and he was not sure that anyone had enough informa-
> tion *to* answer it.[43]

But such common sense had little impact, except perhaps in the president's most secret thoughts. He was resolved to stick to his policy of beginning to bring the advisers home, and by the end of the year a thousand of them had actually been withdrawn.[44] Apart from that he, like everyone else, was waiting for the Diem matter to be resolved. He was not yet ready to lay the problem before the American people, but unintentionally betrayed his own uncertainty by his contradictory assertions. On 2 September he was interviewed on television by Walter Cronkite, and remarked of Vietnam:

> I don't think that unless a greater effort is made by the Government to win popular support that the war can be won out there. In the final analysis, it is their war. They are the ones who have to win it or lose it. We can help them, we can give them equipment, we can send our men out there as advisers, but they have to win it, the people of Viet-Nam, against the Communists.[45]

On the other hand, a week later, in another television interview (with Chet Huntley), asked if he had any reason to doubt the domino theory, he replied:

> No, I believe it. I believe it. I think that the struggle is close enough. China is so large, looms so high just beyond the frontiers, that if South Viet-Nam went, it would not only give them an improved geographic position for a guerrilla assault on Malaya, but would also give the impression that the wave of the future in southeast Asia was China and the Communists. So I believe it.[46]

Friends, enemies and historians have puzzled over this contradiction, asking which statement Kennedy really meant. Unfortunately the truth is that he meant both of them. That was the trouble.

Events in Saigon took their course. The South Vietnamese generals resumed their plotting, and this time secured the approval of the US government ('While we do not wish to stimulate [a] coup, we also do not wish to leave [the] impression that [the] U.S. would thwart a change of government'),[47] Lodge and Harkins continued to quarrel about the right course for US policy, and Washington sent ineffective messages of advice and enquiry. On 1 November the coup began, and ended next day with the surrender and murder of Diem and Nhu.

Kennedy was at a meeting of the National Security Council when he got the news; he turned white with shock and rushed from the room. He had accepted the necessity of a coup, but had not wanted the Ngo brothers to be killed. Yet he had not even managed to make this point clear to Saigon. Perhaps he could not have saved the brothers, but he had certainly not tried hard enough. He felt dishonoured, for Diem, after all, had been the ally of the United States. His end was a grim warning to all those, in Vietnam and elsewhere, who put their trust in Uncle Sam.

Three weeks later Kennedy was dead himself. The crucial decisions in South-East Asia would be taken by his successor, a man of very different views.

Might-have-beens are scarcely proper topics for a historian. It is difficult enough to assess Kennedy's actual record on Vietnam without adding the burden of speculation about what he would have done had he lived. But, surveying that record, it is hard not to see a huge missed opportunity. The essentials of the South Vietnamese problem were already visible, to those who would see, when Kennedy took office: for instance, Ambassador Durbrow's relations with Ngo Dinh Diem were almost as bad as Ambassador Lodge's were to be, and the South Vietnamese armed forces were little less disaffected than they were to be in 1963. Ideally, the new Kennedy administration would have washed its hands of Saigon politics and sought accommodation with North Vietnam as it had sought accommodation with the communists over Laos. In 1962 Hanoi made approaches implying such an arrangement, but was firmly spurned. (No doubt the communists would have double-crossed the Americans, as they did in Laos, but even that would have been better for all parties than what actually occurred.)

In practice, it would have been politically impossible for the Kennedy administration, so narrowly elected and so vulnerable internationally, to attempt any such settlement in 1961 or, before the missile crisis, in 1962. And since the Eisenhower policy of being frank with Diem had failed, it seemed reasonable to try to be nice to him, which meant giving him whatever he asked for.[48] But by the end of 1962 this policy, too, had failed, and Kennedy was in a much stronger position to undertake radical change. The evidence is conclusive that he had despaired of Diem, and compelling that he was moving towards disengagement from Vietnam, but he moved slowly, for the evidence also shows that his advisers, whether military or civilian, found it difficult enough to abandon Diem, let alone the South Vietnamese cause. Kennedy was still not ready to take a new line in public – in a phrase, to level with the people – when he was shot. The sum of his labours over Vietnam, then, is that there had been no real change since Eisenhower's administration, although time was running out.

In view of his death, it must be said that nothing Kennedy was likely to do could have killed the Saigon commitment in the few years that were given to him. Nor should it be assumed that, had he lived, he would have succeeded in sticking to the policy of not sending troops to South Vietnam. It is often overlooked that Lyndon Johnson himself did not go willingly or rapidly down that road: not until March 1965, sixteen months after he became president, did the Marines land at Da Nang. Powerful forces were at work driving the United States towards that fatal commitment. All that can be said is that Kennedy would have been even more reluctant than Johnson to accept it, and might well have looked sooner, harder, and more successfully for an alternative.

Nevertheless, it needs to be recognised that the most compelling reason for his hesitation during life was that an about-turn over South Vietnam would have been a reversal of everything he had stood for and a venture into unknown waters. Such a reversal could be justified only by an abandonment of the Cold War paradigm and the adoption of a new vision of the world. It might have made sense to ask Americans, 'Do you want your sons to die for Saigon?', but such had never been the Kennedy message. Rather, on 26 September 1963, before he got on to the subject of the Test Ban Treaty, he was assuring the citizens of Great Falls, Montana, that

> what happens in Europe or Latin America or Africa or Asia directly affects the security of the people who live in this city. . . . I make no apology for the effort that we make to assist these other countries to maintain their freedom, because I know full well that every time a country, regardless of how far away it may be from our own borders – every time that country passes behind the Iron Curtain the security of the United States is thereby endangered. . . . So when you ask why are we in Laos, or Viet-Nam, or the Congo, or why do we support the Alliance for Progress in Latin America, we do so because we believe that our freedom is tied up with theirs. . . . So we have to stay at it. We must not be fatigued.[49]

To reverse course would entail swallowing a library of words, beginning with his inaugural address. And what would he say instead? That the security of the United States would *not* be affected by retreat from South Vietnam, or anyway not so badly as by fighting an unsuccessful war there? That the great revolutions sweeping the world were largely beyond American or Russian influence or control, and that the United States must have faith that, in the end, its example of democratic peace, freedom and prosperity would have far more effect than any military exertions to steer people the way they should go? That, in a phrase, America was not omnipotent?[50] Such a message would have been very hard to sell to the voters.

There was thus ample reason for Kennedy's caution, hesitation and reluctance; yet the spectacle recalls the anxious deliberations of an earlier president on a matter even more crucial. Had Abraham Lincoln died during his first seventeen months in office he would now be remembered only as the unimpressive figure whose election touched off the American Civil War. It took more than a year of disasters for the United States for him to accept that slavery would have to go, and its abolition be made a war-aim; and months more before he signed the final Emancipation Proclamation. He moved with all deliberate speed, successfully; and so might John F. Kennedy have done.

.   .   .

NOTES

1. The Pentagon Papers: *The Defense Department History of United States Decisionmaking on Vietnam* (Senator Gravel edn, Boston: Beacon Press 1971) (*DD*) vol. i, p. 4.

2. Dean Acheson, *Present at the Creation* (London: Hamish Hamilton 1970) p. 408. Acheson also recommended measures to protect Taiwan and the Philippines.

3. Ibid., pp. 674–7; Arthur M. Schlesinger Jr, *The Bitter Heritage: Vietnam and American democracy 1941–1966* (London: André Deutsch 1967) p. 13.

4. Acheson, *Present at the Creation*, p. 674.

5. Schlesinger, *Bitter Heritage*, p. 13.

6. *DD* i p. 597.

7. Schlesinger, *Bitter Heritage*, p. 9.

8. E.g. Robert S. McNamara, *In Retrospect* (New York 1995) pp. 321–3.

9. I deliberately use this term in the sense given to it by Thomas S. Kuhn in *The Structure of Scientific Revolutions*, second edition, enlarged (Chicago: University of Chicago Press 1970). This is not

the place to argue the point, but I may say that I am profoundly convinced that, in spite of all the obvious difficulties, the categories discovered by Kuhn can be enormously illuminating if applied to such fields of study as the formation of foreign policy.

10. We lack an adequate term for this movement. Neither 'nationalism' nor 'anti-colonialism' is sufficiently comprehensive; 'socialism', 'communism' and 'democracy' are simply inapplicable.

11. Eric Hobsbawm describes and analyses what was happening in his *Age of Extremes*.

12. The Pentagon Papers discuss at length Ho's attitudes, and quote him as justifying a temporary rapprochement in 1946 with the French, as against the Chinese, in the following terms: 'The French are foreigners. They are weak. Colonialism is dying out. ... They may stay for a while, but they will have to go because the white man is finished in Asia. But if the Chinese stay now, they will never leave. As for me, I prefer to smell French shit for five years, rather than Chinese shit for the rest of my life' (*DD* i pp. 49–50).

13. Though I remember D.W. Brogan remarking that what the Americans really needed was a new word for imperialism.

14. *DD* i p. 49.

15. The observer was an expert: he was the son of Ramsay MacDonald.

16. This paragraph and the next rely on *DD* i pp. 291–305.

17. Schlesinger, *Bitter Heritage*, pp. 29–30.

18. Indeed, in one respect he softened it further. In 1954 Ike would have been prepared to go to the rescue of the French after Dienbienphu if his allies would agree to join him (they refused). Kennedy seems never to have contemplated such a contingency.

19. *SP* pp. 59–60.

20. Ibid., p. 80: speech in the US Senate, 8 July 1957. Dean Acheson was so irritated by what he regarded as an insensitive way to deal with the French that he attacked the speech of 2 July in print; for this he was attacked that winter by Jacqueline Kennedy when he met her on a snowbound New York-to-Washington train. See KOH: Dean Acheson.

21. *SP* p. 61. The phrases quoted come from Kennedy's linking commentary on his speeches, and therefore belong to 1959 or 1960; but they accurately express his views in 1955.

22. Ibid., p. 62.

23. See pp. 62–3.

24. *DD* ii pp. 636–7: Clark Clifford, 'Memorandum of Conference on January 19, 1961 between President Eisenhower and President-elect Kennedy on the Subject of Laos'.

25. *PP* ii p. 322: president's news conference 11 April 1962.

26. J.K. Galbraith, *Ambassador's Journal: a personal account of the Kennedy years* (Boston: Houghton Mifflin 1969) p. 267.

27. Ibid., pp. 266–7.

28. Ibid., pp. 341–4; see also *DD* ii pp. 669–71: J.K. Galbraith, 'Memorandum for the President, 4 April 1962'.

29. *DD* ii pp. 671–2: L.L. Lemnitzer, chairman, joint chiefs of staff: 'Memorandum for the Secretary of Defense, 13 April 1962'.

30. Though he was given a hint in February 1962 when two of his best pilots bombed the presidential palace in Saigon instead of Viet Cong in the Mekong delta. Diem and his family escaped unhurt, though three guards were killed. He attributed his escape to 'divine protection'. See Stanley Karnow, *Vietnam* (Harmondsworth: Penguin 1984) pp. 263–4.

31. See David Halberstam, *The Best and the Brightest* (Harmondsworth: Penguin 1983) pp. 349–50.

32. McNamara, *In Retrospect*, pp. 79–80.

33. Halberstam, *Best and Brightest*, p. 243.

34. For Vann, see Neil Sheehan, *A Bright Shining Lie* (London: Cape 1989).

35. Karnow, *Vietnam*, p. 268.

36. Roger Hilsman, *To Move a Nation: the politics of foreign policy in the administration of John F. Kennedy* (Garden City, NY: Doubleday 1967) p. 502.

37. *DD* ii p. 746.

38. Ibid., p. 734.

39. Karnow, *Vietnam*, p. 288.

40. His enemies accused Hilsman of a deliberate leak, but I see no reason to disbelieve his own account (Hilsman, *To Move a Nation*, p. 489).

41. Halberstam, *Best and Brightest*, p. 324.

42. Karnow, *Vietnam*, p. 288.

43. Hilsman, *To Move a Nation*, p. 501.

44. Among them was Colin Powell, a future chairman of the joint chiefs of staff.

45. *PP* ii p. 652: transcript of broadcast with Walter Cronkite 2 September 1963.

46. Ibid., p. 659: transcript of broadcast on NBC's Huntley–Brinkley Report, 9 September 1963.

47. *DD* ii p. 769: CIA to Lodge 6, October 1963. The message opens with the statement that the points it contains have been discussed with the president.

48. Halberstam, *Best and Brightest*, p. 161.

49. *PP* iii pp. 727–8.

50. D.W. Brogan's 1951 article, 'The Illusion of American Omnipotence', was much praised and much quoted but unfortunately seems to have had no effect on policy-making or public attitudes. It was collected in his *American Aspects* (London: Hamish Hamilton 1964) pp. 9–21.

Chapter 8

DEATH AND A PRESIDENCY

On 22 November 1963, during a public visit to Dallas, President Kennedy was killed with two rifle-shots by Lee Harvey Oswald. The murder staggered the world, and left US citizens, in particular, gazing into a black chasm of meaninglessness. Some of them have been trying to come to terms with what happened ever since.

With typical insouciant acuteness Kennedy himself, on the morning of his death, made two remarks which lay bare the heart of what was to happen. In his bedroom at Fort Worth he glanced over the morning Dallas papers, crammed with fulminations against his policies, and murderous threats, and remarked airily to his wife, 'we're heading into nut country today.'[1] He was fatalistic about the possibility of assassination. He had received a good many warnings about the temper of Dallas, but he brushed them aside. The bubble top to the presidential car was not to be used: he wanted the people to see him and, especially, Mrs Kennedy. A few days earlier he had decided to do without the pair of Secret Servicemen who otherwise would have been squatting on the rim of the car: they made him feel crowded. As to the risk of a sniper, he said that anyone determined to shoot him had only to climb on to a rooftop; precautions were therefore pointless. He seems to have expected to die young, and to have had a soldier or a sailor's belief that no bullet would get him unless it had his name on it – in which case it could not be avoided. Were he available for interview beyond Jordan he would probably agree (it would be characteristic) that these points show that he had to some extent contributed to his own death. But this cool assessment was not one that his fellow Americans could share.

Lee Oswald was an inhabitant of nut country. A 24 year old, he was a temporary employee of the Texas School Book Depository in Dallas; his wretched life and flawed character were sinking him deeper and deeper into megalomaniac fantasy just at the time when Kennedy came to Dallas and drove right past the Depository's windows. His state of mind has been admirably summarised by Gerald Posner:

> Failed in his attempts to find happiness in Russia or the U.S., rejected by the Cubans, barely able to make a living in America, frustrated in his marriage, and hounded, in his view, by the FBI, he was desperate to break out of his downward spiral. He had endured long enough the humiliations of his fellow Marines, the Russian and Cuban bureaucrats, the employers that fired him . . . the refusal of V.T. Lee and other Communist leaders to acknowledge his efforts and letters. Lee Oswald always thought he was smarter and better than other people, and was angered that others failed to recognize the stature he thought he deserved. Now, by chance, he had an opportunity that he knew would only happen once in his lifetime.[2]

The essentials of this account of the matter were palpable almost from the moment of Oswald's arrest, an hour after Kennedy's death; but like the death itself, the explanation was unacceptable, in its simplicity, to the American public.

The first attempt to deny the void, or to reconcile the people to its existence, was made through ritual. Lyndon Johnson was sworn in as president with Jacqueline Kennedy standing beside him in Air Force One at Dallas airfield; the photograph, showing Johnson's rugged solemnity, Mrs Kennedy's dazed misery, and the blood on her skirt, was instantly flashed round the world, a token of continuity and of unity in tragedy. The dead president's coffin was received with all honours at Washington; it lay in state in the East Room of the White House, and then under the great dome of the Capitol; hundreds of thousands of mourners filed past it in the night. Next day there was a Requiem Mass at St Matthew's Cathedral, and then a procession to Arlington Cemetery. An English poet caught the mood best:

> . . . In bright grey sun, processionals
> Of pomp and honour, and of grief,
> Crown that dead head
>   With coronals.
> Some stony hearts feel some relief:

But not your heart, America,
Beating so slow and sure and strong,
Stricken in his
          Triumphal car,
Guard Caesar's bitter laurels long

With soldiers' music, rites of war:
He had proved bravely when put on!
The soldiers shoot.
          Rage echoes far
Above the grave at Arlington.
                  (G.S. Fraser)

Psychologically, the immense dignity of the funeral was essential; if it could not completely express the country's grief, it could help the people to regain their mental poise; but still the unanswerable questions would not go away. As Kenneth O'Donnell had asked in anguish on the night of 22 November, 'Why did it happen? What good did it do? All my life I've believed that something worthwhile comes out of everything, no matter how terrible. What good can come out of this?'[3] His was not the only faith to be shaken that day.

Theodore Roosevelt, Woodrow Wilson, Franklin Roosevelt, had all helped to establish a strong tradition of twentieth-century presidential leadership, which had guided all their successors. Kennedy himself had sought and used and relished the presidency precisely for this reason: he sought fulfilment for himself and the American people in gallant leadership. Lyndon Johnson was equally a child of this tradition, and had sought the office for that reason; now, as president, was his chance to show what he could do; but he also understood that what was most necessary was reassurance, which he sought to provide by realising the complete Kennedy programme as rapidly as possible.

A similar impulse lay behind the appointment of the commission headed by the Chief Justice of the United States, Earl Warren, to establish the truth about the assassination. This commission would not have been necessary but for the murder of Lee Oswald while in police custody, two days after Kennedy's death (like his victim, Oswald was carried to Parkland Hospital, and there pronounced dead). This macabre sequel to the assassination was not quite unforeseen: Daniel Patrick Moynihan, then a junior staff member at the White House, had tried in vain to alert his superiors to the risk of such an event, given the known incompetence of the Dallas police; and an attempt had been made to lynch Oswald at the time of his arrest. It now seems clear that Jack Ruby, Oswald's killer, was moved, as he said at the time, by righteous indignation of the kind that, in the South, so naturally expresses itself with a gun. But the American people, already distraught, could not be expected to accept without question the straightforward explanation of what had occurred, or to wait for Ruby's trial to establish the truth, or part of it. Official Washington had few doubts that Oswald had acted alone, for his own reasons (although Bobby Kennedy, in a bewildered moment, asked the head of the CIA if he had killed Jack).[4] The point was to get the people to think likewise. So the presidential commission seemed an excellent idea, and it faithfully carried out its duty – which was not so much to establish who killed Kennedy as how. President Johnson importuned it to report well before the 1964 election; it did so in September, and its findings were in general respectfully accepted. The congressional session of 1963–64 had just been completed. Johnson had rushed through the entire Kennedy programme, including the civil rights bill, which was proclaimed as the dead leader's best memorial. It seemed as if the institutions and national self-respect of the United States had weathered the storm triumphantly.

It was too much to hope for. Kennedy's murder had been too shocking; in the best of circumstances many Americans (including zealous journalists and historians) would have found it impossible to accept that so great an event could have such trivial causes as the odious personality of Lee Oswald and the absence of a Secret Serviceman from the rear of a presidential limousine. But it was not the best of times. The main notes of the Kennedy administration, as it had gradually developed, had been activism at home and abroad, and détente with the Soviet Union – but not with the communist world at large. Lyndon Johnson faithfully continued these policies, and they all backfired on him. He followed up the Civil Rights Act of 1964 with the Voting Rights Act of 1965, thus crowning the work of the non-violent civil rights movement; but it was soon clear that these great achievements were not enough, and that huge social and economic problems, loosely but unbreakably connected with race, still had to be confronted. The mid-1960s were the years of the 'long, hot summers' when rioters in the urban ghettos burned and sacked their miserable surroundings in quasi-revolutionary fury, while the white South seethed with fury at its loss of command. The grand Democratic coalition of North and South, city and country, working-class and middle-class liberals, Blacks and Jews, began to fall apart. And the quest for international stability plunged the United States ever deeper into the war in Vietnam. The Johnson administration was forced on to the defensive, and in the dreadful year 1968 – the year of the murders of Martin Luther King and Robert Kennedy, the year of the greatest riots yet, when the Chicago West Side and parts of Washington, DC, were sacked, the year of the Tet offensive and the violent débâcle of a Democratic presidential convention – it was finally defeated. LBJ did not offer himself for re-election and Richard Nixon defeated Hubert Humphrey, thanks to the defection of large numbers of Democrats to the third-party candidacy of George Wallace. During the Nixon administration (1969–74) things, if possible, got worse, culminating in the extraordinary Watergate affair.

So it is no wonder that many of those who endured the bitter disillusionment of those years, when the US government too often seemed to be wedded to injustice, chicanery and corruption, should begin to question not merely the official explanation of the Kennedy assassination but the accepted account of the Kennedy administration. Lyndon Johnson, it seemed, had systematically deceived the American people; Nixon was a liar without shame. If this was the state of democratic government in 1974, what reason was there to believe that it had been any better eleven years previously, or that Jack Kennedy was superior to his successors? American republicanism was a fraud, manipulated by politicians, generals, big businessmen, organised crime and such sinister institutions as the FBI and CIA for their own ends. In this frame of mind the revisionists got to work.

Assassination theorists got most of the attention. Belief in conspiracies of one kind or another has always been strong in the United States, being attractive as a means either of understanding reality or of evading it. The zeal of the first American revolutionaries had been fed by a belief in a conspiracy between the British and their tools in New England; contending beliefs in an abolitionist conspiracy and one by 'the slave power' largely brought about the Civil War; belief in a Red Peril had all too great an influence on the politics of the twentieth century. None of these alleged plots are now acknowledged by historians; as myths they are among the many aspects of the past which need explanation and interpretation. So it is with the Dallas conspiracy; but in spite of its impalpability it carried all before it for a long time.

The Warren Report offered an easy target to the critics. Paradoxically, had Oswald stood his trial, less might have been discovered about the case, but a verdict of guilty might have been impossible to contest: even after the first O.J. Simpson trial it is hard to imagine what testimony counsel for the defence could have elicited to withstand the scrutiny of a court, or that Oswald himself would have made a persuasive witness to his own innocence. The commission had concerns beyond the bare question of Oswald's guilt or innocence. It had to undertake the historian's task, of giving as complete an account as possible of a particular event; its conclusion was less important than its arguments, its handling of the evidence; and unfortunately but inevitably (as any professional historian would expect) this pioneering work was full of loose ends, illogicalities, blanks and contradictions both in the testimony offered and in the commissioners' analysis. To common sense these did not matter: Oswald's guilt had been established by overwhelming evidence; loose ends could not affect that central point. But to controversialists devoured by scepticism there could be no innocent blunders. Apparent or real weak points in the Warren Report were seized on, at first as evidence of incompetence, later as proof of conspiracy. Either way, the report could be thrown aside (although the critics continued to rely heavily on the research which it published) and innumerable wild fantasies be entertained. Kennedy, it was averred, had been killed by the mob, or by Castro, or by anti-Castro Cubans, or by the CIA, or the FBI, or the Pentagon. The animus of these hypotheses becomes clear if we notice that no one, except possibly the CIA, seriously entertained the idea that Oswald, the former defector to the Soviet Union, the avowed Marxist with a Russian wife, might have been the tool of the KGB.

Lee Oswald's sojourn in Russia had actually disillusioned him with the Soviet system; nevertheless he described himself as a Marxist until the last (or anyway until police interrogation began). He found it impossible to win acceptance into the shrunken regiment of the American far Left, in large part, no doubt, because it barely existed in New Orleans and Dallas, the two cities where he lived after his return from Russia, but also because he was ill educated, conceited and not particularly intelligent. A violent strain in his personality drove him to become an assassin. He tried to murder the right-wing ex-General Edwin Walker before he aimed at Kennedy. At first glance the two crimes seem contradictory, since Kennedy was a liberal president (who had sacked Walker from the army) and was consciously trying to build on the legacy of Franklin Roosevelt and Harry Truman; was, indeed, moving leftwards in 1963 more rapidly and decisively than he had ever expected to. But from Oswald's point of view there was no inconsistency. Whatever his real motives, he could tell himself that to kill either Walker or Kennedy was to strike a blow at capitalism; perhaps he did not realise that Lyndon Johnson was in the car following Kennedy's, or he might have carried this logic a little further.

It was all but impossible for many on the Left to accept this explanation of what had occurred. Dallas was famous for its triumphal capitalists, and notorious as the centre of the most vicious right-wing bigotry in the United States. It could not be coincidence that a liberal president, the advocate of both civil rights and détente with Russia, was killed on a visit to that particular city. This was at first the universal assumption; it lay behind Jacqueline Kennedy's refusal to change her blood-soaked clothes: 'Let them see what they have done.'[5] Then came the unveiling of Oswald, which might be thought to confirm all the libels about the Left that the Right had for generations been propagating. Leftists were killers – nihilists – crazy fanatics – dangerously unAmerican. At any rate Oswald was. The generation which was just emerging from the shadow of McCarthyism, and was still receiving the attentions of J. Edgar Hoover, was bound to question this hideous confirmation of their enemies' paranoid delusions; perhaps were certain to reject it, whatever the evidence; and a few went so far as to distort, invent or re-interpret that evidence so as to eliminate Oswald from the story of the assassination, or at least, if that was impossible, to pass him off as a mere patsy.

As soon as the controversy about the Warren Report was fairly launched (perhaps with the 1966 publication of Mark Lane's *Rush to Judgement* and Edward Jay Epstein's *Inquest*) the woodwork was emptied of cranks, sentimentalists, opportunists, lunatics, hoaxers, criminals, charlatans, flat-earthers and ufologists. So assiduous were their efforts that it is not surprising that to this day most Americans do not believe that Oswald acted alone, though there is no agreement as to who helped him. It is to be hoped that this delusion will die away as the solid information and superior logic of such books as Gerald Posner's *Case Closed* make themselves felt. Meanwhile students of the American people will register the fact that the conspiracy theorists divide broadly into two camps: in one are those who hope that, if all were known, justice would at last be done, and their belief in their country be restored; in the other those whose purpose, from the start, has been to destroy that belief. The sincerity of the critics made them formidable, especially as the American government did in many ways actually fail the people during the 1960s and 1970s. But since there was in fact no plot behind Kennedy's murder (unless we call Oswald a one-man conspiracy) the theorists' efforts could never be more than undertakings to bewilder and pervert the public understanding, whatever their intentions. They tended to weaken American democracy rather than reform it; they tended also, as Posner has forcibly asserted, to 'absolve a man with blood on his hands and to mock the President he killed'.[6] And they distracted attention from the real meaning of the assassination: a meaning so terrible that many Americans snatched at the debate so that they need not confront it, while others, such as William Manchester,[7] denied that it had any meaning at all.

The meaning is the fact that the United States is a country in which a Lee Oswald desired to kill a John F. Kennedy, and was able to do so.

The United States is a vast country, but it is also a village. However diverse its inhabitants, they are all neighbours; their lives perpetually touch each other. Among Oswald's few friends in Dallas was a man, George de Mohrenschildt, who was also a friend of Jacqueline Kennedy's parents. Nor were Oswald and Jack Kennedy connected only by this sort of coincidence and by bullets. Their lives might be read as the negative and positive of the same image.

> Look here, upon this picture, and on this,
> The counterfeit presentment of two brothers . . .

John Fitzgerald Kennedy seemed to be the realisation of the American promise. Young, handsome and rich; intellectual, athletic and sexy; amusing, amused and high-minded: he claimed the presidency like a prince. By his charm, courage and public spirit this Catholic, this heir of Ireland and machine politics and shady business deals, vindicated his people, his faith, his party, and his country's traditions and institutions. He was the best hope which America had to offer to the world.[8] He was too good to be true; Kennedy was far from perfect, and as the facts about his weaknesses emerged, a bitter *déception d'amour* energised many of his posthumous critics; but the legend was sufficiently accurate to justify his hold on the world's affection and imagination.

No promises were kept to Lee Harvey Oswald. If the American system were all it is said to be in the wildest patriotic effusions, the events of his life should have been impossible; in actuality, they were going to prove the truth of President Kennedy's remark, in his inaugural address, that 'If a free society cannot help the many who are poor, it cannot save the few who are rich.'

Neither of Oswald's parents was equal to the demands which life made on them. The father vanished in his children's infancy, the mother failed in two subsequent marriages, found it hard to keep any job for more than a few months, and was quite unable to bring up her sons properly. Lee was never kept at any school long enough to learn much, particularly about socialising. His service in the Marine Corps taught him nothing except how to shoot; he rapidly turned against the Soviet Union after his migration to it; back in America he never kept a job any longer than his mother had. None of this shifts responsibility for his actions from his shoulders to those of society, much-maligned society; from first to last he seems to have been a vile person, who was much luckier than he deserved to be in the number and the quality of the people who tried to help him and his wife. The point is merely that the United States could not save him. In one respect he was very American, forever in quest of the ideal society, the Emerald City. He sought a refuge successively in the Marine Corps, Russia and Dallas; during the last months of his life he tried desperately to get to Cuba, which under Fidel Castro was another delusive embodiment of his hopes. Nothing worked. It is this which explains his Marxism. Here was an intellectual, if

oswald was marxist

not an actual, refuge from a world which would not accept him at his own valuation or give him hope. In the age of the Cold War it was natural for him to turn to communism, the loudly advertised negation of everything which America stood for; as easy as for the young Adolf Hitler to turn to anti-semitism in Habsburg Vienna. As his sexual, social and economic failures pressed harder upon him, he retreated more and more into a world of fantasy where he was a big shot (significant American-ism!) and where revenge and triumph were possible. Chance gave him an opportunity to realise this fantasy: he seems to have been looking forward to making a heroic appearance in the witness box, rather like the assassins of Tsar Alexander II. But it was not his deed which made Lee Oswald a refutation of the promise of American life: it was his existence.

Perhaps this explains his murder. Jack Ruby, an almost touch-ing figure in the story, was almost as much a failure as Oswald. He too wanted to be a big shot. He wanted to be rich, and popular, and welcomed into the circles of the powerful – or at any rate, of the well known. But by 1963 he was no more than the owner of two not very popular strip-joints in Dallas, whose debts were about to overwhelm him. The news of Kennedy's murder came as an appalling blow. Like Oswald, he had taken refuge in a dream, his one being that his country was all that it should be, a place of equal opportunity and success. Kennedy symbolised this. He also symbolised America as a refuge for the persecuted, especially the Jews. Ruby was fiercely aware of the vulnerability of his people, and rejoiced in the number of Jews whom Kennedy had appointed to his administration (though how well informed Ruby was on this point must be doubted, since it appears that he did not know who Earl Warren was). Oswald's rifle shot down his dream at the very time that, in the daylight world, he was facing financial ruin. He haunted the Dallas police station in the hours after Oswald's arrest, and in the end could bear the smug assassin's grin no longer. He should never have been allowed to get near Oswald, but the Texas police department was no more competent in protect-ing the murderer than it had been in protecting his victim. At the best of times Ruby had a lightning temper. 'You killed my President, you rat!' he shouted, and fired. So certain was he that he acted on behalf of America that he expected to be hailed as a hero. He certainly did not realise that he would spend the few years remaining to him, miserably, in jail, persuaded that

Jews were being massacred in the cellars under his prison. He died of cancer in 1967 – in Parkland Hospital.

There can be no denial that these squalid yet pitiful events struck not only at Jack Kennedy's life but also at all his aspirations and ambitions: at everything which he desired and worked for; at his own dream. He believed in the enormous creative potential of political leadership, and believed in himself as a leader.[9] Nor can it be denied that he did his utmost to live up to his belief. A cool, cautious, thoroughly practical politician, forever exasperating his followers by not going as fast and as far as they wanted, he nevertheless strove perpetually to rouse up his fellow-citizens to aspire and dare greatly, to seize the opportunities of American freedom; and he was perpetually receptive to new ideas and new proposals. If there was a contradiction between these traits it was one that could not be resolved, for it defined his character and explains some of his fascination for his contemporaries, especially since it was commonly expressed through wit and humour, those priceless solvents of human difficulties. Whether with formal eloquence and legislative proposals, or with smiles and a waving hand from a moving limousine, this style of leadership captivated his fellow-citizens and defined the presidency in the eyes of his colleagues and rivals. It is impossible to say what a 1961 Johnson or Nixon administration would have been like; what is certain is that after at last reaching the White House neither man could shake off the Kennedy spell. They tried to be themselves and Kennedy as well: all things considered, an impossible undertaking which helps to explain their ultimate failure. But Johnson, in pushing through and expanding the Kennedy programme until it became his own, and the biggest thing of its kind since Franklin Roosevelt's first term, showed himself a great creative politician; nor should the legislative successes of Nixon's early years in office be wholly obscured by the twin débâcles of Vietnam and Watergate. To a substantial degree the record of his two immediate successors vindicated Jack Kennedy's vision of the presidency.

But they did not, they could not, brush away the deepest difficulty. The Kennedy presidency was born of an age when nothing seemed impossible to America; when it seemed wholly fitting to reach for the moon, both actually and metaphorically; when a president and his wife seemed only to be doing their duty by making the White House a place in which to celebrate the greatest achievements of the arts and sciences and lead high society in chic entertainments. A certain sense of America and the presidency never found better expression than when Kennedy invited all the Nobel prizewinners of the Western hemisphere to dinner and received them with the remark that 'I think this is the most extraordinary collection of talent, of human knowledge, that has ever been gathered together at the White House, with the possible exception of when Thomas Jefferson dined alone.'[10] But what had that America to do with Lee Oswald, the dyslexic, ill-educated loser, with his superficial grasp of Karl Marx and the Russian language, and his propensity to beat his wife when he was out of work, which, being essentially unemployable, he usually was?

Tighter gun laws will no doubt eventually reduce the dreadful American homicide rate, though a man like Oswald, if determined, will probably always be able to arm himself. The Secret Service and the FBI may have learned from 1963 how best to protect a president, though Gerald Ford and Ronald Reagan both had narrow escapes which show how much will always lie beyond police control; but these considerations are not to the point. Nor is the point that Oswald and Ruby were members of the under-class: they were not. But the sad stories of their lives direct us to the truth which great writers have mythologised – H.G. Wells, for example, in *The Time Machine*, Ursula Le Guin in *The Ones Who Walk Away from Omelas* – that the glories of Western civilisation rest on a foundation of human despair which can be mitigated by ordinary human kindness (although Oswald rejected that too) but which can probably never be removed by political action. Oswald despaired of America too easily, Ruby clung to his fantasy of it too obsessively, but no yet imagined politics could save them, or the millions like them, from the misery of their condition. Kennedy's vision had sharply limited applicability; seen from near the bottom of the heap it could look like a cruel deception.

No practical politician, least of all an unillusioned soul like Jack Kennedy, expects to create a perfect society. The show can be kept on the road, things can be kept from getting worse, some real improvements can be made. Such is actuality. But democratic politics perpetually holds out the promise of more. The impulse to make rash promises from the stump, the pretence that today's political nostrums hold the secret of immediate and eternal happiness, the temptation, in short, to

215

believe in the omnicompetence of politics, seems to be universal: as true of Russians, Britons and Chinese as of the United States. As an inevitable consequence pressing problems are denied, ignored, or at best palliated. Kennedy and his followers did not avoid that trap.

The 1970s, even more than the 1960s, were years of crisis, as much because of the oil-shock and galloping inflation as because of the defeat in Vietnam and the Watergate affair. The foundations of American politics, as shaped since the Great Depression, were shaken, and the response of the politicians was conspicuously inadequate. Gerald Ford, an old-school conservative, stuck to his creed, vetoed expenditure bills right and left, and lost the 1976 election. Jimmy Carter, a man whose decency at times approached saintliness, rightly discerned a malaise in American life but wrongly supposed that applied Christianity could deal with it: he had no more success with Congress than his predecessor, and his foreign policy was a total failure. His over-anxious intelligence was not what the people wanted, and in 1980 they replaced him with Ronald Reagan, in many ways a brilliant continuator of the Kennedy tradition. Once more Hollywood came to Washington; once more conspicuous consumption and dazzling parties were the order of the day (though Reagan himself liked to retire early); once more a professed devotion to government thrift was combined with large deficit spending; once more the United States sought peace by preparing war. The trouble was that everything was overdone; a sense of proportion, never seriously threatened in Kennedy's day, was summarily abandoned; federal finances were thrown into a chaos from which they have yet to recover, and the disparity between the rich and the poor, which Kennedy had deplored but had not touched, was now positively encouraged and celebrated. Reagan wanted to make the United States feel good about itself again (Kennedy had wanted to get it moving) and his method was to grin at every problem. It was an appalling caricature of the Kennedy style; it corrupted society, where Kennedy had tried to ennoble it; but like every good caricature it contained a grain of truth. The greed and recklessness of the Reagan years seemed to say, 'What's the difference? Eat, drink and be merry, for the poor you have always with you.' Kennedy's leadership (and by implication all political leadership), according to this view, could never have amounted to more than a glittering show;

the reality was and is a world in which the race is to the strong, the lucky, and those with clout at City Hall.

A pessimist might find this message all too true, but the United States was not built by pessimists. Reagan himself was an optimist. George Bush's disastrously mismanaged bid for re-election opened the way for a man who presented himself as a hopeful activist, an ordinary joe, and a claimant of the Kennedy legacy. Bill Clinton too meant to get America moving again in the direction of the schoolchildren's oath of allegiance, which promises 'liberty and justice for all'. He came to power with as many and as serious problems to tackle as any which Kennedy had had to face, and with vastly reduced resources: much had been squandered since 1963 and could never be replaced. Clinton's southern populist syle on the campaign trail was as different as possible from Kennedy's Harvard elegance, but was suitable to both the man and the times; the mingling of high hopes and low politics was in the authentic tradition. Unfortunately Clinton in office showed himself a far less skilful pilot than Kennedy, and Congress was a far less reliable partner in the work of government than that of 1961–63 had been. It is still unclear whether the dynamism of the presidency and American democracy is exhausted.

What, in his time, did Kennedy demonstrate? What difference did he make? In the sphere of American foreign policy and international relations, the answer must be, not very much. This was far from being a bad thing. It is greatly to Kennedy's credit that the going concern which he inherited was still going at his death. He made few mistakes and did little harm: praise which cannot always be accorded a President of the United States. He was lucky: lucky that the Bay of Pigs disaster was no worse; lucky that the missile crisis was resolved successfully; probably lucky that he did not live to face the Vietnamese problem in its fullness. Yet in all areas of American diplomatic activity he showed himself the same: committed, intelligent, hard-working, sane; a quick learner. American strength and prestige were unimpaired at the time of his death; perhaps, compared to the Eisenhower years, they were even enhanced. The Peace Corps and the atmospheric Test Ban Treaty were permanently valuable achievements. In the time given to him he could hardly have done more; perhaps, in the 1960s, no more was possible. Again the parallel with Ronald Reagan is instructive. Both presidents initiated a dramatic arms build-up, and both showed themselves resolute in opposition to what they saw as Soviet adventurism; both, once Moscow had been taught its lesson, showed themselves eager to build a lasting peace, and carried the people with them in the attempt. But Khrushchev in 1963 was personally in a far weaker political position than Gorbachev in 1988, and neither he nor his associates were willing to admit failure and defeat. The Cold War could not have ended in the 1960s, even if Kennedy had lived.

As to the domestic record, the short life and abrupt end of the Kennedy administration makes appraisal even more difficult than judgement of its diplomacy. In a sense that administration lasted until 1969: although there was a rapid change of personnel at the White House, most of the men who led the US government until that year had been chosen by Kennedy, from Lyndon Johnson downwards, or had worked closely with him. Bobby Kennedy left the Cabinet in September 1964 and Robert McNamara, despairing of the Vietnam War, jumped ship (or was pushed) in 1967; otherwise the attrition of Kennedy appointees was little more than would have occurred anyway, and that little was largely to be explained on personal grounds: the extreme difficulty of working for Lyndon Johnson. There was no substantive change of attitude or direction. But that very fact only underlines the need to distinguish John F. Kennedy's individual contribution to the decisions taken between 1961 and 1963; a distinction all the harder to manage because the presidency, and the US government, are larger than the president. Many of the bills which Kennedy signed into law were only marginally his work.

His contribution is clearest in public finance and economic policy. There he did more than keep the show on the road. With the possible exception of Woodrow Wilson no twentieth-century president has equalled Kennedy in his intellectual and practical grasp of this part of government; in this respect he was every inch Joe Kennedy's son. He saw the intellectual merits of the proposals made to him by professional advisers such as Heller and Galbraith; he saw the need to choose between them when their recommendations differed (not for him Franklin Roosevelt's blithe belief that all such contradictions could be evaded); he had enough self-confidence to choose, and more than enough political horse-sense to know how to effect his decisions. He was a Keynesian in economic policy, but a tight-fisted conservative in finance; and this, far from being the weakness that his more academic counsellors supposed, was exactly what America needed. The tax cut was an economic stimulus that helped carry on the boom into the Johnson years; but Kennedy's thriftiness, by keeping public expenditure under control, promised also to keep down inflation and thereby prevent boom from eventually turning into bust. It was to be extremely unlucky for the United States that neither Johnson, nor Nixon, nor (above all) Reagan, shared Kennedy's hard-headedness on this point.[11] Kennedy regarded the strength of the dollar, the balance of trade and the balance of payments as serious matters and shaped his policy accordingly. Given the strength of underlying contrary tendencies it would be too much to argue that his policies would have averted the crisis of the 1970s (by which time he would in any circumstances have left office); but it can be fairly asserted that in his time they worked, and worked, as they were meant to, a great deal better than Eisenhower's. As with foreign policy, those who know how easy it is for things to go wrong will agree that this was not nothing; an achievement, and not a small one. Kennedy prosperity was genuine, and was largely Kennedy's work.

It is unnecessary to repeat the argument of Chapter 6 about Kennedy and civil rights, but perhaps it is worth re-emphasising the point that both praise and blame are somewhat wide of the mark. The United States had reached a moment of decision, and to emerge from it successfully a Civil Rights Act and a Voting Rights Act were both essential. Nixon had a well-attested hankering for the southern racist vote, but even he, had he been elected in 1960, would have been forced to sponsor a Civil Rights Act, or risk losing the 1964 election. Lyndon Johnson got the Kennedy Act through Congress, and the Voting Rights Act of 1965 too. The Kennedy record is instructive chiefly for what it tells of the relations between Washington, the civil rights movement and the southern state governments, and of the characters of the leaders involved. Then was a time of crisis which tested people and institutions relentlessly, and showed them for what they were. It would be difficult to argue seriously that the Kennedy brothers emerged from the test discreditably.

The reform of mental health provision was uniquely, because almost exclusively, a Kennedy achievement: it would not have happened had anyone else been elected president in 1960 (though had Senator Kennedy pushed such a proposal as Senator Kefauver pushed his drugs bill, it would probably have got on to the statute books eventually). It was the sort of thing that Kennedy particularly liked. It pleased him to be well briefed about sensible proposals for improvement and reform, and to launch them with suitable eloquence, and to see them successfully through Congress. His attitude recalls that of the eighteenth century's enlightened despots, and had he lived in quiet times no doubt he would be remembered as a humane and practical statesman, with no delusions that the Kingdom of Heaven was just round the corner, but with a firm belief in the capacity of democratic leadership to continuously improve the world. As it was, he lived from crisis to crisis, and this individual ambition could only manifest itself intermittently, above all in his speeches.

He was no utopian. When, during the Berlin crisis, it became necessary to extend the draft and prolong conscripts' tours of duty, somebody said to Kennedy that it was unfair. 'Life is unfair,' he replied, uttering a truth which both his good fortune and his bad had taught him. For this reason he was not dismayed by what he knew of the lower depths which bred his assassin. He sat lightly to his religion, but not so much that he did not know about original sin. America and American institutions could never be perfect, but they could always be improved, and democratic politics was the best way to go to work. Kennedy seems to have been equally impressed by the power of the presidency and by the creativeness of the human intelligence, and delighted to exercise them both. No doubt he relished his political success for the normal reasons of ambition, pride and vanity: it would have been astounding if he had not, and his open enjoyment of power is surely preferable to the creeping Jesus in President Eisenhower, who would never admit even to himself that ambition drove him to the White House; or to the desperate see-sawing of President Johnson between grotesque self-aggrandisement and equally grotesque self-abasement. But although psychology has its fascination, what counts is what a president does with himself and his power while in office. He can, if he chooses, spend most of his time asleep, like President Coolidge, the preferred exemplar of President Reagan.

For his part Kennedy took to heart the example of the Roosevelts. Their deeds were inspirations, and as Theodore Roosevelt famously said, the White House was a bully pulpit.

Kennedy's time was short, so his completed deeds were few, but his words were many, and Oswald's bullets ensured that his presidency would be remembered above all for its eloquence, and that eloquence's effect.

He has often been sneered at for being only a man of words; a man whose fine speeches led to nothing and who, anyway, did not even write them. The accuracy or inaccuracy of these observations need not be debated: either way, they are beside the point. As a matter of fact, Kennedy could not possibly have composed all his speeches and messages: he was too busy, and so have been all modern presidents. But he took an active part in shaping all the more important of them, a part which seems to have steadily enlarged as his experience lengthened and his self-confidence grew. Nor is the writing of a speech the most important part of it. The orator's art consists in taking his script, or in improvising it, and using it to convey his passion and his vision to his audience. Martin Luther King was the supreme exponent of the art in the 1960s, but Kennedy came not far behind (and learned to appraise and appreciate King as a fellow-craftsman). He developed slowly as a public speaker, but his performance at Berlin shows that by the summer of 1963 he had little left to learn:

> There are many people in the world who really don't understand, or say they don't, what is the great issue between the free world and the Communist world. Let them come to Berlin! There are some who say that communism is the wave of the future. Let them come to Berlin! And there are some who say in Europe and else-where, we can work with the Communists. Let them come to Berlin! And there are even a few who say that it is true that communism is an evil system, but it permits us to make economic progress. *Lass' sie nach Berlin kommen*! Let them come to Berlin.[12]

There was a paradox here: this essentially cool man distrusted inflamed emotions, and was almost appalled by the roaring, rapturous response he evoked from the crowd: he did not like to be told that no one had been so successful there since Hitler. This, and other speeches in the same fateful year, nevertheless established him securely as the greatest orator in the presidency since Franklin Roosevelt. It was the power which he put into his speeches, as much as the words them-selves, which ensured him a permanent place in history, and perhaps even in literature.

The success of his oratory is thus a historical fact which needs analysis and explanation, for it lies somewhere near the heart of the Kennedy story (as all would agree) and may well throw light on the function of oratory in the modern presidency (a topic which seems made for Mr Gary Wills). Failing that, a more summary treatment must suffice. And the truth seems to be that Kennedy's words were deeds, like those of all the great orators. First as a presidential candidate and then as president it was his business to rally the troops and set them marching. Read cold, today, his campaign speeches have a bizarre quality: they seem oddly unreal and out of touch; they suggest that all too familiar phenomenon, the professional politician, the veteran campaigner, pumping out routine views to small gatherings of the faithful in cold and draughty halls: a ritual activity grown almost pointless. But that was not what actually occurred. Millions of Americans were looking for leadership, guidance, counsel, inspiration. It was the hunger of a great people at the height of its strength and glory, which was yet aware of dangers, difficulties and the possibility of decline. All the politicians of that remarkable time, from Eisenhower to Humphrey, Nixon to Stevenson, Rockefeller to Lyndon Johnson, felt this pressure upon them and tried to satisfy it; Kennedy happened to do so best. This was in large part because of his individual qualities of youth, charm and earnestness; but he also succeeded because he and his team systematically trawled the speeches, books and journalism of the day for usable ideas and proposals – and for jokes. In this way Kennedy entered the presidency, for good and ill, as the spokesman of his generation:

> the torch has been passed to a new generation of Americans – born in this century, tempered by war, disciplined by a hard and bitter peace, proud of our ancient heritage – and unwilling to witness or permit the slow undoing of those human rights to which this nation has always been committed, and to which we are committed today at home and around the world.[13]

Had he done nothing else, he would at least, in his speeches, have consolidated the American world view into something apparently rational, solid and noble.

In fact he did more than that. He convinced his friends and followers (and even some of his opponents and critics) that the agenda set before them was practicable and necessary. This is what matters to posterity. The hesitations and blunders of the man in the Oval Office are unimportant: it was the confident tone of the leader on the podium or the television set that gave impetus to the political process. It is likely that, had he lived, Kennedy himself would have reaped the harvest; as it was, Lyndon Johnson, by virtue of his own special gifts (which included his own sort of eloquence), won a bumper crop, of which Kennedy's words had been the seeds, because Kennedy had consciously and deliberately made himself the prophet of his age. He thereby illustrated one of the permanent possibilities open to presidents of the United States.

He was not, he could not be, invariably consistent in message and tone. Inevitably, in speeches made in the South, Kennedy sounded more nationalistic than he did in New England (it is instructive to contrast his last two, undelivered speeches, one intended for an audience of conservative businessmen in Dallas, the other for enthusiastic Democrats in Austin). But as all his speeches would be reported, and many would be televised nationally, he could not afford to depart too radically into inconsistency or mere demagogism, and anyway did not want to. It was his abiding purpose to stimulate the American people, to make them think, to inspire them to noble effort. Again and again he and his speechwriters achieved this; most famously in the inaugural address but perhaps, in the long run, more impressively in such orations as his Yale Commencement Address,[14] or his American University Commencement Address (he was at his best on campus) on the new possibility of détente.[15] Other speeches were effective because they showed a strong-willed, intelligent, competent president in command of events, or interpreting them credibly: his radio and television speech on the Test Ban Treaty did both.[16] His oratory thus enhanced Americans' self-respect, calmed their anxieties and aroused their courage, their willingness to try new things. Kennedy could be extraordinarily exhilarating, even though, on great occasions, he favoured a sober, unemphatic, even solemn manner. At other times he had a wonderfully light touch, and the people relished it.

It was in this way, and for these reasons, that they took Jack Kennedy to their hearts for good and all. It is for these reasons that he is an inspiration to them still, and for these reasons that the veteran journalist, Walter Lippmann, said on the fourth anniversary of the assassination that he was glad of the Kennedy legend, for 'I think that it contains that part of the truth which is most worth having. This is the conviction, for which he set the example, that a new age has begun and that men can become the masters of their fate.'[17] Kennedy was not given time to do much else, but in this respect he left his mark on the presidency. Ronald Reagan made Americans feel comfortable, but only Kennedy, in the past half-century, has renewed their belief in themselves and their government. It was a rare achievement, and the more necessary for its rarity. Whatever their merits and their other deeds, most of his successors are remembered for their dreadful failures. Kennedy is remembered as a president of hope; he was shot down by a soldier in the army of despair, but it is more than well that before then he had had time to demonstrate the possibility of such leadership.

. . .

NOTES

1. William Manchester, *The Death of a President* (New York: Harper & Row 1967) p. 121.
2. Gerald Posner, *Case Closed: Lee Harvey Oswald and the assassination of JFK* (London: Warner 1994) p. 220.
3. Manchester, *Death of a President*, p. 416.
4. Schlesinger, *RK*, p. 616.
5. Manchester, *Death of a President*, p. 348.
6. Posner, *Case Closed*, p. 472.
7. Ibid., p. 471.
8. 'I have a dream,' he said when greeting Martin Luther King at the White House on the day of the march on Washington.
9. In Kennedy's eyes the Bay of Pigs was by far the worst event of his career because it shook his belief in himself.
10. *PP* ii p. 347: remarks at a dinner honoring nobel prize winners of the western hemisphere, 29 April, 1962.
11. Gerald Ford, who did, failed to understand the other half of the equation, and gave no promise of positive economic leadership; rather the reverse, which largely explains his defeat in the 1976 election.
12. *PP* iii p. 524: remarks in the Rudolph Wilde Platz, Berlin, 26 June 1963.
13. *PP* i p. 1: inaugural address, 20 January 1961.
14. See p. 107.
15. *PP* iii pp. 459–64: commencement address at American University in Washington, 10 June 1963.

16. Ibid., pp. 601–6: radio and television address to the American people on the Nuclear Test Ban Treaty, 26 July 1963.
17. Quoted in Ronald Steel, *Walter Lippmann and the American Century* (London: Bodley Head 1981) p. 543.

CHRONOLOGY

1917	(29 May)	Born in Brookline, Massachusetts.
1931–35		Attends Choate School.
1936–40		Student at Harvard College.
1938–40		Joseph P. Kennedy serves as ambassador to Britain.
1939		Serves as one of his father's embassy secretaries.
1940	(July)	*Why England Slept* published.
1941	(25 September)	Enlists in US Navy.
1943	(2–8 August)	*PT 109* incident.
1944	(12 August)	Death of Joseph P. Kennedy Jr.
1945	(1 March)	Discharged from Navy on account of incapacity incurred on active service.
	(April–May)	Covers founding of United Nations at San Francisco for *Chicago Herald-American.*
1946	(November)	Elected to Congress for Eleventh District of Massachusetts (North Boston) by 69,000 votes to 26,000.[1]
1952		Elected junior Senator from Massachusetts, defeating Henry Cabot Lodge Jr by 1,460,000 to 1,390,000.
1953	(12 September)	Marries Jacqueline Lee Bouvier (1929–94).

1956	(January)	*Profiles in Courage* published; wins Pulitzer Prize.
	(August)	At Democratic national convention, narrowly defeated for vice-presidential nomination.
1957	(27 November)	Birth of Caroline Bouvier Kennedy.
1958		Re-elected to Senate by 875,000 votes to 307,000.
1960	(July)	Nominated by Democratic convention for presidency.
	(8 November)	Elected president, defeating Richard Nixon by 34,226,731 votes to 34,108,157.
	(25 November)	Birth of John Fitzgerald Kennedy Jr.
1961	(20 January)	Takes office as president; gives his inaugural address.
	(1 March)	Peace Corps founded.
	(14–19 April)	Bay of Pigs disaster.
	(4 May)	*Freedom Rides begin.*
	(25 May)	Proposes to send a man to the moon before 1970.
	(30 May–6 June)	Visits Europe: meets De Gaulle in Paris, Khrushchev in Vienna, Macmillan in London.
	(6 June)	Radio and television reports on his meeting with Khrushchev.
	(25 July)	Television report on Berlin crisis.
	(7 August)	Signs Cape Cod National Seashore Park Act.
	(11 August)	Issues NSAM-65, committing USA to support a large increase in size of South Vietnamese army.
	(12 August)	*At midnight, the communists begin to build the Berlin Wall.*
	(24 August)	Kennedy statement on Berlin.

(30 August)	*USSR resumes atmospheric nuclear testing.*
(25 September)	Sets out disarmament programme in speech to UN.
(17 October)	*Khrushchev withdraws his Berlin deadline.*
(30 October)	*USSR tests 50 megaton nuclear bomb.*
(2 November)	Kennedy announces that USA is preparing to resume nuclear testing.
(9 November)	Tells Tad Szulc that he is under 'terrific pressure' to order Fidel Castro's murder.
(13 November)	Pablo Casals concert at White House.
(15 November)	At meeting of National Security Council, decides not to send combat troops to Vietnam.
(14 December)	Sets up President's Commission on the Status of Women.
(18 December)	Joseph P. Kennedy has a disabling stroke.
1962		
(1 March)	Announces on television renewed US nuclear testing.
(22 March)	Breaks with Judith Campbell, after White House lunch with J. Edgar Hoover.
(6 April)	'Jubilant' at steel wages agreement.
(10–13 April)	Steel crisis.
(28 May)	*'Black Monday': stock market plunges.*
(7 June)	News conference: announces tax-cutting policy.
(11 June)	Receives honorary degree at Yale; gives Yale address on economic mythology.

(23 July)	*Geneva Protocol on Laotian neutrality signed.*
(25 September–1 October)	James Meredith affair.
(15–28 October)	Missile crisis.
(6 November)	Congressional elections.
(20 November)	Issues 'stroke of a pen' order on non-discriminatory housing policy.
(18–19 December)	Meets Macmillan in Bahamas to resolve Skybolt crisis.
(29 December)	Inspects Cuban Brigade at Miami.

1963

(24 January)	Tax message.
(29 January)	Special message on education, containing 1963 education bill.
(28 February)	Proposes his first civil rights bill.
(3 April)	*Martin Luther King begins Birmingham marches.*
(12 April)	*King sent to Birmingham jail.*
(10 June)	Honorary degree at American University: peace speech.
(11 June)	*First Buddhist monk immolates himself in South Vietnam.* George Wallace 'stands in the door', but University of Alabama is successfully integrated. Kennedy gives television address on civil rights: promises a strong civil rights bill. *Medgar Evers murdered.*
(19 June)	Sends civil rights bill to Congress. Evers funeral: receives the family at White House.
(23 June–4 July)	Visits Europe: Germany, Ireland, Italy.

(26 June)	Speeches in Berlin.
(25 July)	*Nuclear Test Ban Treaty agreed in Moscow.*
(26 July)	Gives television address on the treaty.
(7–9 August)	Birth and death of Patrick Bouvier Kennedy.
(21 August)	*Ngo Dinh Nhu raids the pagodas in South Vietnam.*
(28 August)	The march on Washington; receives civil rights leaders at White House.
(15 September)	*Four little girls killed in a bombing in Birmingham, Alabama.* Kennedy publicly blames George Wallace for the killings.
(19 September)	White House conference on mental retardation opens.
(24 September)	Senate ratifies Test Ban Treaty; Kennedy leaves Washington for a western tour.
(25 September)	House of Representatives passes tax cut.
(29 October)	House Judiciary Committee reports out civil rights bill.
(1 November)	*Ngo brothers murdered in Saigon.*
(16–18 November)	Trip to Florida.
(21 November)	Flies from Washington to Texas.
(22 November)	Assassinated in Dallas by Lee Harvey Oswald.
(25 November)	Buried at Arlington Cemetery.

. . .

NOTE

1. Some figures are corrected to the nearest thousand.

BIBLIOGRAPHICAL ESSAY

The amount of primary material now available in print for the study of Kennedy and the Kennedy administration is substantial. There are Kennedy's three books, *Why England Slept* (reissued London 1962); *Profiles in Courage* (New York 1956); *A Nation of Immigrants* (New York, first published 1958, reissued 1964). Kennedy in Congress had always been active in the matter of immigration policy, and as president he made proposals which became the basis of the Immigration Act of 1965, which transformed US law. According to Robert F. Kennedy, he was working on a revision of his little book at the time of the assassination. No doubt that means that Sorensen was.

I have found the three Kennedy volumes of *The Public Papers of the Presidents of the United States* (Washington, DC 1961–63) invaluable; also worth consulting is the collection of his pre-presidential speeches, *The Strategy of Peace* (New York 1960). The campaign of 1960 may be followed in *The Speeches of Senator John F. Kennedy: presidential campaign of 1960* (Washington, DC 1961) and in *Joint Appearances of Senator John F. Kennedy and Vice President Richard M. Nixon* (Washington, DC 1961). '*Let the Word Go Forth*': *the speeches, statements, and writings of John F. Kennedy 1947 to 1963*, edited by Theodore C. Sorensen (New York 1988) is a work of piety rather than scholarship, but is not without its uses.

The *Public Papers* include transcripts of all Kennedy's presidential news conferences, but these have also been published separately in Harold W. Chase and Allen H. Lerman (eds) *Kennedy and the Press* (New York 1965) with an introduction by Pierre Salinger. It is instructive and amusing to compare Kennedy's tone and manner of expression when speaking to reporters (a skill in which he delighted) with the tone and manner of his formal orations and messages to Congress. Still another contrast is provided by Edward B. Claflin (ed.) *J.F.K. Wants to Know: memos from the president's office, 1961–1963* (New York 1991) also introduced by Pierre Salinger. Students will find much valuable documentation in the Pentagon Papers: *The Defense Department History of United States Decisionmaking on Vietnam*, vol. i (Senator Gravel edn, Boston 1971). The Warren Report, *Report of the President's Commission on the Assassination of President John F. Kennedy* (Washington, DC 1964), for all its inadequacies, is the only possible starting-point for a study of Kennedy's death and its significance.

There are many memoirs by Kennedy's associates. In a class of its own is Edwin O. Guthman and Jeffrey Shulman (eds) *Robert Kennedy in his Own Words* (New York and London 1988). This volume contains all the lengthy interviews of Bobby Kennedy conducted for the oral history project of the Kennedy Memorial Library. The interview sessions were evidently cosy occasions, but a great deal of valuable material was elicited, and the early date of many of the interviews (1964) meant that Bobby did not have the time, or perhaps the political motive, to doctor his memories. The same cannot be said of his memoir of the missile crisis, *Thirteen Days* (London 1968), which was written, though because of his murder not quite completed, in 1968, when he was running for the presidency; it remains essential reading.

Benjamin C. Bradlee, *Conversations with Kennedy* (London 1976) is of the greatest value, being essentially Bradlee's diary of his friendship with Kennedy during the White House years. It has not been superseded by Bradlee's autobiography, *A Good Life* (New York 1995), though that is not without interest. John Kenneth Galbraith, *Ambassador's Journal: a personal account of the Kennedy years* (Boston 1969) is a combination of diary and memoir, in which the immediacy of the diary, to the book's great benefit, generally prevails over the deliberation of the memoir. No source comparable to these two books has yet emerged, although one day Arthur Schlesinger Jr's White House diary, kept at Kennedy's suggestion, will, I suppose, be published.

Apart from Bobby, no member of the Kennedy family has published a memoir; it sometimes seems that no member of the administration has failed to do so. Pride of place still belongs to the first to appear: Arthur M. Schlesinger Jr, *A Thousand Days*

(Boston 1965), and Theodore C. Sorensen, *Kennedy* (New York 1965). Schlesinger was near, but not of, the inner circle at the White House, and his intense romantic loyalty to the president, his wife and his brother undoubtedly affected his perception and his presentation; but these limitations were more than compensated for, in my opinion, by his lively intelligence, his great literary ability, and his outstanding professionalism as a historian. He made brilliant use of his opportunities. These merits are even more in evidence in his life of Bobby, *Robert Kennedy and his Times* (London 1978). Both books are indispensable, but British readers must be warned that the hardback London edition of *A Thousand Days* was stupidly and needlessly abridged by the publisher, and should not be relied on. Sorensen was as near the president as anyone, and his account of his association with Kennedy, which swells into a history of the administration, is essential, but it reads too much as if it were a campaign biography, conceding nothing to Kennedy's critics and occasionally making claims which cannot be accepted; furthermore, when compared to Schlesinger, Sorensen's lack of scholarly experience is apparent. But the central point is that after thirty years these two somewhat flattering portraits remain complementary and convincing likenesses: on most important points they told the truth and presented it accurately.

No one looking for a corrective to these rosy pictures of Kennedy will find it in memoirs by other members of his administration. I would give a lot for the considered and detailed views of Lyndon Johnson, but they were never recorded, and were probably never formulated: Johnson's attitude to Kennedy was so bound up with his ambitions and insecurities, and his way with facts was so manipulative, that he could not be detached or even sincere in his judgements. All Kennedy's other associates were devoted to him and his memory, and write about him and his presidency as about the most golden years of their lives. Even Harris Wofford, who in his *Of Kennedys and Kings* (New York 1980) is admirably objective and level-headed, and who was the only person to leave the presidential entourage on a matter of principle, remains in the end a strong admirer – much to Kennedy's credit. Lawrence F. O'Brien, *No Final Victories* (New York 1974) is an enjoyable book by a relaxed professional who kept his self-respect through all the stresses of the Kennedy years, the Johnson years and Watergate.

Authors such as Pierre Salinger, *With Kennedy* (London 1956), Evelyn Lincoln, the presidential secretary, *My Twelve Years with John F. Kennedy* (New York 1965), Paul B. Fay Jr, Kennedy's close friend and Undersecretary of the Navy, *The Pleasure of his Company* (New York 1966) and Kenneth O'Donnell and David F. Powers, '*Johnny, We Hardly Knew Ye*' (Boston 1972) would have been uniformly adulatory even if they had not been writing under the close supervision of the Kennedy family. Their books contain much valuable detail, but should be used with caution. The same must be said of a very different work, Judith Campbell Exner, *My Story* (New York 1977), in which one of Kennedy's discarded lovers spills the beans. The book is almost ludicrously unreliable, and in places is unconsciously very funny, but it gives us details of life in the White House that Mrs Lincoln did not see fit to mention, and truth of a kind can, with care, be winnowed from it. Of larger historical significance are Dean Rusk, *As I Saw It* (New York 1990), in which the former Secretary of State somewhat redeems his reputation, and Robert S. McNamara, *In Retrospect* (New York 1995), in which the former Secretary of Defense inflicts further damage on his (but which contains a first-rate appendix on the missile crisis). Roger Hilsman, *To Move a Nation* (Garden City, NY 1967), though highly instructive, is perhaps too self-serving.

Kennedy has not so far had much luck with biographers. The best complete account is the two-volume work by Herbert S. Parmet (*Jack* and *JFK*, New York 1980 and 1983), of which the first volume is excellent, but the second a disappointment: possibly Mr Parmet was too close in time to the events which he describes. Even the first volume has been eclipsed by Nigel Hamilton, *Reckless Youth* (New York 1992), which gives a brilliantly convincing account of Kennedy as a boy and a young man. Unfortunately Mr Hamilton found it impossible to be fair, let alone sympathetic, to Joseph and Rose Kennedy. The later volumes of his projected full-scale biography have yet to appear. Richard Reeves, *President Kennedy* (New York 1993) is an enjoyable chronicle of Kennedy's years in the White House; it must not be confused with Thomas C. Reeves, *A Question of Character: a life of John F. Kennedy* (London 1991), a hostile account which seems to me now to suffer fatally from lack of a sense of proportion.

On particular incidents in Kennedy's career, Nigel Hamilton's

Reckless Youth is the best treatment of the *PT 109* affair, but Robert J. Donovan, *PT 109* (New York 1989) is still well worth reading. For Kennedy's early political career James MacGregor Burns, *John Kennedy: a political profile* (New York 1960) is still essential, less for the information it contains – the wool was pulled firmly over the author's eyes on several matters, for example the writing of *Profiles in Courage* – than for Burns's acute political insight and excellent style. Theodore H. White, *The Making of the President* (New York 1961) is still a must for the campaign of 1960, although in retrospect it is clear that the book's chief significance is that it was an early and immensely successful piece of Kennedy myth-making (it also launched a few myths about presidential elections, but that is another story). The missile crisis and its antecedents have been more exhaustively studied than any other aspect of Kennedy's presidency; Michael R. Beschloss, *Kennedy v. Khrushchev: the crisis years 1960–63* (London 1991) is the best and most comprehensive treatment. With the exception of Kennedy's policy on civil rights his domestic record has been comparatively neglected by scholars; Irving Bernstein, *Promises Kept: John F. Kennedy's New Frontier* (New York 1991) is an honourable exception. My cousin, Gerard T. Rice, has written an admirable study of the Peace Corps, *The Bold Experiment* (Notre Dame, IN 1985). On economic policy Herbert Stein, *The Fiscal Revolution in America* (Chicago 1969) is an excellent place to start, though its central thesis looks increasingly odd with the years. Jim F. Heath, *Kennedy and the Business Community* (Chicago 1969) is also very good.

On civil rights, the essential book is Taylor Branch, *Parting the Waters: Martin Luther King and the civil rights movement, 1954–63* (London 1988). It is difficult to know what other titles to recommend from a vast number. Carl M. Brauer, *John F. Kennedy and the Second Reconstruction* (New York 1977) should be read. To catch the flavour of the times it is plainly necessary to read some of King's writings, especially perhaps the *Letter from Birmingham City Jail*. That document, and many others, will be found in *Eyes on the Prize: the civil rights reader* (London 1991). James Silver, *Mississippi: the closed society* (London 1964) contains an eye-witness account of the Meredith affair, and much else. E. Culpepper Clark, *The Schoolhouse Door: segregation's last stand at the University of Alabama* (New York 1993) is equally enlightening.

On Kennedy and Vietnam, apart from works already mentioned, it is essential to read David Halberstam, *The Best and the Brightest* (New York 1972) and Neil Sheehan, *A Bright Shining Lie* (London 1989). In the years since 1963 voices have never ceased to assert that Ngo Dinh Diem and his regime could and should have been saved by wise American policy; taken in conjunction with the Pentagon Papers, Halberstam and Sheehan will persuade all but the most obstinately blind that this contention is absurd, and that anyway Washington was incapable of formulating wise policy. John M. Newman, *J.F.K. and Vietnam: deception, intrigue and the struggle for power* (New York 1992) is a vigorous defence of Kennedy's policy, but is, I think, too ingenious to be convincing.

To discuss Kennedy's assassination is to re-enter nut country. It is doubtful if in any circumstances the American public would easily have accepted the 'lone gunman' theory, once the initial shock had worn off; but the circumstances were grotesque even beyond the simple fact of the murder. The killing of Lee Oswald was bad enough, but in the years that followed all events seemed to conspire to shake Americans' faith in their government and its utterances. Scepticism and the paranoid style gradually spread and deepened, until the majority concluded that the Warren Commission's conclusions were nothing but a cover-up. I remember coming to believe in the possibility of some sort of conspiracy, as the various weaknesses in the report were brought sharply into view. But what none of the critics and sceptics realised was that although the Warren Commission had failed to produce a watertight theory of exactly *how* Oswald had killed the president, it had succeeded in showing that he was certainly the murderer: attempts to show that he was just a patsy, or that he had a double (as if the conventions of cheap fiction operated in the real world) could never overcome this central point. By the 1990s certain technical advances made it possible to reject all other theories as based on a faulty reading of the evidence, or on no evidence at all; and Gerald Posner, *Case Closed* (New York 1994), a systematic investigation of Oswald and Ruby, cleared up all other points, and should be read by all interested students. Oliver Stone's notorious movie, *JFK*, is most certainly *not* the place to begin: it is a peculiarly distasteful piece of historical falsification, and probably set back public acceptance of the truth by several years.

William Manchester, *The Death of a President* (New York 1967) is much the best and most moving account of the murder at Dallas and the events which immediately followed it.

Finally, for overall accounts of the Kennedy presidency, students cannot do better than turn to James N. Giglio, *The Presidency of John F. Kennedy* (Lawrence, KS 1991) and to Richard Neustadt, *Presidential Power and the Modern Presidents* (New York 1990).

INDEX